THE LONG ROAD HOME

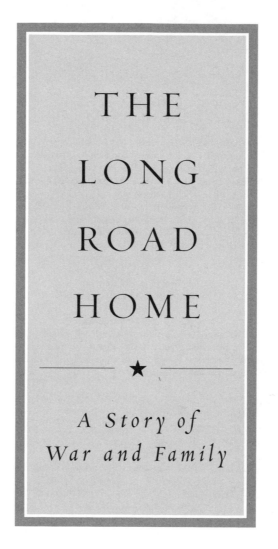

THE
LONG
ROAD
HOME

★

A Story of
War and Family

MARTHA RADDATZ

G. P. PUTNAM'S SONS   NEW YORK

⅏P

G. P. PUTNAM'S SONS
Publishers Since 1838
Published by the Penguin Group
Penguin Group (USA) Inc., 375 Hudson Street, New York, New York 10014, USA •
Penguin Group (Canada), 90 Eglinton Avenue East, Suite 700, Toronto, Ontario M4P 2Y3,
Canada (a division of Pearson Penguin Canada Inc.) • Penguin Books Ltd, 80 Strand,
London WC2R 0RL, England • Penguin Ireland, 25 St Stephen's Green, Dublin 2, Ireland
(a division of Penguin Books Ltd) • Penguin Group (Australia), 250 Camberwell Road,
Camberwell, Victoria 3124, Australia (a division of Pearson Australia Group Pty Ltd) •
Penguin Books India Pvt Ltd, 11 Community Centre, Panchsheel Park, New Delhi–
110 017, India • Penguin Group (NZ), 67 Apollo Drive, Mairangi Bay, Auckland 1311,
New Zealand (a division of Pearson New Zealand Ltd) • Penguin Books (South Africa)
(Pty) Ltd, 24 Sturdee Avenue, Rosebank, Johannesburg 2196, South Africa

Penguin Books Ltd, Registered Offices:
80 Strand, London WC2R 0RL, England

Library of Congress Cataloging-in-Publication Data

Raddatz, Martha.
The long road home : a story of war and family / Martha Raddatz.
p.   cm.
ISBN 978-0-399-15382-2
1. Iraq War, 2003– —Personal narratives, American.   2. Raddatz, Martha.
3. Soldiers—United States—Biography.   I. Title.
DS79.76.R33   2007   2006037332
956.7044'3092—dc22   [B]

Printed in the United States of America
1   3   5   7   9   10   8   6   4   2

Book design by Lovedog Studio
Maps by Jeffrey L. Ward

*For the men and women of the U.S. military
and the families who support them.
And for my own family—Tom, Greta, and Jake.*

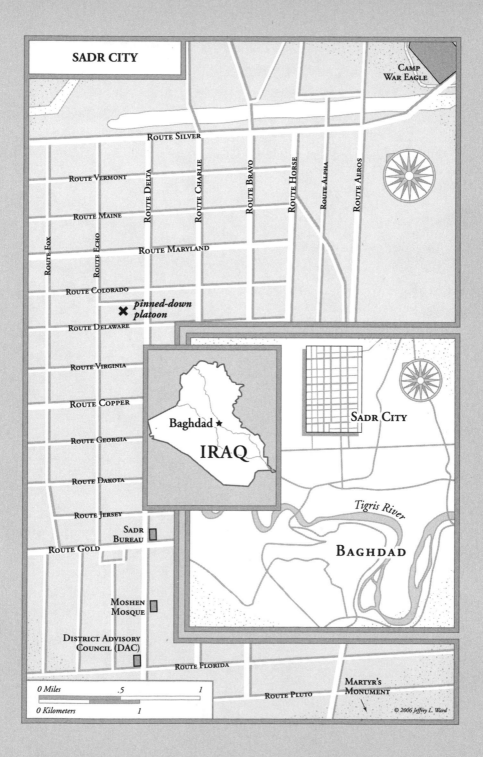

SADR CITY

CAMP WAR EAGLE

ROUTE SILVER

ROUTE VERMONT

ROUTE MAINE

ROUTE DELTA
ROUTE CHARLIE
ROUTE BRAVO
ROUTE HORSE
ROUTE ALPHA
ROUTE AEROS

ROUTE FOX
ROUTE ECHO
ROUTE MARYLAND

ROUTE COLORADO

✗ *pinned-down platoon*

ROUTE DELAWARE

ROUTE VIRGINIA

ROUTE COPPER

Baghdad ★

IRAQ

SADR CITY

ROUTE GEORGIA

Tigris River

ROUTE DAKOTA

ROUTE JERSEY

BAGHDAD

SADR BUREAU

ROUTE GOLD

MOSHEN MOSQUE

DISTRICT ADVISORY COUNCIL (DAC)

ROUTE FLORIDA

0 Miles   .5   1

0 Kilometers   1

ROUTE PLUTO

MARTYR'S MONUMENT

© 2006 Jeffrey L. Ward

Some guys have seen things that no one ever wants to see. . . .
I understand now what it means when you go to a veterans'
ceremony and you see the old veterans get together and hug
and cry, and you never really understood it. I understand
it now.

—Lieutenant Colonel Gary Volesky

BLACK
SUNDAY

≈ *1900 hours*

April 4, 2004

Sadr City, Iraq

WHERE THE LIGHT SHONE THAT EVENING, it illuminated only gore and the clenched faces of soldiers unaccustomed to pain.

There were so many young men, more than thirty, and they had arrived so unexpectedly that the cramped concrete aid station was quickly overrun. The overflow lay outside, soldiers naked and bleeding, on the cooling sands of Camp War Eagle. Dry wails or an occasional whispered plea of "Sir" came from those who could muster a voice, as the medics moved among them. Others were silent, breathing in staccato gasps, as if rationing what little air they had left.

With no electricity and with darkness beginning to settle, the medics relied on the dust-caked headlights of Humvees circled around the aid station to help guide their fingers to the source of each trauma. The splayed black hole of a gunshot wound here, the rip of shrapnel there. Narrow beams from flashlights allowed them to probe more carefully the chunks of splintered bone, extract bits of steel, and bundle and bind wayward intestines.

On a signal from the medics, two of the most catastrophically wounded survivors were swaddled in sleeping bags and rushed to the roaring belly of a nearby helicopter.

Standing amid the chaos was Colonel Robert Abrams, commander of the brigade to which these men belonged. The son of legendary Vietnam War general Creighton Abrams (for whom the army had named its biggest tank), the younger Abrams was drolly referred to by some soldiers as "the natural-born killer." But like virtually all the three thousand soldiers he now commanded, Colonel Abrams had never once in twenty-two years of service heard a gun fired in battle, never seen a soldier wounded in combat or watched a soldier die. He would see it all this night.

Abrams moved from one wounded soldier to the next, grasping hands and offering crisp reassurances. "You'll be fine," he said again and again, feigning confidence as he looked at the wrecked bodies all around him. "You'll be okay."

The massive hand of Staff Sergeant Robert Reynolds, whom the men called "Big Country," grabbed Abrams's pant leg as he passed. At six-foot-six and 280 pounds, the sergeant was considered the First Cavalry Division's "go to" squad leader—a soldier who made things happen. Colonel Abrams bit back his horror as he stared at the sergeant. He was stripped from the waist down, his genitals smeared red and buttocks glowing white. A loaf-sized chunk of Reynolds's inner thigh was blown off, laying bare the remaining tangle of veins and tendons. Reynolds strained to tell his commander about the brutal assault on his men that he'd barely survived. Abrams bent down, his ear close enough to hear

Reynolds above the din of the aid station. Emotion and pain shook Reynolds's voice.

"There were hundreds of them, sir."

Separated from the wounded soldiers, on a stretcher next to the outside wall of the aid station, Captain Trent Upton saw what was unmistakably a dead soldier. Medics who first examined him had pulled the soldier's camouflage top and T-shirt up and over his face, pinning his arms in a grimly unnatural position. Upton, who was supposed to be keeping track of the dead and wounded, called quickly for the chaplain. Ramon Pena, like almost all the soldiers at Camp War Eagle, was so new to this base that he hadn't even known where the aid station was located, and had to be guided there when the word came that a platoon had been ambushed. Now the chaplain looked down at the soldier stiffening in front of him and remembered the prayer he had recited to the men of Alpha Company just an hour before, when they had left the base on their ill-fated rescue mission.

Lord, protect us. Give us the angels you have promised and bring peace to these soldiers as they go out. In the name of the Father, the Son, and the Holy Spirit.

These words haunted the chaplain as he took hold of the dead soldier's hand and watched as Upton gently pulled down the T-shirt and uniform top covering the face. Pena didn't know the soldier, but Upton recognized him instantly. It was Specialist Stephen Hiller, twenty-four years old, from a small town in Alabama. Hiller had just announced that his wife, Lesley, was pregnant again.

Upton knelt at Hiller's side and put a hand on his shoulder as the chaplain, clutching Hiller's fingers in his own, administered last rites. Then the men covered the young soldier in a thick flowered blanket—the kind found in nearly every Iraqi home.

Colonel Abrams stood nearby frozen for a moment as he watched Chaplain Pena and Captain Upton move between the dead and the wounded. With the muffled sound of tank fire close by and soldiers still trapped in the city, Abrams, cursing, mumbled a quiet plea. *"Damn, this is bad, this is really bad, but please, God, I hope this is all of them. Let this be all of them."*

LESS THAN FOUR MILES AWAY, at the center of the action, Lieutenant Shane Aguero and his platoon were huddled on a rooftop as the smack of automatic weapons grew louder in the narrow alleyway below. Humvees burned in the distance—the same vehicles his men had escaped not long before. Frenzied crowds now surrounded the vehicles.

Aguero was only dimly aware of a thick line of blood making its way down the left side of his face as he watched the tracer rounds streak across the deepening gray sky. Despite the approaching waves of armed militia, or perhaps because of them, the lieutenant's eyes were drawn briefly to the sight of a bird—a sparrow, he thought—arcing low and untouched beneath the gunfire. For some reason, the bird carried Aguero's thoughts back home, away from the battle, away from his soldiers now trapped in this Sadr City firefight, to the warning his wife had given him when he left her outside their home near Fort Hood, Texas, just a few weeks before.

"In every war," she had cautioned, "there is always a platoon that gets pinned down. Don't let it be your platoon."

★

Chapter 1

ELEVEN

HOURS

EARLIER

0800 hours

April 4, 2004

Camp War Eagle, Sadr City

"WHERE THE HELL IS AGUERO?"

Captain Troy Denomy had been in Iraq only four days and already he was irritated with his soldiers. In ten hours the seven-hundred-soldier infantry battalion to which Denomy's company belonged would officially take over command in this huge, impoverished Baghdad neighborhood of two and a half million people called Sadr City. At exactly 1800 hours the 2-5 Cavalry battalion flags would be unfurled, salutes exchanged, and the transfer of authority completed. But things were not off to a good start. Twenty soldiers from Denomy's First Platoon had been assigned security duty that morning for Iraqi sewage trucks, escorting the "honey wagons" through ankle-deep liquid waste that ran through the streets. Their Humvees were supposed to be lined up and ready to head out the gate of Camp War Eagle, the forward operating base on the city's outskirts.

It wasn't like his platoon leader to be late, Troy Denomy thought. Lieutenant Shane Aguero was a solid soldier who had worked under Denomy back at Fort Hood for six months prior to this deployment. Aguero was familiar with the routine of these sewage runs, having arrived in Sadr City several weeks before his captain. This teeming Shiite neighborhood had suffered more than any other during the Sunni-dominated reign of Saddam Hussein. Once called Saddam City, its infrastructure was rudimentary at best; the principal means of sewage removal here was evaporation. Securing honey wagons wasn't exactly warrior's work, but it was part of the effort to improve the quality of life for Iraqis. Suck up a little waste, help turn on a few lights, and at the end of the day the soldiers figured they'd have a far better chance of eventually getting out of this miserable place. And maybe diminish the incentive for their being shot at in the meantime. The patrols had the added benefit of providing the soldiers a gut check on the mood of the streets.

Denomy was a natural leader who'd earned considerable respect for surviving the crucible of Army Ranger School. Before that he'd been a history major at a small southern college, where he was captain of the soccer team and a regular at his fraternity house. The army had made all that possible through school loans. The last eight years' service had been payback—a fair exchange as far as Denomy was concerned.

Now the young captain made his way past the two-story concrete headquarters. Almost all the buildings looked alike on the barren terrain of this forward operating base. The decaying rows of rectangular barracks had once housed units of Saddam Hus-

sein's intelligence service. Mottled buildings that smelled like rotting cream lined up next to wide dirt paths packed with dried
weeds. Denomy still could see no sign of the four Humvees, or
of Aguero's platoon. He was irked but, on second thought, not
surprised: It was a chaotic time, to say the least. Denomy's battalion was moving into Camp War Eagle at the same time the battalion from the First Armored Division was pulling out. The heavily
armored Bradleys, the few that had been brought on this mission,
were still rumbling through the camp that morning, and massive
supply trucks were being unloaded near the motor pool, where the
vehicles were housed, after the long ride in from Kuwait. Three
hundred twenty-five miles of sand and sweat. Gear and ammo and
the few personal items that the soldiers were allowed to bring were
dumped wherever space was available. Some of the new arrivals
were sleeping inside and on top of vehicles; others were in a
maintenance bay until the departing soldiers cleared out.

Denomy had been one of the last commanders to arrive at
Camp War Eagle. His superiors had allowed him to stay behind
in the battalion's home base of Fort Hood, Texas, until the birth
of his first child in March, a boy named Merrick. Five days later,
Denomy found himself in the middle of the Kuwaiti desert, preparing to enter Iraq with most of the 136 soldiers under his command. A handful of junior and mid-level officers had gone into
Iraq early to start the transition process, Shane Aguero among
them. But 90 percent of Denomy's men had arrived in Sadr City
with their captain just four days before.

The farewell from Fort Hood had been wrenching for everybody, but especially so for Troy Denomy. Merrick was born the
Saturday before he left for Kuwait. Because his wife, Gina, had
had to have a cesarean section, she couldn't leave the hospital until the following Monday. She arrived home with the baby midday, sore and exhausted; by four in the afternoon the Denomys

bundled up Merrick again and headed for church. A friend had helped arrange a hasty baptism for Merrick because Troy was scheduled to leave the next day. It would be the only night he would spend with his wife and son at home before his yearlong deployment.

Troy and Gina cradled Merrick between them that night, professing love in halting whispers and crying so hard the baby was wet with his parents' tears. It was the first time in three years of marriage that Gina had seen her husband cry. There had never been any cause before, she reasoned: Nothing bad had happened, no one close to them had ever died, and they had never been apart for more than a few weeks.

Now there seemed to be no end to the tears. By Tuesday morning Gina was dizzy at the thought of Troy leaving. To make matters worse, all departing soldiers were to gather with their families at the Fort Hood gymnasium, the "Abrams gym," to say goodbye later that evening. Everything in the military seemed to be a shared event, even when you ached for privacy.

"How am I going to cope at the farewell ceremony?" she asked her husband.

Troy looked into Gina's blue eyes and outlined a plan. "We are going to go to the gym and you can hang out for a while, but you're not going to want to see kids clinging to their dads and all that sadness for long. So I am going to give you the biggest kiss of your life, and then I want you to walk away with the baby and not look back."

Gina didn't argue. Hours later, standing in the refrigerator-cold air of the gym, Troy kissed his wife—yes, the biggest kiss of her life—and then Gina turned and walked through the crowded gym, past all the sobbing families, and out into the steam of the Texas night.

When Troy arrived in Kuwait a few days later, the pain of that goodbye still lingered. It was the hardest thing he'd ever been through. And now, just days later, here he was living in an enormous tent with twenty other soldiers nearly eight thousand miles away. Mercifully, the tents were air-conditioned: even in these days in mid-March, the temperature was reaching eighty degrees. The showers and bathrooms were in portable trailers, as clean as one could expect with so much sand and dust. There were even a Subway and a Burger King. Conditions weren't so bad, considering. But what really made it all bearable was the Internet. A handful of computers had been set up in a trailer so the soldiers could keep in contact with their families. The lines were long and the connection was slow, but Troy was determined to get a message to his wife.

> Gorgeous,
>
> Got in safely with no issues. The very next morning at 0600 I had to go to a range to shoot! That night, I completely collapsed. How are you feeling. I assume that you are still pretty sore. I hope that my Mom is taking very good care of you. Everyone congratulated me about Merrick and sends hellos and their best wishes. I miss you and Merrick and not a minute goes by without me thinking of the both of you.
>
> Love you tons and miss you. Give Merrick a hug and kiss for me and tell him that his daddy loves him.
>
> Troy

For those last few weeks in March, while he was training in Kuwait, Gina and Troy were able to communicate fairly regularly by either e-mail or phone. Gina provided updates on Merrick's progress, right down to how many diapers he was filling a day. Troy laughed at how much pride and delight such mundane details could bring.

As a security precaution, soldiers weren't allowed to reveal on the phone or computer the exact day they were leaving Kuwait and heading into Iraq. But Gina knew what was about to happen when Troy told her during a late-night phone call, "I might not talk to you for a few days." She was a nervous wreck for the week after that, fearful whenever she watched TV and saw news of a convoy attacked en route from Kuwait to Baghdad. On the second day of April the tears came again, when Troy finally managed to get a phone line to let Gina know he'd arrived. Since then he had been so busy he hadn't had another moment to call, and the lines for the computers were so long that he did not even try e-mailing. Gina was just happy he was safe, starting a mission that had been described to the wives as largely a peacekeeping mission, in an area of Iraq that had seen little violence since the war began one year before.

For the soldiers arriving after weeks in the Kuwaiti desert, it was a stunning transition. One of Denomy's fellow captains, Steve Gventer, wrote in his journal after riding through Baghdad on the way to Sadr City on March 31:

> The desert suddenly became a full-fledged city with the traffic typical of a New York, Boston or Dallas. . . . My sixty-vehicle convoy was escorted through the city, past some of Saddam's old palaces. It had a feeling of seeing history—the same buildings we watched on FOXNEWS getting tomahawked were right before my eyes, and as we traveled further there were huts, next to BMWs and rusted junk cars. The people seem friendly and I yell "Mahaba" (hello) and smile a lot. This usually gets a wave especially from the kids. The neighborhoods are so dirty and street markets have

live sheep and sides of beef (the live sheep are chosen as a lobster might be in the US and slaughtered on the spot—the head set on a table). Life here seems to be less meaningful or death more commonplace as evidenced by the dead body from a car wreck I passed today—bloody and in the open on the highway, no slowing of traffic, just common.

Like Captain Gventer and the others, Denomy knew almost nothing about Sadr City. To make matters worse, a directive from the Office of the Secretary of Defense—that no soldier should have "boots on the ground" in Iraq for more than a year—had had the unintended consequence of depriving Denomy's unit of a carefully coordinated transition. The soldiers from the 2-2 Cav (Second Squadron, Second Armored Cavalry Regiment) had been in charge the previous year, but they had reached the end of their twelve-month deployment and left weeks before the main body of Denomy's unit arrived; the 1-2 Cav (First Squadron, Second Armored Cavalry Regiment), responsible for another part of Iraq and with little experience in Sadr City, had been sent to fill the gap for a month until the 2-5 Cav took over. The result was that Denomy's soldiers never had a chance to conduct the thoroughgoing "right seat, left seat" rides that allow for the experienced unit to pass along to its replacements what they need to know before assuming command.

There was one thing the new soldiers did know, however: There had been only one violent incident in Sadr City the previous year. On that occasion, between fifty and a hundred Iraqi insurgents had ambushed a scout platoon, killing one soldier. He was the only soldier to die in hostile action in that area during the entire first year of the Iraq war.

But the day before—April 3, during his first foray beyond the gates of Camp War Eagle—Denomy hadn't liked what he saw.

His reconnaissance platoon was stopped at a major intersection by members of the Mahdi Army, a local militia loyal to the cleric Moqtada al-Sadr. His father, a revered Shiite cleric, had been murdered along with two of his older sons in 1999 by Saddam Hussein's government. Moqtada, the fourth of his sons, was now the de facto ruler of Sadr City.

The militia had caused only minor trouble in the past, but now they were refusing to let the U.S. forces pass through a makeshift checkpoint. Denomy's interpreter explained that the Mahdi Army was protesting the closure of al-Sadr's *Al-Hawza* newspaper by Paul Bremer, the director of the U.S. Office for Reconstruction and Humanitarian Assistance as well as the head of the Coalition Provisional Authority; Bremer had charged the paper with inciting violence. When Denomy tried to keep his convoy moving, the militiamen lay down in front of the vehicles and formed a human chain ten rows deep, locking arms and preventing them from passing.

A minute later, Denomy understood the reason for the human barricade. On the other side of the rows of militiamen, huge groups of protesters were coming into view. Men, women, and children, thousands of them, were carrying poster-sized portraits of al-Sadr and banners written in Arabic. Most of the men were carrying swords.

From the Humvee behind Denomy, Staff Sergeant Franklyn Doss looked around at his twenty soldiers, then back at the thousands of marchers. *This must be how Custer felt,* he thought, *just before the Battle of Little Bighorn.*

Captain Denomy had a similar thought, and he acted on it swiftly. Denomy had no idea where the marchers were heading, but his gut told him to turn his convoy around and head back to camp. No need to incite a mass of sword-carrying militiamen.

Later that night Denomy learned that the protest had ended peacefully, but some of the other units patrolling in town afterward reported sporadic but unsettling incidents. Shane Aguero's platoon had driven off the main roads and down back alleys to get a more intimate sense of the city. Everyone they encountered had voiced disdain for Americans, spitting and hurling invectives, if not rocks. Some of the newly arrived soldiers were mystified. Aguero's gunner sergeant Yihjyh Chen, known as Eddie, a burly native of Taiwan who'd moved to Saipan as a teenager, just shrugged when another sergeant asked why they were being treated with such disrespect. "Whatever," Chen said. "I guess they don't realize we're just here to help." Nothing much fazed Eddie Chen.

The incoming battalion commander, Lieutenant Colonel Gary Volesky, had told Denomy that there seemed to be an increasing number of young men gathering in groups in Sadr City, and an increase in anti-U.S. rhetoric as well. The battalion commander was a strong believer that flare-ups could be avoided by behaving respectfully toward the local population while continuing to try to provide the sorts of services that might make a difference. This was one of the reasons Denomy was so eager to get Aguero's platoon out the gate that morning; but he also wanted to get a sense of what his men were getting into. The battalion was only hours away from assuming command; there was no time to lose.

Denomy sent out the word. "Go find Aguero."

The slumbering bray of roughly two hundred soldiers, who had worked night shifts, echoed through the maintenance bay some fifty yards from the headquarters, temporary housing quarters for the new arrivals. Even though he was scheduled for a daylight patrol, Lieutenant Aguero was among them, his lanky frame curled into a cockeyed fetal position on a thin foam mat, his knees apart so as not to further inflame his throbbing joints. The slender wire-rimmed glasses through which he perpetually squinted were stuffed inside his helmet and within easy reach. Aguero could sleep through the sounds of passing tanks and weapons fired on a nearby shooting range, but there was one noise that always kept him awake: snoring. So when he had retired that night, he donned combat-strength earplugs to drown out the grinding noise. It did the trick—so well, in fact, that he never heard his wristwatch alarm.

Aguero felt a boot in his backside.

"What the hell?" He wiped the sleep from his eyes, grabbed his glasses—and figured out why he'd been so rudely awakened.

"Shit," he said. "The patrol." He pulled on his body armor, jammed his helmet over a fringe of matted black hair, and ran over to the motor pool.

If anyone in the First Cavalry Division embodied the nomadic military life, it was Aguero. The son of a retired army command sergeant major, he had been born on a military base in Panama thirty years before. The lifestyle was second nature to him, and he considered himself far too geeky for the popularity contests he saw in his high school, so it surprised no one when he enlisted. By the time Aguero was in college, he was married with children. His wife, Amber, a self-professed geek, had found a soul mate in Shane. Nothing made them happier than spending the evening in their small apartment outside Fort Hood, eating pizza and battling high-tech monsters in Champions of Norrath on the video screen long after their two kids were tucked in bed. The couple had an easygoing, joking banter that belied a serious and deep connection. Neither could imagine life without the other.

Most of the men in Aguero's platoon were up and waiting on him when he emerged from the maintenance bay. Platoon Sergeant First Class Jerry Swope, a country boy from Missouri, had already started loading up the four Humvees for the sewage run. Swope had slept on the hood of his Humvee the previous night—staying off the ground kept him clear of rodents and crawling insects, but it didn't exactly provide the best night's sleep—and hadn't bothered with breakfast or a shower. Swope figured it was better not to have a full belly when inhaling steaming mounds of garbage so early in the day. Within minutes of leaving Camp War Eagle, great waves of liquid sludge would be lapping at the doors of his vehicle, so a shower seemed a wasted effort. He would save that for tonight.

Swope would be in the last Humvee, Aguero in the first. Both vehicles were up-armored M-1114s, weighing a ton more than the standard Humvee and built to include such upgrades as two-hundred-pound steel-plate doors and ballistic-resistant glass. The two vehicles between them were "add-on armor" M-998s. They were soft-skinned Humvees with additional armor-protection kits installed, usually out in the field after they had been manufactured. They were more vulnerable and had less power than the up-armored vehicles, but they were considered well suited for a peacekeeping mission. Each of the Humvees carried five men—plenty of manpower to serve as security escort for three small trucks—as well as crates of water bottles and MREs, meals ready to eat, in the back. And each vehicle contained a combat lifesaver kit, which was packed with all of the essentials for emergency first aid.

Aguero mumbled a quick apology as he brushed past Troy Denomy before climbing into his Humvee. Denomy gave the lieutenant a quick slap on the back and headed over to headquarters.

"Okay, let's go," Aguero grunted. He climbed into the passenger seat of the lead vehicle and signaled for his driver, Specialist Jonathan Riddell, to roll.

Also in the vehicle were Sergeant James Fisk and an Iraqi interpreter, Jassim al-Lani,* dressed in the same desert-camouflage uniform the soldiers wore. Sergeant Chen was behind the .50 caliber weapon in the turret, only his legs visible to the others. Chen was already cracking jokes, but Aguero was in no mood. He'd been up half the night, and the stench of feces still permeated his nostrils and clothing. He had a vague sense that things in Sadr City weren't quite as stable as advertised, and had told his wife, Amber, as much when he managed to get a phone line out the day before. "This place is hot and nasty," he complained. Shane Aguero hated escorting the sewage trucks, hated the anti-American slurs, and was disgusted driving through a city so packed with people and filth. But it never mattered how you *felt* in the army. It was part of your job; it was what you had signed on to do.

Like it or not on this Sunday morning, the soldiers of the First Platoon headed out the gate to do it all again.

*Not his real name.

★

Chapter 2

PALM

SUNDAY

8:00 a.m. CDT

April 4, 2004

Fort Hood, Texas

EVERYTHING SEEMS LOUDER in the middle of nowhere. Maybe it is the stretch of the land or the spread of the sky across this army post, but if the wind is blowing your way, the peal of church bells, even the prerecorded kind, is as powerful a sound as incoming tank fire. It is enough to rouse even those who have no intention of attending Sunday services.

Fort Hood sits in the hill country of Bell County, Texas, a 340-square-mile facility located sixty miles north of the capital city of Austin, fifty miles southwest of Waco, its main post in the town of Killeen.

There are ten chapels on Fort Hood for some 65,000 men, women, and children. There is "Comanche Chapel," rising from "Tank Destroyer Boulevard"; there are "First Cavalry Division

Chapel" and "Iron Horse Chapel" on "Battalion Avenue"; and over on "Tank Battalion Boulevard" are several more. Not that there were many tanks or battalions left at Fort Hood on this Sunday morning. Its population ebbs and flows, depending on where, when, and for how long the men and women of the First Cavalry Division and the Fourth Infantry Division are deployed. Named after the Confederate general John Bell Hood, Fort Hood is home to both divisions, as well as the III Corps headquarters, thus earning its billing as the "largest armored training installation in the free world." Fort Gates, as it was originally called, was established in the mid-1840s to defend against the Apache, Comanche, and Kiowa Indians, who fought hard to regain their land from white settlers.

The First Cavalry Division traces to the mid-1850s, when cavalry troopers, as they were known, rode the western frontier, engaging in bloody battles with Native Americans, smugglers, and thieves. One hundred fifty years later the soldiers of the "First Cav" still answer the call of "Charge!" with Stetsons flying and pistols firing as their horses stampede down Fort Hood's parade fields to re-create the rich history of the division.

But now the First Cav was on a yearlong deployment to Iraq, the 21,000 cavalrymen and much of their equipment gone.

Indeed, the division was made up overwhelmingly of cavalry-*men*. Women have made tremendous strides in the military, but because the army is largely a ground force and women are prohibited from ground combat units, only about 15 percent of the army is female. Thus, entering Fort Hood during wartime in the twenty-first century is not entirely different from what it would have been like walking on post a century before. It is a place dominated by wives, women whose sorority has the cruel requirement of living apart from the men they love, knowing that the separation can suddenly and violently be made permanent. One might see them walking together in groups, with their children trailing behind, or on a Saturday morning struggling to mow the neat patches of lawn that border their ranch-style houses—houses often with a second car in the driveway, a big pickup or a sporty roadster: dusty monuments to absent husbands, fathers, best friends. It's a scene replicated at Army and Marine Corps installations across the country.

Sundays were hardest, the day when the absence of a husband was keenly felt. The sound of the church bells seemed to prompt the memories of backyard barbecues, lounging on the couch together, or just playing ball with the kids. Memories that would often leave the women weepy and distracted.

Connie Abrams was struggling with all those recollections this morning. This was the fourth consecutive Sunday she'd spent without Abe, her husband of twelve years, and she was still trying to get used to life without him.

Abe—First Brigade commander Colonel Robert Abrams— had left for Iraq in mid-March to prepare for the arrival of his 3,000 or so soldiers. There were six brigades in the First Cavalry Division, colonels commanding each one of them. Within each brigade there were usually four battalions of about 700 soldiers, commanded by lieutenant colonels. Connie knew that today one of Abe's favorite battalion commanders, Lieutenant Colonel Gary Volesky, was officially taking command of his area of responsibility (AOR), a place called Sadr City that Connie knew little about. Gary and his wife, LeAnn, were friends of the Abramses; LeAnn's house was just a few blocks from Connie's.

It would still be another ten days before Abe officially took charge of his brigade. The transfer of authority from the outgoing brigade to Abrams's brigade was being done on a staggered basis so that the handover to the new forces didn't happen all at once. Until the transfer of authority, Abe was shadowing the departing brigade commander in Baghdad. The same was true for his boss, division commander Major General Peter Chiarelli, now doing the "right-seat ride" with the commander of the outgoing First Armored Division.

As brigade commander, Abe had easy access to international cell phones, as well as to the special DSN (defense system network) lines that had been installed in all the brigade commanders' homes at Fort Hood. This made it possible for Connie and Abe to talk regularly—all Connie needed to do was pick up the line, dial a ten-digit number, and she was connected to Abe's brigade headquarters in Baghdad. Once Abe took command, Connie knew he would have far less time to talk; in the meantime, though, the regular conversations had helped her through the first few weeks of loneliness.

Connie was born into a military family, to a father who had served during wartime. Connie vividly remembered when she was just a small girl, her mother, Irma, receiving a call over the MARS, or military affiliate radio station, from her dad while he was doing his second tour in Vietnam. It was her parents' tenth wedding anniversary, and Connie sat wide-eyed listening to her mother speak to her father, Staff Sergeant Bennett Clevenger, for the first and only time during his deployment. Huddled in a small communications room in the jungles of Southeast Asia and surrounded by soldiers who could hear both sides of the dialogue, Connie's father sent anniversary wishes with military precision as his voice crackled over the high-frequency radio lines.

"How's it going? Over!" Connie heard her mom shout into the phone. There was a long pause and then her father's voice. "Everything's fine! How are you? Over!"

And now here Connie sat, more than thirty years later, in bed with her phone and laptop computer that kept her instantly connected with her husband.

Connie was also accustomed to moving—in fact, she went stir-crazy if a few years passed without a change of location—and to watching neighbors come and go; she reconciled the disappointment she sometimes felt with the knowledge that, at some point down the road, they'd probably be reunited on some new and equally desolate army post, with a chance for friendships to pick up again where they'd left off.

But this separation from Abe was something different. Until now they'd never been apart for much more than a month. This deployment was expected to last twelve to sixteen months. Longer than she could stand to think about. Connie tried to take some comfort in the promise that they'd all been told they could expect an easy deployment. "A babysitting mission," that's how they'd described it. Abe repeated the phrase time and again. "This is not going to be a dangerous deployment, honey," he'd say. "We're going to be fine."

To a stranger, the weeks leading up to Abe's departure would have looked anything but loving. Connie constantly picked fights with her husband, bickering over minor things—socks left on the bed, overflowing garbage cans, the dog that hadn't been brushed. Abe couldn't do anything right. In a good moment Connie would catch herself and try hard not to snap—but inevitably she'd pick up on one small detail or another, and the two would be bickering by midday. Abe wasn't one to sit back when Connie was itching for a fight. Always the colonel, even at home. To Abe, there was no argument he didn't think he could win, no detail too trivial for his attention. Neighborhood kids who would show up at the Abramses' house to babysit eight-year-old Robbie would find the colonel waiting at the door to give a formal brief on what was expected. "Copy that?" Abe would bellow. "Yes, sir!" But Robert Abrams's public bravado failed to intimidate his wife.

As the day of his departure grew closer, Connie finally said, "It's time for you to go, because I'm ready to kill you." She wasn't the only one—many of the other wives felt the same way. "They need to leave," they confided to one another. "We need to get on to the next stage." Connie knew it was terrible to waste the little time she had with Abe, but she *wanted* to be angry with him in order to protect herself—to close herself off so it didn't hurt so much when he left.

Once Abe was gone? What Connie wouldn't have done for one more day of Abe pacing the house, leaving his clothes around their bedroom and towels on the floor. When she watched his bus pull out of Fort Hood on March 12, it hit her hard.

A whole year. This is going to be horrible.

The first few days were the worst. Suddenly Connie Abrams was responsible for everything—Robbie most of all. They'd been straight with him about how long Dad would be away, but Connie knew he really couldn't comprehend the time and distance. She wondered whether she could keep it all together. There was a lot to manage. How many days had gone by? Not enough to start counting yet.

The real key to keeping sane, she knew, would involve her tight circle of friends at Fort Hood. Connie had been told time and again that she acted nothing like a colonel's wife, and she took it as a compliment. Blond and bubbly, a bit crass, and with no qualms about speaking her mind, Connie made newcomers feel comfortable within minutes. An overstuffed glass candy dish and regularly rotating snacks on the coffee table were hints that anyone who crossed her doorstep was welcome to stay and chat. Her arched eyebrow and an ear leaned close let you know that she was willing to give you the real lowdown.

But what mollified Connie more than anything since Abe's departure was the Family Readiness Group, the army's support network for families left behind. It was the link between the soldiers and their loved ones. The FRG, as it was called, helped families with paperwork, social gatherings, and—God forbid—the injury or death of a soldier. It was the network that tied everyone together. The FRG was like a large extended family, the people with whom you spent weekends and holidays and shared hard times. It was also the group that got together to support the troops, the organization that put together care packages. Most days the FRG meant socializing, planning events, and keeping morale high among wives and kids. Connie had always been involved, and as the colonel's wife she was even more dedicated to helping all the families get through this deployment.

Even so, on Palm Sunday Connie found herself lying in bed while Robbie watched cartoons, missing Abe powerfully and repeating the mathematical mantra of those left behind: *Let's see, if it is 9:00 a.m. here, it must be 6:00 p.m. in Baghdad.* Daylight savings time had kicked in that morning, so what had been a ten-hour difference was now diminished by one hour. She warmed to the thought that, thanks to the clocks, her husband was now somehow an hour closer.

When she finally dragged herself into the kitchen, Connie Abrams turned on the television, which was tuned to a news channel. She sometimes had all three televisions on throughout the day—CNN on one, Fox on another, MSNBC on the third. Connie wasn't the sort who could put the war out of her mind; she wanted to know everything she could about what was going on in Abe's world. When she heard a reporter say something about *grisly murders in Fallujah,* she snapped down the volume to make sure Robbie wouldn't hear.

The news was a bracing reminder that parts of Iraq were still not under control. There were more details on the shocking story out of Fallujah, where, four days earlier, American contractors had been burned, mutilated, and their bodies hung from a bridge. Abe had assured Connie that Fallujah was a long way from the relatively peaceful neighborhoods where he was now based, but the mental images of those blackened corpses still horrified her.

Robbie startled Connie with a burst of laughter from the other room, followed shortly by a plea for his mother to hurry up and get ready. It was Brunch Day, after all, the regular Sunday "date" with the other wives she'd instituted as soon as Abe left for Iraq.

After a slow shower and a tall cup of coffee, Connie climbed out of her baggy sweats and slid into a short black dress and summer sandals. At houses nearby, Connie's two closest friends— Casey Sanders and Kelly Lesperance—were going through the same ritual: donning their best dresses, sprucing up the kids, and heading for the officers' club.

The club was just up the road from Patton Drive, where the Abramses lived. Beth and Pete Chiarelli's house was at the end of the quiet, winding lane. The Chiarellis had one of the biggest houses on post, which always amused Beth. "When all of your kids are young and at home, the army gives you the tiniest houses on the post; and when the kids are grown and off on their own, you get the biggest house on the block." The size of your house in the military had everything to do with rank, of course, and almost nothing to do with family size. Pete Chiarelli was a two-star general, and only rarely would anyone attain that rank before he or she turned fifty.

Almost everyone living in this quiet section of Fort Hood joked that it resembled the bland black-and-white neighborhood depicted in the movie *Pleasantville,* a satire of American suburbia in which kids are perfectly behaved and the neighbors exceedingly kind. Beth thought of Patton Drive as a time warp, a place where kids played in the streets and walked to school, and where neighbors really did borrow sugar and eggs from one another. Beth herself wouldn't think twice of walking down the street in the evenings, having wine with girlfriends, then walking home again, unescorted. Beth loved the calm, the familiarity and safety of living on post. Soldiers with automatic weapons manning checkpoints around the gated facility added a layer of protection the rest of the country did not have. It could sometimes be an annoyance driving in and out, but as a result, the most serious crime anyone at Fort Hood could remember was a stolen bicycle.

When her husband left for Iraq, Beth Chiarelli had counted up the number of times she had moved: twenty-five in thirty-two years of marriage. Twenty-five moves! Yet whatever place the Chiarellis called home, Beth had a way of making it as inviting and comfortable as any family's lifelong home. Her affinity for antiques helped, and like many an army home, the Chiarellis' was decorated with treasures and mementos from a life of travel, each with a story attached.

Beth had never dreamed of marrying anyone in the service. Growing up in the suburbs of Portland, Oregon, the daughter of the vice president of a steel company, Beth Kirby had little exposure to the military. Only one young man in her neighborhood had gone off to Vietnam, and she had barely known him. She met Pete Chiarelli in 1968, during her freshman year at Seattle University. Pete had drawn a high lottery number, so the draft was not an issue. But to pay for college, Pete, a butcher's son, had joined ROTC to help with the bills. Beth didn't even know what ROTC *was;* they never discussed it, and she never saw him in a uniform.

They married shortly after graduation, in a big Catholic ceremony in Portland. Pete's mother managed to pry out a piece of rice that had lodged in the ignition of her son's 1972 Camaro as the young couple tried to drive away. Neither Beth nor Pete had expected that he would stay in the military. A political science major, he dreamed of becoming a lawyer. But the promise of a three-year stint teaching at West Point and another two years to earn a graduate degree in international relations made a military career seem far more appealing to him. And it was clear to his superiors from early on that Pete Chiarelli would be a star in the army.

Beth loved being a mother—to two boys and a girl—and she and Pete regularly combined her passion for cooking with his for entertaining. She came to treasure and take pride in the military life. There were thousands and thousands of military wives doing the same thing, getting little outside recognition for the tremendous burden they bore during deployments. She loved her husband and was incredibly proud of his service—but what really made it all worthwhile, what made it *work,* she believed, was the sisterhood of army spouses that formed the backbone of the army, that held it all together.

Beth had spent years making her way into the sisterhood, and now in her fifties she finally felt confident enough to offer advice to the younger women. She watched as they struggled to come to terms with their roles and responsibilities. And she knew well the story of Pete's own father during his years as a soldier in World War II, a story that Pete had not discovered until he was sixteen. Pete was reading some yellowed newspaper clippings about his father's heroics during the war. The elder Chiarelli had received a Silver Star in 1945 for helping to remove a stuck tank while under enemy fire. At the bottom of the article, young Pete came across a line that stopped him cold: ". . . married to Dorothy Chiarelli." Pete ran upstairs to his father, whom he considered just shy of a saint, and said in shock, "Dad, this is *not* Mom! Who *is* this?" The elder Chiarelli sat his son down and explained that when he arrived home in Seattle after the war, he was greeted by his twin brother, who informed him that Dorothy had run off and was living with another man in town. Young Pete was stunned by the story, but he would never have had any desire to meet his father's first wife; he hated her for hurting his dad. His father harbored no such bitterness. In order to get a divorce in the Catholic Church, and remain in good standing in the Church when he remarried, he would have had to obtain an annulment; that would have required that the elder Chiarelli accuse his wife of adultery. He refused to do it; it was bad enough that his first marriage had been a casualty of the war, he reasoned. He didn't want to make things even uglier.

Living at Fort Hood more than a half century after World War II, Beth knew this was the kind of sad scenario that could happen in wartime, but she believed that open communication and a strong support system at home would make such trouble much less likely. All Beth really wanted to accomplish in her role as "first lady" of the division was to make things easier for the families on post and, in turn, of course, to help the soldiers.

Like Connie Abrams, Beth was able to talk to her husband regularly. The general had a direct line to his home, and when the phone rang in his now empty home office at Fort Hood, Beth knew who was on the line.

Just before the troops deployed to Iraq, the Chiarellis invited some of the officers over for dinner. Beth borrowed a large round table from the officers' club and squeezed in a good crowd. Gary Volesky, out of uniform and looking uncomfortable, arrived with his wife, LeAnn. Beth smiled when they came to the door, and stifled a laugh at the sight of Gary's skinny neck bound in a string tie for the evening. He was clearly not happy with his attire, or with the prospect of spending the evening at the home of his two-star commander. But Pete's ebullience and Beth's natural warmth put almost everyone who visited them at ease. At the end of the evening, as Beth started to clean up, Gary Volesky approached her. "Mrs. Chiarelli, I'm going to tell you something," he said. "I didn't really want to come tonight to the general's house. But I have to tell you: I had a really good time." Whenever Beth thought of Gary, she thought of that night.

Gary's wife, LeAnn, had felt the same unease when the evening began. With deployment only a few days away, she viewed outside parties as obligations—distractions that kept her from spending time with Gary. They had spent the last few days sitting on the couch, holding hands, and saying little. But that night, when LeAnn saw how happy her husband was around the soldiers with whom he'd soon be living, she felt better about letting go. She explained it to a friend:

"When you marry a soldier, you have to realize that he is married to the service, and that you are basically the other woman. You get your time with him when he is done with his duties and responsibilities with the service. And you cherish those times. You just have to take that to heart. And if you don't you are going to be a miserable, miserable person."

Once Gary had gone, LeAnn was less inclined to go to church, so when Sunday came and the church bells tolled, she simply rolled over. Gary and LeAnn took their faith very seriously, but LeAnn wanted to take it easy this morning and let Alex, her six-year-old son, sleep in. Besides, Alex had done plenty of praying the night before. Since his dad had headed to Iraq, Alex approached his prayers with near zeal.

Each night before bed, the boy would start off with a traditional prayer but then turn it into a prayer all about his father. "Please don't let Daddy get shot by the bad guys or get hurt or get killed." Or, "Please don't let Daddy get bit by any giant scorpions. Don't let him fall in a hole and get lost. Don't let him drown in the water."

LeAnn listened patiently to her son trying to cover all the bases, but she would sometimes interrupt his prayers to allay Alex's concerns. "Alex, there's not much water there for him to drown in, and there are no giant scorpions." Alex would glare at his mother unconvinced and continue. "Please don't let Daddy drown in a *little* bit of water; please don't let him get bit by a *medium* scorpion or a *little* scorpion." LeAnn took to calling these "the adventures and prayers of Alex."

She tried not to talk about what the boy's father was doing in Iraq, but when pushed she would just say, "Daddy is over there helping people."

Alex's nightly prayers would either make her smile or send her to bed in tears. Like many of the wives, she found that Sunday was the day she was most likely to break down. She understood both sides of military life—she'd been in the service herself, and left a few years before Alex was born. LeAnn liked to stay busy, and she would meet other wives for lunch and shopping outings or work on her numerous craft projects. When she didn't have plans she would start to get blue, and having Alex home from school over the long weekends could be exhausting. Having friends who had kids in the school on post, and husbands in the same unit—people who really understood what it meant to have a bad day when your husband is deployed—helped her keep sane. It also meant there was almost always someone willing to take turns with the kids. That way everyone got a break.

WHEN GARY AND LEANN VOLESKY moved to Fort Hood in May 2002 and Gary took command of his unit, the couple decided that this was going to be "an us thing," a chance for them to contribute and gain from the army experience. Like Connie Abrams, LeAnn devoted herself to being an FRG leader. She did everything from planning family barbecues and outings to counseling women who were depressed or having a tough time managing their jobs and families.

On this Sunday morning, Alex wandered into his mother's bedroom just before nine o'clock, his cotton pajamas stained with crayon and a soft sweat. LeAnn caught herself looking at his dark blond hair and vivid brown eyes, startled at how much Alex looked like his father. Gary Volesky often joked about his own rough looks, the angular face and sharp nose, yet Alex was an achingly appealing child to everyone who met him. LeAnn couldn't resist his pleas for her to hop out of bed and log on to the computer so he could write to his father. Alex had been born nearly three months premature, and at six years old he still could not read. But he would instruct his mother what to write—"Tell him I miss him very much and I love him very, very, very much and I want him to be very careful"—then watch intently as his mother would start to type. "No no no, not that," he would say. LeAnn would stop what she was doing and back up on the screen, even though she knew Alex had no idea what she was writing.

LeAnn didn't watch a lot of TV, but when she did it was never the news. That drove Connie Abrams crazy. "How can you not want to know everything that's going on?" But LeAnn didn't want to obsess more than she already was obsessing over her husband's deployment. She had already noticed a change in her husband's demeanor once he arrived in Iraq. "Lee, something's wrong," he told her. "It's not the way they said it was going to be." Gary had thought the mission would be nothing more than peacekeeping. Now he sensed instability. LeAnn hated to hear him sound edgy. He had good instincts and had made his own as-sessment of Sadr City. She knew Gary would have an even better sense of things once he took command.

She thought of that conversation from just days before while she dashed off Alex's e-mail to his father this Sunday morning. Her eyes locked on the time on the computer screen, and she counted forward. Nine o'clock in the morning in Texas, six o'clock in the evening in Iraq. The transfer of authority was over. Gary's long road home had officially begun.

A mile or so away, Connie and little Robbie Abrams were just arriving at the officers' club for brunch. Her dress still sticky from the heat, Connie looked up with a hoot when she saw her friends Kelly and Casey walk in with their children. "I've cor-rupted you," she said, noting their outfits. "You've come over to the dark side." Kelly and Casey had always kidded Connie about her affection for dark colors. On this steamy Sunday morning, as they sat down for their now ritual meal, all three women wore black.

Chapter 3

--- ★ ---

SUNDAY

AT

SUNRISE

≈ *0600 hours*

April 4, 2004

Sadr City

LIEUTENANT COLONEL GARY VOLESKY hadn't noticed the nearly full moon fading into the sand behind him. He was walking briskly toward his headquarters, toward the rising sun, which was just now sending faint sparks above the horizon. He had gotten up even earlier than usual this morning, grabbed some chow, and then headed back to the two-story sand-colored concrete building that was being set up to serve both as an officers' sleeping quarters and as his battalion's Tactical Operations Center, or TOC. Alongside it was an open concrete courtyard where the soldiers had planted a basketball hoop. Volesky mounted the metal stairs that ran up the outside of the building to the second floor.

In its incomplete state, the operations center consisted of only a large, boxy room whose walls were plastered with maps. In the center sat a single table covered with radios and more maps.

This was the day Volesky had been preparing for since the previous December. At 1800 hours, the 2-5 Cav—the battalion under Volesky's command—would officially take responsibility for Sadr City. A transfer-of-authority ceremony would be held in front of the headquarters, with Volesky presiding as the officer set to take command.

Ceremony notwithstanding, the authority transfer would be less than ideal. With the battalion that had been responsible for Sadr City for the previous year, the 2-2 ACR (Armored Cavalry Regiment), having left about a month earlier, and the unit that was to turn the area over to the 2-5 Cav that evening, the 1-2 ACR, having filled in only temporarily, Volesky, in fact, already knew more about Sadr City than many of the officers who were on their way out: He'd arrived in Baghdad nearly a month earlier with an advance team of senior staff, including his young intelligence officer, Captain Dylan Randazzo.

The 2-5 leadership team started having regular briefings on the situation in Sadr City as soon as they arrived, but Volesky and Randazzo wanted to know more and had made inquiries of their own. Each night the senior staff gathered to discuss what they had learned that day about the environment in which they would be operating and the challenges they were likely to face.

The more they learned about Sadr City, the more they realized that they had been deployed to a sprawling, critically important part of Baghdad that was in a state of flux. It no longer appeared to be one of the safest places in Baghdad. Volesky had come to understand that the 2-2 ACR had generally followed a hands-off policy in Sadr City. That would not be his approach. He was determined to know more about what was going on beneath the surface calm.

The new commander would have to wait his turn, however. Until 1800 hours, he and his men had essentially been guests of the 1-2 ACR, depending on them for accommodations and communications support. He was getting his own operations center set up, but he couldn't do much more until he had full command authority. He was looking forward to the transfer that evening for another reason: The battalion flag-raising ceremony would be good for the morale of the 2-5 soldiers who'd just arrived and didn't yet feel at home in their new post.

Even though he was not yet officially in charge, Volesky was wasting no time getting as many patrols into Sadr City as possible. Volesky was one of the most highly respected battalion commanders in the U.S. Army—smart, even cerebral, but with a true warrior's sensibilities. He was completely loyal to his soldiers. They knew it, and they would follow him anywhere.

Volesky wanted to understand Sadr City from within, to conduct the most effective military operations possible. Arabic-language training he had had years before added to his ability to get a sense of his surroundings. His intelligence officer, Captain Randazzo, a small, wiry Italian-American, was key to helping Volesky's team know what they faced. Volesky and Randazzo both had their suspicions that the year ahead in Sadr City could prove to be far more difficult than the past year had been. After the October 2003 ambush, during which a soldier was killed when scores of insurgents ambushed a scout platoon, conditions had reportedly stabilized. But in the past few days there had been a series of incidents inside and outside Sadr City that suggested tensions were rising again.

Captain Denomy's checkpoint confrontation during the Mahdi Army protest parade the night before was especially troubling in this regard; it had gotten Randazzo out of bed even earlier than usual in order to update his intelligence analysis. He'd been steeping himself in the nuances of Sadr City for several months, having begun even before the plans to send his battalion there had been finalized, but the reports he had read about the district were often contradictory and inconclusive. For much of 2003, in the aftermath of the U.S. invasion, the assumption had been that Sadr City was unlikely to represent much of a threat to U.S. forces. Because of the grievous suffering of this Shiite district under Saddam Hussein, U.S. officials had expected the population to be largely cooperative. If any Iraqis were to greet the Americans warmly as "liberators," surely Sadr City's population would be among them.

The October 2003 ambush had therefore come as a surprise. Since they hadn't yet identified Shiite militants as a problem in Iraq, the U.S. leadership hadn't established a plan of action to deal with such confrontations. When order was quickly reestablished in Sadr City, U.S. military operations had returned to a business-as-usual approach. American commanders had continued to focus on Saddam Hussein loyalists—or former regime elements (FREs), as the military called them—and paid little attention to the militants in Sadr City, and in any case, the place was quiet again.

The immediate future would depend largely on the actions and attitude of Moqtada al-Sadr, and his Mahdi militia. Al-Sadr, Randazzo learned, was only a middle-ranking Shia cleric, without the religious education or training to interpret the Koran and issue edicts, or fatwas. His authority in Sadr City derived only from his lineage. The 1999 assassination of his father, Mohammad al-Sadr, and his defiance of Saddam Hussein, were the reasons "Saddam City" had been renamed "Sadr City" after Saddam Hussein was removed from power.

In the years following his father's death, Moqtada al-Sadr had played brilliantly on his image and reputation to develop his own base in Sadr City, constantly expanding his power through a mixture of intimidation and outreach. The political organization he developed in Sadr City, known as the Sadr Bureau, soon overshadowed all other local governmental and community institutions, but beyond that U.S. commanders knew little about its workings or importance, even after spending nearly a year in Baghdad. What mattered to the U.S. military in the short run was that in the months following the October ambush, al-Sadr was able to maintain order in Sadr City, thereby permitting the overstretched American commanders to turn their attention to more overtly troubled areas.

In January 2004, two months before his unit's deployment, Dylan Randazzo had come to Iraq to do advance reconnaissance of the area. He'd read all the reports about the October ambush, which had been blamed on Moqtada al-Sadr loyalists, but the 2-2 ACR officers who briefed him insisted that the situation had calmed considerably in the intervening months.

Randazzo was somewhat reassured, and on his return to Fort Hood, he reported that Sadr City might not be quite as volatile as he had initially feared. But to be safe, Randazzo drew up what he called a "worst-case scenario," to be used as part of the battalion's preparation and training. It involved a platoon on patrol finding itself suddenly isolated and under fire in the city, surrounded by several hundred hostile insurgents, taking casualties, without communications, and in need of rescue. For a peacekeeping mission, Randazzo's scenario seemed a bit far-fetched, but as an intelligence officer, he had been trained to think in pessimistic terms.

Within days of his arrival in early March 2004, Randazzo saw that his worst-case planning had been time well spent. Moqtada al-Sadr was far more powerful and much less predictable than Randazzo and his fellow officers had originally believed. It was obvious that the Sadr Bureau had infiltrated every aspect of life in Sadr City. Though informally organized, the "Bureau" was the place to go for everything from jobs to building permits. The Iraqi police force trained under the supervision of the Sadr Bureau, and it was to Sadr loyalists that the police reported. The Bureau also oversaw schools, community activities, and the distribution of social welfare benefits. Whether or not al-Sadr commanded the respect and genuine loyalty of the population was not clear. Anyone who spoke out publicly against him faced severe punishment. Randazzo couldn't help noticing that al-Sadr was building a system of control in Sadr City that was not unlike that imposed by Saddam Hussein's regime. The Sadr Bureau employed section chiefs, who kept a close eye on the population in their areas of responsibility, much as Saddam's own spies had done during his rule. Al-Sadr's militia, the Mahdi Army, clearly ruled the district.

In their nightly meetings during those first weeks in March, Volesky, Randazzo, and the other battalion officers shared their Sadr City observations and insights, but the picture was maddeningly unclear. "In one area it seemed as if the majority of the people responded very well to our presence," Randazzo wrote. "In other areas there was a feeling that some of the people were more skeptical about us being there." The 2-5 Cav was up against the same problems facing the U.S. military across much of Iraq: a lack of knowledge about the true political situation and about the nature of potential military threats, compounded by a critical shortage of human intelligence from reliable informants on the ground.

Randazzo was getting more nervous by the day. The Mahdi

Army was becoming increasingly aggressive. The armed militia-men who guarded the Moshen Mosque were boosting their presence, expanding their perimeter of operations, and carrying more weapons. The local clerics were becoming demonstrably more anti-American in their Friday sermons and proclaiming loudly that the Mahdi Army was the force to be reckoned with in Sadr City. Randazzo reclassified the Sadr Bureau in his intelligence analysis from a "possible threat" to his battalion to a "likely threat."

If the 2-2 ACR units had erred in not responding to Moqtada al-Sadr and his increasingly aggressive posture, Volesky was deter-mined not to repeat the mistake, and he ordered more presence patrols around the Moshen Mosque as a show of U.S. force. At the nightly leadership meetings, he argued that the 2-5 patrols needed to be highly disciplined. The point wasn't to be confrontational, but to show that U.S. soldiers were alert and on guard.

During the last week of March, in the final days and hours pre-ceding the arrival of Volesky's full battalion, the situation in Sadr City took another turn for the worse. U.S. administrator Paul Bre-mer closed down the *Al-Hawza* newspaper. This prompted a noisy protest outside the newspaper offices by al-Sadr supporters, who chanted "No to occupation!" and burned a U.S. flag. New and much larger demonstrations followed each day, including the pro-tests that Troy Denomy had witnessed the night before that had brought ten thousand people into the streets. Equally troubling were the riflemen who had assumed sniper positions on some of the rooftops.

Randazzo reported that several of his new contacts were call-ing Sadr City "a volcano ready to explode."

As dawn broke over Sadr City on Sunday, April 4, Captain Randazzo huddled in the makeshift Tactical Operations Center to make plans for the day ahead. Volesky walked outside to the metal landing and surveyed his new surroundings. In the early-morning light the nearby buildings, the sand, and even the sky had the same parched yellow tint, blending together in a drab sepia tableau.

Volesky could see vehicles already beginning to move across the dirt field below him. He wanted to send out as many patrols as possible on sewage runs and other missions, but he knew it was a time for extra caution. He and Randazzo would go out themselves for a firsthand look, and they agreed to stay in touch throughout the day.

By mid-morning, the day had unfolded without event. Volesky radioed Randazzo. "Deuce," he said, "I'm looking around, driving all over the city, and everything seems normal. People are walking in and out of shops and selling things on the street. Are you getting anything different?"

"Negative," Randazzo answered. "I am not getting anything different, and the reports have been the same across the board."

In the early afternoon of April 4, Randazzo returned to the headquarters to be on hand when patrol leaders arrived with their situation reports and threat assessments. One by one, they came back with the same news: relative quiet, nothing significant to report. Relieved, Volesky turned his attention to the organization of his new operations center, where his staff was mounting map boards and installing antennae and other communications equipment.

At about 1700 hours a call came in to the operations center from Lieutenant Shane Aguero, whose platoon was one of the last still on patrol in Sadr City at this hour of the day. He radioed in to say that he had encountered some armed militiamen in the vicinity of the Moshen Mosque and confiscated some of their weapons. He needed guidance on how to proceed. Randazzo consulted with Volesky, who told Aguero to return the weapons to the militiamen if he had no reason to believe they were engaged in hostile activity. But Aguero was told to let the militiamen know they should limit their activity to providing mosque security within the perimeter. Aguero did as he was told.

At 1730 hours he called back and said he was ready to return to the base at Camp War Eagle. Volesky paused. With the transfer of authority only half an hour away, he wanted to confirm the situation in the city was under control. He gave Aguero one final order.

"Lieutenant," he said, "swing by the Sadr Bureau on your way back. Then report to me when you return."

Chapter 4

★

CONTACT

≈ *1600 hours*

SLUMPED IN THE PASSENGER SEAT of his Humvee, Lieutenant Shane Aguero fingered the thin chain pooled in the sweat of his neck. Although raised Catholic, Aguero was taking no chances. In addition to the gold cross and the Saint Jude medallion, a Hebrew mizpah dangled from the chain. Its jagged edge was a perfect mate for its twin, which his wife, Amber, wore. In addition, a rosary was stuffed into Aguero's right pocket and, in his left, the smooth stones of a set of Islamic prayer beads.

It was near the end of the daylong escort mission, an exhausting mission for the entire platoon. The soldiers had spent the day riding around in the two-and-a-half-ton steel Humvees, clanking hard through dumpster-sized potholes filled with sewage. The eighty-degree heat, the weight of the body armor, and the snug fit of the helmets only added to the discomfort.

At one point Aguero, in the lead Humvee, had glanced up to find a group of children pressing into their path.

"Whoa, whoa," Aguero said to his driver, Specialist Jonathan Riddell. "Easy!"

Aguero had lived all over the world, had seen his share of poverty. To him the kids looked the same in every down-and-out place on the planet—stained little hands signaling thumbs-up, hair matted red from the dust, smiles already marred by decaying teeth. It was a heartbreaking blend of innocence and the hard edge of a survivor's cunning. "Mister, mister," they shouted eagerly at the soldiers waving from inside the Humvees. These missions were part of what Aguero's brigade commander, Colonel Robert Abrams, called "community outreach."

It was pretty obvious what it was this community of two and a half million people needed most: sewers. The "what the fuck"— the soldiers' term for liquid waste—was splashing up over everything. The men called it "what the fuck" because the first time any of them had the disgusting experience of stepping, knee-deep, in it, they'd invariably shout, "What the *fuck?*" It quickly became soldier lingo in Sadr City, blending into one long word:

"Watch out for the *whatthefuck* on the right."

Sergeant First Class Jerry Swope, in the last Humvee of the four-vehicle convoy, had been deep in sludge all day. He was still stunned that the dilapidated outdoor markets sold vegetables, fish, and bread right next to streams of what was essentially the remains of the previous night's meals. Watching the big sewage truck suck up waste from goats, donkeys, humans, and God knew what else had left what felt like a marble of puke in Swope's throat.

This mission certainly hadn't been what twenty-three-year-old Sergeant Eric Bourquin had envisioned when he joined the army. Bourquin, riding in Swope's rear Humvee, had been living on his own since before his sixteenth birthday. A few years after he left home, in the middle of a late-night party, he had decided on the spur of the moment to join the army. For the *fun* of it. He loved the idea of being an infantryman and going off to a war zone. He had a strange fantasy that some bad Iraqi would take a few wild shots at him and his buddies sometime during his deployment—then it'd really feel like he'd been at war. Instead, he was stuck in Sadr City guarding truckloads of turds.

Communications problems had made today's patrol feel even longer. After leaving Camp War Eagle early in the morning, the soldiers had a hard time making contact with the Tactical Operations Center back at the base. By lunchtime, radio communication had worsened, so the soldiers returned to Camp War Eagle for a quick stop to fix the gear. It was a fortunate stop for Staff Sergeant Josh York, who had suffered through the morning with a bad case of "Mookie's revenge," the stomach ailment that seemed to strike every soldier new to Moqtada, or "Mookie," al-Sadr's city.

"Ready to roll!" someone yelled after the communications gear had been repaired and the soldiers had downed a quick meal. The convoy headed back out the gate so quickly that York was left behind, still doubled over in the latrine.

Once the convoy rejoined the three sewage trucks, the mission began to run into trouble. The townspeople had been threatening the Iraqi truck operators with verbal taunts and menacing gestures, and the Iraqi operators were getting spooked. The soldiers tried to reassure them, but at one point the Iraqis became so frightened that they tried to bolt. A near-comical scene followed—four American Humvees chasing three sloshing sewage trucks down a wide roadway.

The soldiers were eventually able to convince the drivers to get back to work. By late afternoon, though, the soldiers were ready to part ways with the Iraqis for the day, knowing the sewage escort was scheduled to run for the entire week.

"See you tomorow," Aguero told the drivers, through Jassim al-Lani, the interpreter.

The Iraqis shook their heads, speaking emphatically and conveying obvious apprehension.

"The fear is too great," Jassim explained. "They think they will be killed for collaborating with the Americans. They are all quitting."

At one level, Aguero would've been thrilled at the prospect of his sewage duty coming to a close; but the threats to the workers were disturbing. The platoon leader ordered his men to begin the ten-minute drive back to base, where he would report to his commanders what had happened.

Five minutes later, as they passed the Moshen Mosque, Specialist Carl Wild, in the second Humvee, saw a quick movement out of the corner of his eye. His staff sergeant was Trevor Davis.

"Sergeant Davis," he said, "I saw a guy back there with an AK-47."

Davis's response was immediate and emphatic. "Turn around," he shouted. "Turn this thing around!" His driver made a wide U-turn and headed straight back to the mosque. Before the Humvee was fully stopped, Davis jumped out and walked directly toward the man with the weapon.

"Come here," he screamed. "Come here right now! Put the weapon down! PUT the weapon down NOW!"

Jassim ran over to try to calm the situation. Stone-faced, the man with the weapon rocked back and forth, refusing to drop the rifle, staring with obvious fury at the soldiers, gradually backpedaling to the mosque behind him. Several other armed men emerged from the mosque.

"Security," they explained, with Jassim translating. "We are mosque security. We store the weapons in the mosque." Jassim also reported that the men seemed surprised to be confronted in this way, as though the rules of the street had somehow been changed. The platoon formed a horseshoe around the armed men, while an entourage of clerics retreated into the mosque.

Eventually Aguero was able to convince the men to turn over their weapons to an Iraqi police commander who'd been summoned to the mosque. But the scene remained extremely tense, so Aguero called back to headquarters to discuss the situation. From Volesky and Randazzo, he learned that the standing policy allowed Iraqis to carry weapons inside the courtyard perimeter of the mosque. Aguero explained that the first man had initially been seen outside the perimeter. Nonetheless, after a brief discussion about their options, Volesky instructed the lieutenant to return the guns. There seemed to have been no hostile intent, and Volesky preferred not to create trouble if it could be avoided.

Aguero did as he was told, apologizing to the Iraqis and explaining that he and his men were new in town and hadn't meant to overstep. But the effort to placate tensions seemed to have the opposite effect: As the patrol was leaving the mosque, Corporal Shane Coleman turned to see one of the Iraqis standing out front with a sword. With Coleman watching, he ran the blade of the sword inches from his throat, glaring menacingly at the Americans. The meaning was perfectly clear, and impossible to miss.

Aguero and his men were irritated by the order to retreat, having spent more than a few anxious minutes confiscating the weapons in the first place. So when Aguero told them they'd be making one more pass to check out the Sadr Bureau, thirty-four-year-old gunner Sergeant Eddie Chen seemed to speak for many of the soldiers.

"Fuck yeah!" Chen said. "Let's roll by there! It'll be great! We'll go piss them off!"

Aguero's platoon had been driving past the building periodically throughout the day. There'd been no violence or rock throwing, but the steely faces of the Sadr militiamen standing outside had sent their own message: The Americans should keep moving.

Now Aguero could see that the crowd in front of the Sadr Bureau had grown significantly, but as the convoy approached, the people scattered across the road. He saw a small group of men on the side making emphatic if contradictory gestures. Some were signaling for the soldiers to turn back; others seemed to be waving the platoon forward reassuringly.

Aguero thought it odd. He radioed Davis, in the vehicle just behind him, and told him to proceed. Davis acknowledged Aguero's command, then noticed something overhead. An enormous image of Moqtada al-Sadr was plastered to the side of one of the buildings. Its scale, and the sinister sneer on the cleric's face, held Davis's eye for several seconds.

By the time he looked back—in just that moment—everything had changed.

The streets were deserted; in no time at all, the people on the streets had vanished.

Where the hell did everyone go?

For the next hundred yards the Humvees proceeded along empty streets. Garbage blew past the pockmarked buildings. Colorful blankets hung on window ledges. But the people were simply *gone.* For what seemed the longest time, only the occasional sound of a barking dog or the bleating of a goat interrupted the silence.

Then SFC Swope, in the trail Humvee, heard something else. Short popping sounds. It took a second for his brain to acknowledge what his gut understood more or less immediately.

"Holy shit, man!" he said in his slight southern drawl. "Is that gunfire?"

Swope craned his neck toward the rear, looking for visual confirmation. He heard another burst of gunfire, heard, too, the almost instantaneous *ping* of bullets glancing off the side of his vehicle. Swope's Humvee was under fire.

It was now nearly 1800 hours. The transfer of authority was just minutes away.

Swope and Bourquin jumped into the street, along with several men from the other two Humvees—they'd heard the rounds and, when they saw Swope's Humvee stop, had followed his lead.

Another burst of enemy fire—probably from an AK-47—made it clear that Swope hadn't overreacted. "They're firing at *us!*" he yelled. He pointed to a wall across the street. "Over there, now! Return fire! Return fire!"

The soldiers raised their rifles—M-16s and M-4s—and began squeezing off rounds, pummeling the low concrete wall on their left, from where the shooting was coming. When the gunfire stopped momentarily, Swope moved around the vehicle, signaling to the men to form into teams—some crossing the street, others staying beside the vehicles to provide cover and support. They advanced now, weapons raised, the soldiers hoping to isolate and disarm the assailant or assailants—at this point they didn't know how many there might be—with the intention of taking them to the local Iraqi police station to be arrested. This was by-the-book, standard training-manual procedure.

But the militiamen weren't playing by the book. Once most of the U.S. soldiers were on the street, the militiamen opened fire again, this time from both sides of the street. Rounds were now ripping all around the vehicles. But it was impossible to see the shooters. Behind the wall? On the rooftop?

The soldiers were firing as soon as they heard a burst, but the bursts were everywhere, it seemed. It was clear they were greatly outnumbered. *Where have these people come from?* Swope wondered. *How has this happened so fast?*

IN THE LEAD VEHICLE, Aguero hadn't heard the rounds, and he had continued forward, unaware of what was happening behind him until several minutes had passed. Now he heard the gunfire; when he looked in the mirror, he saw that the three trail vehicles had lagged and were some twenty yards behind him and right in the middle of a firefight.

"Go back! Go back!" Aguero yelled. SPC Riddell jammed the Humvee into reverse and hit the gas, as Aguero got on the radio to the battalion's Tactical Operations Center.

"Lancer Fourteen, Lancer Fourteen, this is Comanche Red One!" Aguero said, using his call sign. "We are in contact! We are in contact!"

"Is it celebratory fire?" the TOC radio operator asked.

"No, this is no celebration. We are receiving fire. Repeat. We are receiving fire!"

Seconds later, Aguero saw a black-clad figure balancing a Soviet-designed belt-fed automatic weapon, sending a steady stream of bullets in rapid succession. The rounds started bouncing off the side of Aguero's vehicle. As Aguero's gunner, Eddie Chen, began returning fire, Swope jumped back in his vehicle to give his own update to the TOC.

"Where are you?" a battalion officer asked.

"On the north side of the Sadr Bureau, on Route Delta."

Swope then turned, opened the door of the Humvee, aimed his automatic weapon at an enemy position, and laid down a torrent of fire. Up front in Aguero's Humvee, Sergeant Chen was propped up against his .50-caliber machine gun, scanning the nearby buildings for movement. Chen was firing thunderous rounds at the rooftops, moving the turret from right to left and back again. Screaming profanities as he aimed, his upper body exposed above the Humvee, Chen gripped the big gun tighter, his body reverberating with each blast.

Up and down the line, the men in Aguero's platoon were returning fire almost continuously now, but the amount of incoming fire was increasing unabated. The number of visible enemy militiamen was rising too. Faces would appear on roofs, in alleyways, on the tops of buildings; moments later there'd be a muzzle flash; then the faces would disappear.

With rounds popping off on all sides, and the ranks of the enemy growing by the minute, Swope quickly realized the vehicles were providing limited protection to his dismounted troops. The sheer number of people—hundreds of them—firing at the platoon was astonishing. Swope had no doubt about the threat they faced, about the *reality* of it; even so, he couldn't help feeling like this was just a bad war movie. After all the drilling and training and rigorous preparation that came from fifteen years in the army, *this*—live rounds coming at him and his men—was worse than anything he'd ever imagined.

"Get back in the vehicles and let's get the fuck outta here!" he hollered. Aguero echoed the call. Swope had just shut the heavy door of his armored Humvee when the powerful smack of an RPG, or rocket-propelled grenade, a shoulder-launched weapon with the power to tear apart a tank, momentarily lifted the Humvee off the ground.

Barely audible above the gunfire, Aguero screamed into the radio: "Head north! Head north!" Swope and Aguero knew they had to keep the convoy moving forward—relying on training that taught them to "assault through the ambush"—to try to get out of what they perceived to be the "kill zone." The soldiers were badly outnumbered and in the open, but Aguero did not even consider turning the convoy back the way it had come.

When a pilot is caught in a thunderstorm, he's trained to fly straight through it rather than circling back around. Turning while inside the clouds only increases the amount of time spent in the storm. Shane Aguero, likewise, knew that reversing direction while in the kill zone was likely to put his soldiers at even greater risk. Yet one block farther into the kill zone there wasn't even a glimmer of blue sky on the other side. The platoon fired incessantly, yet the waves of people kept coming and the enemy fire intensified the farther north the Americans moved.

"Shit!" Eddie Chen yelled from the gunner's perch above the Humvee. "They're everywhere!" It seemed now that the whole town had come into the streets, armed for battle. Chen continued to fire, the deafening recoil of the .50-cal rattling the vehicle down to its axles, its huge expended shell casings—nearly five inches long—raining down on his comrades below.

Aguero grabbed the radio and called the TOC again. "We are taking heavy fire!"

One vehicle back, Staff Sergeant Davis, too, was astonished by the scale of the assault—hundreds and hundreds of people with weapons. He couldn't imagine it getting any worse.

But it could, and it did. The *ping* of small arms was suddenly punctuated by the smoking trails and concussive roar of a stream of RPGs. Small explosions were set off in trash piles, and hand grenades were being lobbed from above.

Along Route Delta, it was as though the people of Sadr City had taken everything from their houses, markets, and shops and dumped it onto the roadway to keep the convoy from moving. Kiosks, refrigerators, engine blocks, axles, rolls of concertina wire, wooden furniture, heaps of debris, and piles of rotting meat now made for a deadly obstacle course. Flaming piles of trash formed a red-hot wall along potential escape routes. Thick, putrid smoke rose from what an hour before had been a thriving marketplace.

It was becoming more and more obvious to Aguero and Swope that this ambush was part of a larger plan.

With tires now flattened by bullets and shrapnel, the vehicles lurched down the roadway, banging into curbs and piles of debris, as gunfire and grenades were directed at them from both sides of the street. The commanders and their drivers—Lieutenant Shane Aguero and SPC Jonathan Riddell in the lead; SSG Trevor Davis and nineteen-year-old PFC Derrick Perry following; Sergeant Stanley Haubert and PFC John Taylor in number three; and, in the rear, SFC Jerry Swope and SPC Joshua Rogers—tried desperately to navigate serpentine trails through and around the hunks and heaps that cluttered the road, all the while scanning rooftops and windows and alleyways in all directions and trying to maintain radio contact with the TOC.

"Go! Go!"

"Up there! Eleven o'clock ! Shoot at eleven o'clock!"

"Keep driving! Drive over it!"

"We are under constant fire!"

"Go! Go! Go!"

From his position in the lead, Aguero no longer had visual contact with the rest of his platoon. The big side mirrors on his Humvee had been blasted off, one still dangling by heavy wire. Up in the gunner's turret, Sergeant Chen continued shouting a string of profanities between bursts of his .50-cal. The noise was so intense that it was hard for Aguero to hear Swope over the radio.

"You good?" he yelled.

"We're okay. We're good," Swope replied. "Keep going. Keep going."

Aguero was about to respond when a deep, low thud reverberated in the Humvee. He felt something heavy drop into the vehicle right behind his seat, covering him in a spray of sweat and blood. Then he saw—it was Sergeant Eddie Chen.

"He's hit!" screamed Sergeant James Fisk.

Chen had landed facedown in the lap of Jassim, the Iraqi interpreter. Blood drained from Chen's nose and mouth in narrow streams.

"How bad? How bad?" Aguero shouted.

Fisk probed frantically for a pulse and found none. "He's not breathing, sir." The bullet had found its way through the side of Chen's protective vest, ripping and spinning through his upper body.

Jassim, trained in first aid, slipped his hand under Chen's body armor and found the entrance wound. Spreading his hand across the warmth of Chen's chest, he thought he felt a heartbeat—just one. Then nothing.

He knew Chen was dead—already he was turning pale—but Jassim tried to revive him. Fisk, meanwhile, jumped up to the empty gunner's position and began firing, the .50-cal still streaked with Chen's blood.

Unable to see behind him, Aguero now had no choice but to open the door and lean out of the Humvee. No other vehicles were in sight. Desperate to find the rest of his platoon, he got on the radio but got no response.

"Stop!" he yelled to Riddell. "Turn! Turn!" Riddell yanked the wheel to the right, rumbling up onto the sidewalk. Jassim held fast to Chen's body as it rolled with each bounce. Ten yards, twenty yards, and then the vehicle jolted to a stop. What looked like a large yellow hot dog stand stood in the middle of the sidewalk. There was no getting around it.

In the number-two vehicle, Sergeant Trevor Davis and the others were more than 150 yards behind Aguero. Davis had been trying to stay close to his platoon leader, but his M-998 Humvee, with its "add-on" armor, had far less power than Aguero's M-1114 armored version, which meant the M-998 couldn't make it over the obstacles or through them. Davis was watching the gap between his vehicle and Aguero's widen, when a round from an AK-47 pierced his front windshield. As PFC Perry yanked the wheel abruptly, the round ricocheted into the steel of Davis's

M-16 rifle. His hands were stung by bits of shrapnel but were still whole. But now the M-998 wouldn't move.

Swope pulled alongside Davis's vehicle. "Why're y'all stopped?" he yelled. "Let's go! Let's get out of here!"

"Sergeant, it won't go," Davis hurriedly explained. "We're stuck."

Swope saw the problem: The Humvee was wedged on a concrete barrier, the front wheels dangling just off the ground.

Swope called Aguero over the radio. "Number two is down," he said. Davis, meanwhile, started gesturing and yelling at the number-three vehicle. PFC John Taylor, the driver of number three, rolled forward, butted up against the Humvee in front of him, and set his foot to the gas. Davis's vehicle started to move, rocking forward with each push. It was working. The rear tires of Davis's Humvee were powering forward. His driver, PFC Derrick Perry, ground the gears, mounting a final surge up the barrier when the vehicle stopped moving completely.

The engine groaned to a halt; the electronics inside dimmed and went dark. In the back of the M-998, Staff Sergeant Darcy Robinson flipped the switches frantically to see if he could get it started. Still nothing. The vehicle was dead.

Aguero, still stuck behind that hot dog stand in the road, couldn't catch up to the rest of his platoon fast enough, and he didn't understand why the rest of the convoy wasn't following. Jumping out of the vehicle, Aguero sprinted more than a hundred yards through the sparks of AK-47 rounds to where the vehicles behind his Humvee had come to a halt.

Only then did he see the concrete block under Davis's M-998. With bullets and grenades all around him and a vehicle disabled, Aguero had to make a quick decision.

"Okay, move! Get out of there!" he yelled, ordering everyone from the disabled vehicle into the two others directly behind it. The soldiers were grabbing bundles of ammo, weapons, and water from the number-two Humvee when they noticed the engine of number three starting to smoke. Taylor pressed lightly on the gas, and the engine dropped like a bomb from the chassis. It lay burning on the sidewalk.

"Un-fucking-*believable!*" shouted Aguero.

Aguero and Swope scrambled together a plan. Under continuing fire, with two vehicles now inoperable—and four flat tires on the two Humvees that were still running—the situation was desperate, the options limited. What should have been an easy ten-minute drive had turned into mass chaos. His soldiers were battered and shell-shocked; several were wounded, at least one of them gravely.

Aguero told Swope to call the TOC for guidance. As Swope grabbed the radio, a young soldier approached with what seemed the obvious solution.

"Whatever we do, sir," he said, "we have to get the fuck off the street."

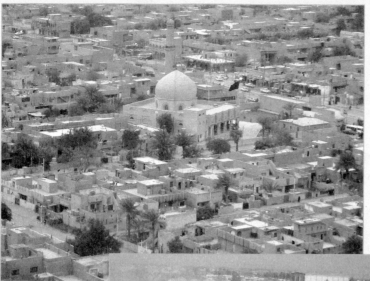

Sadr City— where more than 2.5 million people live in a six-square-mile area. (U.S. ARMY PHOTO)

Camp War Eagle. (PHOTO BY MARTHA RADDATZ)

Members of Moqtada al-Sadr's Mahdi militia drive through the streets of Sadr City, 2004. (PHOTO BY SERGEANT FIRST CLASS REGINALD BUTLER)

U.S. Humvees along Sadr City's Route Delta in the summer of 2004. Raw sewage still lines the streets. (PHOTO BY MARTHA RADDATZ)

An open LMTV truck—already taking gunfire, its right rear tire flattened—enters Sadr City on Route Delta at sunset on April 4, 2004. Staff Sergeant Robert Miltenberger, who will later receive a Silver Star for his heroism, can be seen facing outward on the right side, just behind the vehicle's cab. He is administering first aid to Private First Class Lucas Fournier and Specialist Tomas Young, whose lives he will be credited with saving. In the back of the truck, his face visible, Sergeant Robert Chivas opens a packet of bandages. On the left, with his weapon pointed outward, is Specialist Matthew Milks, and in the gunner's turret is Specialist Loren Haller. Eleven of the sixteen men on the truck were wounded, many of them seriously. Tomas Young was left paralyzed. (PHOTO BY WATHIQ KHUZAIE/GETTY IMAGES)

Tanks line one of Sadr City's main roads days after the April 4 battle. (PHOTO BY SERGEANT JOHN WANCZOWSKI)

Sadr City children run past a burning U.S. Humvee of Lieutenant Shane Aguero's pinned-down platoon on Route Delta. Aguero and his soldiers have taken refuge nearby. (PHOTO BY AHMAD AL-RUBAYE/ AFP/GETTY IMAGES)

The alley where Lieutenant Aguero's platoon was pinned down. The house where the men took refuge is the tallest brick structure on the left. (PHOTO BY LIEUTENANT COLONEL S. JAMIE GAYTON)

Lieutenant Shane Aguero at Camp War Eagle, 2004. (PHOTO BY STAFF SERGEANT LEE ANN SUNN-WAGNER, U.S. AIR FORCE)

Sergeant Benjamin Hayhurst on the alleyway rooftop, moments after being shot in the shoulder, April 4. (PHOTO BY SPECIALIST CARL WILD)

Specialist Carl Wild (left) and Sergeant Eric Bourquin at Camp War Eagle after their extraction from the alley. (COURTESY SPECIALIST CARL WILD)

The aid station at Camp War Eagle on the morning of April 5. Soldiers sift through piles of bloody boots, helmets, uniforms, and body armor belonging to the dead and wounded. (PHOTO BY LIEUTENANT COLONEL ROBERT GERHARDT)

Lieutenant Colonel Gary Volesky in Sadr City, 2004. (PHOTO BY MARTHA RADDATZ)

Major General Peter Chiarelli and Lieutenant Colonel Gary Volesky in Sadr City. (U.S. ARMY PHOTO)

Gina, Troy, and Merrick Denomy, 2004. (COURTESY DENOMY FAMILY)

David and Rhonda Mathias with sons Levi (left) and Reuben. (COURTESY MATHIAS FAMILY)

Specialist Stephen "Dusty" Hiller with his newborn daughter, Storm, in October 2003.
(PHOTO BY LESLEY HILLER)

Sergeant Eddie Chen (in turret) and Sergeant Eric Bourquin departing Kuwait for Iraq, March 30, 2004.
(COURTESY SERGEANT ERIC BOURQUIN)

Corporal Forest Jostes in Sadr City.
(PHOTO BY LIEUTENANT JOSEPH ESENSTEN)

Specialist Ahmed Cason (left) and Sergeant First Class Reginald Butler at Butler's house, Fort Hood, Texas, before departing for Iraq.
(COURTESY SERGEANT FIRST CLASS REGINALD BUTLER)

Specialist Robert Arsiaga.
(COURTESY FIRST CAVALRY
DIVISION)

Specialist Israel Garza.
(COURTESY FIRST
CAVALRY DIVISION)

Sergeant Michael Mitchell.
(COURTESY BILL MITCHELL)

*Specialist Casey Sheehan (left)
and Specialist Justin Johnson at
Fort Hood in 2002.* (PHOTO BY
LIEUTENANT JOSEPH ESENSTEN)

Lesley Hiller (holding flag) is comforted after the funeral of her husband, Specialist Stephen Hiller, April 14, 2004. (AP IMAGES)

Sergeant Eddie Chen's gravestone at Arlington National Cemetery. (COURTESY MICHAEL PATTERSON)

Sergeant First Class Jerry Swope (facing camera, left) and Staff Sergeant Robert Miltenberger (facing camera, right) are presented with their Silver Star medals, September 30, 2004. (U.S. ARMY PHOTO BY SPECIALIST ERIK LEDREW)

Memorial service at Camp War Eagle on Sunday, April 11, 2004. The helmets and boots are those of the seven soldiers from the 2-5 Cav who were killed on April 4. The eighth soldier killed on that day was from C/2-37, First Armored Division. (PHOTO BY LIEUTENANT JOSEPH ESENSTEN)

Chapter 5

★

THE

RESPONSE

≈ 1800 hours

ONLY MOMENTS AFTER OFFICIALLY taking command of
his battalion—a transfer of authority suddenly stripped of cus-
tomary ceremony—Lieutenant Colonel Gary Volesky sat huddled inside his Tactical Operations Center, listening to the sounds
of war. Each frantic radio transmission from Lieutenant Shane
Aguero and his men was punctuated by the lethal, pounding gunfire now ripping through the platoon.

It was the third such transmission that left Volesky reeling.

"Attention, TOC!" barked Major Alan Streeter, Volesky's operations officer. "Quiet!"

Through the static of the radio came the voice of the platoon
sergeant first class, Jerry Swope. "We have one urgent casualty,
two vehicles that won't move, and we're under heavy fire!" Swope
paused. "What's the guidance?"

Charlie Company commander Captain Troy Denomy was at

the TOC for the battle update briefing. Shane Aguero's platoon, known as "Comanche Red," was one of three platoons under Denomy's command. The captain had seen Aguero out the gate that morning. These were his soldiers in danger, and when he heard Swope's report, he didn't hesitate.

Denomy grabbed the radio. "Abandon your vehicles and establish your defense," he ordered. "Get off the street!" The two remaining Humvees would help provide cover for those soldiers whose vehicles were now inoperable. The vehicles would move alongside the men until the platoon could find a location to set up a defense.

"We're coming for you," Denomy assured his men. "Help is on the way."

LEANING OVER a large map spread on the table before him, Volesky traced the platoon's location through a fine layer of dust. Aguero's platoon was equipped with a GPS-guided system that would ordinarily relay its precise location to a monitor in the operations center. But because the battalion had just arrived, the tracking device hadn't yet been connected to headquarters. Instead, Volesky was using the simple grid coordinates the platoon had given when they first reported hostile fire.

He was grateful, at least, to have all his company commanders, including Captain Denomy of Charlie Company and Captain George Lewis of Alpha Company, there with him in the TOC, but he could not believe this was how they were all spending the first moments of their command. *Already we've got contact, we've got casualties, we're planning a rescue mission.*

Volesky turned to Denomy and Lewis. "Get your guys ready," he said. "Fast."

Outside headquarters, the movement had already begun. Staff

Sergeant Joshua Rountree was closely following the radio traffic at the Charlie Company command post. The temporary post consisted of nothing more than two Bradley fighting vehicles with their rear ramps down and a tent between them. As soon as Rountree heard the conversation between Captain Denomy and SFC Swope, Rountree knew that a rescue was imminent and that the designated Quick Reaction Force for the evening, the "Comanche Blue" platoon, had to be notified immediately. Without waiting for confirmation, he began to pack up.

"Get everyone ready," he yelled, "'cause I know Captain Denomy's gonna want us to roll!" Rountree spotted Staff Sergeant Josh York, who'd been with Aguero's platoon earlier in the day but had been bent over in the latrine with stomach trouble when the convoy went back out.

"Hey, York!" Rountree yelled. "Come over here and listen to this radio. It's your guys in the city!"

Lieutenant Clay Spicer, the twenty-five-year-old executive officer for Charlie Company, was in his quarters, a conference room he shared with other young officers, when Denomy radioed him. "Red Platoon is getting ambushed, and I need to get out there," Denomy said. "Get a vehicle ready." Spicer could hear it in his captain's voice. This was *bad*.

Spicer leaped off his cot and threw on his combat gear. Earlier in the day he'd accompanied Denomy on a series of get-acquainted visits to police stations and government offices in Sadr City; Spicer, who had arrived several weeks before Denomy, was helping his company commander get the lay of the land. Now Denomy would be going out again, this time prepared for a fight. Spicer ran to the motor pool to begin assembling convoys for the rescue run into the city.

As soon as Volesky ordered the rescue mission, Captain George Lewis bolted down the stairs to tell his platoon leaders to get men, equipment, and vehicles ready to move. It was a far cry from what Lewis had assumed he'd be doing that night. Lewis, the commander of 2-5's Alpha Company, had expected the evening's battle update to be another tedious staff meeting. A few days earlier Lewis had e-mailed a friend. "Our nightly meetings are sucking the life out of me. Every night at 1800 or 1900 we have a meeting that lasts two to three hours. That's one thing our battalion is very good at—having lengthy meetings." Lewis had risen through the enlisted ranks to become an officer, but he still identified closely with enlisted soldiers. He had scant patience for the endless reporting requirements and staff consultations that went with so many command positions.

Lewis returned to the TOC after talking to his platoon leaders and squeezed in next to Denomy, Volesky, and the others to discuss the evacuation plan.

"I want all units to move into the city along a single corridor," Volesky explained. They'd estimated the distance from the base to the stranded platoon to be about four miles; Volesky felt that traveling on one corridor would limit the risk of another unit becoming stranded. Once the rescue teams made their way to the vicinity of Aguero's platoon, they would approach from different angles in order to secure the streets surrounding the area.

Volesky's instructions were interrupted by another call on the radio.

"Lancer Fourteen, Lancer Fourteen!" It was SFC Swope again. "We have a litter-urgent soldier in need of immediate medical care!" Everyone in the TOC knew Swope to be steady under pressure. The trace of emotion in his voice provided an additional, unstated piece of an already urgent message: There was a soldier who might not make it. The men in the TOC didn't yet know that it was Eddie Chen, or that the Iraqi interpreter was desperately trying to revive him, but they now knew that someone was in very bad shape.

Volesky glanced down at the floor. "Litter-urgent" meant that if help didn't arrive the soldier would be dead within the hour, perhaps sooner. Never before, in twenty years in the service, had Gary Volesky lost a soldier in combat. Back at Fort Hood he'd given reassurances—in his mind, *promises*—to look after these men and to bring them all back home. His command was just minutes old, and he already felt he'd broken that promise.

But there wasn't time for regret. Not now. What was needed was a plan that would result in the rescue of Comanche Red platoon. Volesky did not want another radio call like the one he'd just heard.

The evacuation of the nineteen men in the platoon would be a major mission, involving hundreds of soldiers. "We have to overwhelm them," Volesky said, turning to the assembled officers and aides. "I'm going in myself, behind Charlie Company. Get me A-Train and Martinez," referring to his driver, Sergeant Michael Adkins, and his gunner, Staff Sergeant Matthew Martinez. This was an operation the battalion commander wanted to direct from the scene as much as possible. Captain Dylan Randazzo, who was doing his best to keep the intelligence flowing, told Volesky he wanted to come along to relay the latest information back to the TOC. He told his deputy, Lieutenant James Egan, to take charge of the TOC intelligence shop, and he began to gather his gear. Egan stopped him and looked Randazzo directly in the eyes.

"Sir," he said, "you know you can't go. We need you here."

Frustrated, Randazzo hurled his equipment into a corner. He knew Egan was right, but Denomy was a close friend, and this could be tough combat, and Randazzo wanted to be at his buddy's side.

He spotted Denomy across the room and walked over to embrace his friend. "Good luck, man," he said. He didn't need to say how much he wished he was going along. Denomy could see it in his eyes.

VOLESKY NEEDED to be certain his superiors were apprised of the situation, but it was an awkward chain of command. He was now officially in charge of his battalion, but the higher-ranking officers in the First Cavalry Division had yet to take charge. The 2-5 Cav was part of the First Brigade, the brigade commanded by Colonel Robert "Abe" Abrams, which was in turn under the First Cavalry Division, commanded by Major General Peter Chiarelli. Because First Brigade would not assume responsibility for the area until April 10, Volesky reported to the Second Armored Cavalry Regiment, assigned to the First Armored Divison. That meant that even though their soldiers from the First Cavalry Division were in a firefight, Major General Chiarelli and Colonel Abrams could only observe the action until their counterparts from the previous unit transferred command. But both men were of course well aware of the battle that was under way. Chiarelli was temporarily headquartered in a huge tent at Camp Liberty, the sprawling U.S. military base on the west side of Baghdad. Abrams was closer to Camp War Eagle, but he was still about four miles away, due south of Sadr City. The TOC called Abrams at his headquarters, Ironhorse base, to tell him Aguero's platoon was in trouble. Within twenty minutes the colonel and nine of his soldiers were roaring up the road toward Sadr City, pushing the Humvees to sixty miles an hour. He would not be able to direct the fight, but Abrams wanted to be with his soldiers.

Abrams radioed Chiarelli at Camp Liberty to pass on the news.

"Sir, 2-5 got into a fight," Abrams said. "There's at least one kid who is in bad shape, and his platoon is still pinned down."

Like Abrams, Chiarelli instinctively wanted to take command, but he was temporarily subordinate to Major General Martin Dempsey, commanding general of the First Armored Division. But these were the soldiers Chiarelli had brought over from Fort Hood; they were his responsibility. He told Abrams to call him back the moment he reached Camp War Eagle. Breathing deeply, Chiarelli, a powerful presence in his desert camouflage and high suede tanker boots, walked outside the tent to compose himself. He was an enormously emotional man. The thought of even one soldier dying ripped him apart. Chiarelli called Major General Dempsey, offering his support and assuring Dempsey he was comfortable with whatever decisions he made. "I know my soldiers are in good hands with you, Marty." Chiarelli walked back inside the tent and straight to the radios, listening intently for news from the rescue teams.

Volesky also had his staff place a call to Lieutenant Colonel Robert White, whose tank battalion had been patrolling Sadr City for the last year, and was holding a position at the old Martyr's Monument on the south end of Sadr City. Volesky requested they send a patrol north toward Aguero's platoon. The Crusaders (a long-standing name for the company, but controversial in Iraq, to say the least) acknowledged the call and promised to ready their Quick Reaction Force—QRF—without delay.

The 2-5 QRF back at Camp War Eagle, Charlie Company's Third Platoon, under the command of Lieutenant Dan Hines, left the base first—"balls to the wall," as Hines ordered. Denomy's own convoy pulled out a couple minutes later. The convoys headed southwest on the street the U.S. military had designated Route Aeros, skirting the eastern edge of Sadr City. Specialist Seth

Wiebley was driving Denomy's Humvee. They would travel about two miles, then turn right onto Route Florida into the heart of the city. Lieutenant Colonel Volesky and his team—including his headquarters commander, Captain Darrel Gayle—were right behind them. Volesky had left his operations officer, Major Alan Streeter, and Major Martin Dannat to track the battle from the TOC and oversee the preparation of the additional convoys, including Captain Lewis's Alpha Company. With their fellow soldiers in danger, hundreds of soldiers at the base were clamoring to join in the rescue mission.

A wide gray veil of smoke hung over Sadr City as Volesky sped down Route Aeros, his driver trying his best to keep up with Denomy's convoy. The faint sounds of gunfire echoed in the distance. With the sun beginning its descent, Volesky was still trying to imagine what his units were about to encounter. As he was pulling out of the front gate at Camp War Eagle, Major Streeter had radioed from the TOC with the latest news: An Iraqi police liaison had just called to say that the Mahdi Army, Moqtada al-Sadr's militia, had taken over all the police stations in Sadr City.

Volesky was no longer dealing with an isolated ambush of a single platoon; he was facing a coordinated citywide assault. What had begun as a rescue mission would now have to be conducted as a full counterattack to retake the police stations as well. Volesky was sending his troops into urban combat against God only knew how many heavily armed insurgents. And darkness was approaching fast.

Chapter 6

——— ★ ———

THE AID
STATION

—————

1810 hours

CAPTAIN DAVID MATHIAS WAS TRYING to coax himself to take another bite of the gray lump on his plate when he saw a group of soldiers, six or seven of them, heading out of the chow hall with radios close to their mouths. They were talking quickly and moving even faster, looking as if they were heading for something important. He shook his head—probably a broken-down truck or a visiting general.

Mathias went back to navigating his plastic fork around the flies. It wasn't the young doctor's nature to get mad, complain about the food, or yell about the heat, the flies, or being away from his wife. But this place could push anyone's patience.

The food *was* awful, no question about it. *Exactly what is this I'm eating?*

He'd been in Iraq for only four days and still couldn't quite grasp what he was doing there. He was a pediatrician, not a combat doctor. He had never even seen a gunshot wound, and he had no experience treating serious traumatic injuries. Mathias took care of the *children* of soldiers, not the soldiers themselves. And he had only ever done that in the safety of a U.S. Army clinic back in the States. His most trying days had been spent vaccinating wailing infants or stitching up the bumped foreheads of whimpering toddlers. He was a soldier, yes, but you'd have never known it to look at him. Fresh-faced, lean, quick to smile, he looked like a tall child playing army in his father's camouflage. Even at thirty, Mathias radiated innocence, with huge brown eyes beneath long lashes.

The son of missionaries, David Mathias had joined the army to help pay for his seven years of medical education in Michigan. He had liked the idea of serving his country, but as a pediatrician he had never imagined he would be deployed and certainly had never thought he'd see a war zone.

It was at a dinner with several other army physicians and their wives just before the invasion of Iraq that the reality hit. One of the doctors, the son of a four-star general, told his friends that his father thought they'd all be over in Iraq soon. It came like a punch to the gut for Mathias. He couldn't eat another bite. His wife, Rhonda, pregnant with their first child at the time, could barely speak. Every day after that, he would get nervous going to work, expecting his orders would come. Every time Dave called home, Rhonda feared it was to deliver bad news.

The call finally came in 2003, a little more than a year ago, and now, here he sat in Sadr City, while Rhonda was back in El Paso expecting their second child. They wanted a large family and were determined not to let the deployment slow them down. And they'd been blessed—Reuben had just turned one, and "Sibby" (the name he and Rhonda used for Reuben's soon-to-arrive sibling) was due in seven months.

Dave and Rhonda were the best of friends. Skeptics needed to be around them for only a few minutes to see how well matched they were. They hated being apart, and before this deployment they had never been separated for more than a few weeks. The loneliness ate at both of them; they found the strength to endure it through their faith, through daily prayer.

What was making this separation even more difficult for David Mathias was the kind of work he was doing. It seemed a waste of his training: There were hundreds of thousands of kids outside the gates of Sadr City who could use his help, but his job was to stay at Camp War Eagle. There had been minimal injuries in the previous year, and from what he'd been told, they could expect more of the same. So Mathias figured he'd be spending his year treating intestinal problems, dehydration, insect bites, and the like.

There had been some moderately good news, though: Improvements were being made to the aid station where he worked. The squat block of concrete had only one exam room, no flooring, and no windowpanes. But the commander had requested the building be doubled in size; at the moment it could hold only eleven patients at a time. The expansion was a long way from being finished, however.

ANOTHER COUPLE of soldiers ran across the chow hall; before Mathias could figure out what the trouble was, somebody yelled. It was another of the battalion doctors.

"Doc! Doc, we need you! Some soldiers have been hit in the city." Mathias dropped the rest of his dinner into the trash and headed to the aid station.

CHAPLAIN RAMON PENA was on his way to a staff meeting when he saw Lieutenant Colonel Volesky leaving his evening battle update. Pena noticed he looked ready for battle himself, dressed in full combat gear and moving toward a line of Humvees. The battalion commander approached the chaplain and, speaking in almost a whisper, said that soldiers had been injured—one was possibly dead—and that Pena should go to the aid station to wait. Stunned, the chaplain mumbled a prayer as Volesky headed off, then started looking around for the small medical facility. Camp War Eagle had barely been set up, and the place still confused him. Pena wasn't sure which way to walk. "Excuse me, the aid station? Where is the aid station?" he asked in his thick accent to more than one passing soldier before being pointed in the right direction.

As Pena approached the aid station, the insignia of a cross stitched on his uniform, a small group of soldiers called him over—a rescue team, moments away from heading into battle. "Sir, will you pray with us?" the soldiers asked. The young men were pale and frightened—not fearing death so much, but more afraid of how they would perform in battle.

Pena bowed his head, his hands clutching the shoulders of the men next to him. They prayed for courage. They prayed for strength. They prayed for the soldiers now pinned down in Sadr City. Then, in a slow, comforting voice, the empathy plain on his face, he concluded:

"Give us the angels you have promised and bring peace to these soldiers as they go out. In the name of the Father, the Son, and the Holy Spirit. Amen." As Ramon Pena watched, the soldiers hurried off to their vehicles, each with an automatic weapon slung over his shoulder.

THE FIRST PERSON Pena saw when he entered the aid station was David Mathias. Pena, originally from Venezuela, had been transferred to Fort Hood shortly before deployment; Mathias had been training in El Paso. They were friendly but didn't know each other—or anyone, really—very well. The chaplain did have experience with emergency medicine, though, having worked in a hospital in Chicago, where trauma and chaos were a daily occurrence.

Mathias was feeling unsettled, trying to prepare himself for what lay ahead. *I have no idea what is about to come through that door,* he kept thinking. Mathias was moving around the aid station with the other doctors and medics, organizing supplies, laying out surgical gloves, and going through boxes of medicines that had yet to be unpacked. There was only so much they could do.

CAPTAIN TRENT UPTON was the S-1 officer charged with personnel, readiness, and management, which this evening essentially made him responsible for overseeing the aid station. Though they'd never had what would pass for a crisis situation, Upton had to be prepared to record who came into the aid station, who left by helicopter, who died, and who walked out. If there were any casualties, it would be Upton who would put together the reports, which would then wind their way through the ranks. Eventually a casualty assistance officer, back in Fort Hood, would use that report as the basis for the difficult task of contacting next of kin. With the Internet and twenty-four-hour news services, every effort would be made to ensure that the spouse or a family member was notified as soon as possible.

Rumors were already circulating; Upton didn't know what to believe. Could somebody really be dead? Who might it be? And how many more were injured? Ten minutes before, Upton had been waiting to make a telephone call to his wife so he could wish her happy birthday. Now he was waiting for wounded. He tried to prepare himself for the horrors that might soon be confronting him, but he just couldn't imagine that a soldier in *his* battalion was dead. Was it a friend?

MATHIAS AND PENA exchanged a few words with Upton and then walked outside to the front of the unfinished building, kicking up dust as they paced back and forth. Piles of gravel, a rusted cement mixer, and stacks of floor tiles had been left outside by construction crews. The fading light was bringing down the temperature after a steamy day. The men were quiet, looking off into the distance, when they began hearing sounds of gunfire. They each knew they were listening to a battle.

That's when it hit the chaplain: *We are in a war.* And the casualties of war, the wounded soldiers who soon would be coming toward him, would make that reality even clearer.

Chapter 7

★

THE

ALLEYWAY

1810 hours

THE GUNFIRE GREW STEADILY WORSE as Shane Aguero sprinted along Route Delta, ducking behind vehicles and debris, then moving forward again, his rifle raised, as shards of concrete sparked and sprayed from the impacting fire all around him. He knew he had to find someplace secure where his men could establish a defense, and find it fast. Then they'd try to hold their position till the QRF arrived.

He saw it, off to his right: an alleyway, perhaps about seventy-five feet from where his two disabled M-998 Humvees were sitting, smoking and shot to hell on one of the city's main thoroughfares. The lieutenant screamed back to his men—eighteen total, plus the interpreter, Jassim, some pulling equipment and ammo out of the vehicles, the others laying down cover.

"Get everybody fuckin' out of there! Let's go! Into the alleyway!"

The two Humvees that were still operable were the up-armored M-1114s—Aguero's, which had been in the lead, and Jerry Swope's, which had been bringing up the rear of the convoy. Flat tires notwithstanding, they started moving forward to pick up the men from the broken-down vehicles. There was room for only ten or twelve of the men—the others would have to run alongside the Humvees, stooping for cover as they made their way to the narrow alley. But several soldiers chose to go on foot, taking their chances, rather than ride in Aguero's Humvee. Aguero's gunner, Sergeant Eddie Chen, dead or very nearly so, was still in the back of the vehicle, spread across the lap of Jassim, the interpreter, who was still making a futile attempt to revive him. To the soldiers, Chen was a perennially upbeat soldier who woke up every morning belting out country-and-western tunes. The men preferred not to climb into a vehicle where Eddie Chen's blood was sloshing across the floorboards.

Specialist Justin Bellamy, gunner in the disabled third vehicle, ran toward Swope's Humvee. In his haste to get to safety, Bellamy had left his big M-240 machine gun inside the M-998 Humvee. Swope stopped him with a shout.

"Hey, Bellamy, your weapon!" A look of sheer terror crossed Bellamy's face when he realized he would have to run back to get it. "We'll cover you," Swope shouted. "Run!"

Bellamy doubled back and, fast as he could, pulled down the high-powered machine gun, then sliced the strap that attached the AT-4, an antitank weapon, to the side of the Humvee. The M-240 fired up to 950 rounds per minute; the AT-4 fired armor-piercing rockets; this was firepower they'd need and, just as important, weapons they couldn't afford to have fall into the hands of the Sadr supporters. Trevor Davis had the same thought about the radios: Reaching inside the vehicle, he disabled the built-in communications gear as he'd been taught, zeroing out critical coded information. Then he grabbed the AT-4 from Bellamy

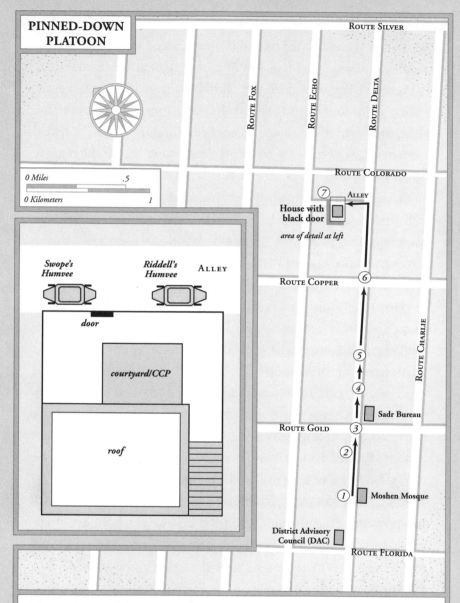

PINNED-DOWN PLATOON

ROUTE SILVER

ROUTE FOX

ROUTE ECHO

ROUTE DELTA

ROUTE COLORADO

⑦ ALLEY

House with black door

area of detail at left

ROUTE COPPER

⑥

ROUTE CHARLIE

⑤

④

Sadr Bureau

ROUTE GOLD ③

②

① Moshen Mosque

District Advisory Council (DAC)

ROUTE FLORIDA

0 Miles .5
0 Kilometers 1

Swope's Humvee   Riddell's Humvee   ALLEY

door

courtyard/CCP

roof

---

1. Lieutenant Shane Aguero's platoon encounters armed men at Moshen Mosque, but no shots are fired.

2. The platoon is first hit with enemy fire.

3. The soldiers head north to escape what is now a kill zone.

4. Sergeant Yihjyh "Eddie" Chen is hit.

5. Staff Sergeant Trevor Davis's Humvee dies when it hits a concrete block. The soldiers are forced to abandon the vehicle.

6. A second Humvee breaks down; all soldiers head for an alley off Route Delta.

7. Specialist Jonathan Riddell leads the platoon to the first *black* door.

© 2006 Jeffrey L. Ward

with a grunt and hoisted it onto his back, along with two boxes of ammo. The weight of it all left him bent over at the waist.

Aguero directed Riddell to pull his Humvee into the alleyway, yelling from the street: "Stop at the first door after you take the right, the corner building." A corner building offered a broad view of the streets below and a far greater area from which to lay down fire.

Riddell rounded the corner and turned his armored Humvee into the alley. It was a colorless street, lined with small concrete houses and beat-up cars. A tangle of bootlegged electrical wiring ran every which way, swaying overhead from homemade wooden poles. Riddell began looking for a black door—in the chaos of the street, he'd misheard Aguero's order. Riddell found it hard to concentrate, his legs shaking and his friend dying in the seat behind him, after gasping for air his lungs wouldn't hold. So instead of stopping at the first door, as he had been told to do, Riddell drove ahead, certain Aguero had told him to find a *black* door. Which, to his great relief, he found—the fourth doorway, more than two hundred feet down the alley. *A black door, the first black door.* If Riddell hadn't spotted this black door on the left, he probably would've kept driving until he found one.

Riddell maneuvered his Humvee into a blocking position on the east side of the door. Moments later, Swope's hobbled Humvee turned up the alley, bouncing and scraping against the cars parked just two or three feet on either side before it came to a stop in front and to the west of the black door.

Trailing behind were Aguero, Swope, and the others, moving across Route Delta and into the mouth of the alleyway, returning fire when possible, as grenades popped from rooftops and small-arms fire rained down from every direction. It seemed that hundreds of eyes were watching, but all from the shadows. There was no other traffic on the street, and the shuttered businesses on this main roadway were lost in a smoky haze of trash and burning tires.

Trevor Davis and Shane Coleman took up the rear, scanning rooftops as they worked their way along the narrow roadway. An Iraqi sniper came at them from street level, firing off a few high-velocity rounds before ducking out of sight on Route Delta. He was a persistent shooter. Between bursts, Davis and Coleman zig-zagged back and forth along the alley until they reached Swope's Humvee. Here they set up to return fire.

"Come on, motherfucker," Coleman muttered, lining up his automatic weapon. "Come around, come around."

Davis put the heavy antitank weapon he'd been carrying into the back of Swope's Humvee and grabbed the M-240 machine gun. His hands still tingled, streaked with blood from the round that had hit his M-16. He braced himself against the Humvee. Then, the instant the sniper came around the corner, Davis delivered a heavy stream of lead. The Iraqi twirled right, then left, and fell, his rifle clattering beside him. Davis had been firing his weapon repeatedly since the ambush, but mostly at unseen targets. This was the first time he had aimed directly at another human being and watched him die; he was surprised at how little it troubled him. He had three kids at home—maybe that was the difference, knowing that it was kill or be killed. Nothing theoretical about it. He'd shot the man, and he was happy about it. So was Coleman.

"Yeah! Sergeant D!" he said, high-fiving Davis. "That's what I'm talking about!"

RIDDELL'S BLACK DOOR was metal, about five feet across and five feet high, attached to a wall of concrete about a foot taller. Beyond the wall, a small courtyard led to the entrance to a three-story house. Gray concrete; everything in Sadr City was concrete, Riddell thought. Shane Aguero, baffled initially that Riddell had failed to stop at the corner, soon realized that this was an ideal spot. It was one of the tallest buildings in the alley, which gave them good sight lines of the street below in both directions.

The gunfire had diminished somewhat when the platoon first headed into the alleyway, but now the enemy had regrouped, and the intensity of the fire was starting to pick up again. Aguero instructed four of his soldiers to secure the house with Jassim's help. That's when he realized Jassim was still sitting with Sergeant Chen's body more or less on his lap, trying to revive him, though it seemed clear he was gone. He waved Jassim over, and the interpreter gently moved Chen aside and climbed out of the Humvee. Aguero put a hand on his shoulder—Jassim was soaked through with Chen's blood—and explained the urgency of the situation. As Jassim headed toward the black door, Aguero instructed the platoon medic, Specialist Pedro Guzman, who had been in a different vehicle when Chen was struck, to take over tending to the gunner.

Jassim, shaken but determined to help, took up his position, while the soldiers banged hard on the metal door. "Open up! Open up!" he shouted in Arabic. After a moment he repeated, "OPEN UP!" The soldiers echoed the order in English.

There was no response.

"Open the fuckin' door or we'll break it down!" Still nothing. Standing entirely exposed to the gunfire, without body armor or helmet, Jassim mustered all the volume and authority he could.

"LET US IN OR WE'LL KILL YOU!"

Shane Aguero counted to five and then moved.

"Clear it! Clear it now!" Aguero shouted. Sergeant Eric Bourquin pointed his weapon, blew off the lock, and busted down the door. Staff Sergeant Darcy Robinson, Sergeant Benjamin Hayhurst, and SPC Joshua Rogers followed him over the threshold, rifles cocked. The men scanned the room.

Two Iraqi men stood frozen in panic; three small children sobbed and shook in the arms of an old woman. From an adjacent room, several other women could be heard whispering urgently. Despite the rain of gunfire and grenades at the end of the alley, the family had just sat down for their evening meal. Some still sat hunched over steaming plates of food, terrified and pleading. One of the men offered water to the soldiers, but Bourquin pushed him back. With a badly wounded soldier just outside the door and an assault still under way, the sergeant was raging with adrenaline. He didn't trust them. The soldiers forced the men to the floor, binding their wrists and ankles and moving them into a back room. The women and children were hustled into another part of the house, under guard but not restrained.

Bourquin, Robinson, Jassim, and several others then went room to room, methodically looking through the house for weapons and possible enemies. Once they cleared the second floor, they spread out and began setting up defensive positions.

"I found access to the roof!" Robinson yelled to the men below. A stairway led to an open third-story space surrounded by a short sand-colored brick wall. For the first time, Aguero felt they'd caught a break: The roof would provide a strong defensive position for the platoon, and the four-foot wall offered a bit of cover as well.

The soldiers began hauling ammo and guns inside the house, and a "casualty collection point" was set up in the narrow courtyard, a place to coordinate care for the wounded while they waited for evacuation.

IN THE ALLEY, the two armored Humvees pulled within several feet of each other to form a tight defensive box, noses pointed inward so the gunners could have a clear shot at either side of the alley. The walls along the alleyway provided cover from the north and south, assuming the neighbors didn't join the fray. Sergeant Swope remained in the passenger seat of his M-1114, updating the Tactical Operations Center with coordinates. "We're parked down an alleyway left off of Delta as you head north. We are still under fire." The message behind Swope's dispatch to the TOC was simple: *You need to get us out of here*. Coleman stayed up top in the turret behind the .50-cal, facing Route Delta, where the enemy was concentrating, and where the noise of artillery and grenades was growing louder and louder. Shane Coleman gripped his weapon tightly, feeling that this situation was about to get a whole lot worse.

Swope glanced over at the second Humvee and saw SPC Riddell jump from the driver's seat and run around to the back passenger door of the vehicle. Riddell was calling urgently for help. Before Swope could move, Sergeant Bourquin bolted from the house; together they carried Sergeant Chen out of the vehicle. Chen's body armor and helmet had been removed, revealing a wide red stain across the front of his desert camouflage uniform.

The two soldiers struggled to carry the two-hundred-pound sergeant inside, his head and arms bouncing in a dead man's flail. Without emotion Swope keyed his radio and relayed Chen's status to the TOC: "We have one soldier probable KIA."

Bourquin and Riddell carried Chen across the small courtyard to the casualty collection point. They had not heard Swope's radio transmission, and even if they had they would have ignored it. Bourquin leaned close to Chen.

"Wake the fuck up, Chen," Bourquin yelled.

Riddell, hands shaking, tilted Chen's head back, pinched his nostrils, and blew one, then two short breaths through his parted lips.

Placing the heel of his hand in the center of Chen's chest, Riddell pushed hard and fast. "One, two, three . . . One, two, three . . ."

Inside the house, high-pitched laughter came from a television—cartoons of some kind. The sound enraged Eric Bourquin.

"Turn that shit down!" he screamed, to no one in particular. Then he turned back to his comrade and begged him to respond.

"Fuckin' wake up, Chen, man! Chen, wake up!"

Riddell began the mouth-to-mouth again. None of it did any good. There was no sign of life. Pedro Guzman, the medic, told Bourquin and Riddell that he would continue the CPR, even though Guzman knew it was too late.

JUST OUTSIDE THE COURTYARD, Lieutenant Aguero spotted Staff Sergeant Stanley Haubert holding a hand aloft, his fingers bloodied and dangling unnaturally.

"Aw, shit," Aguero said.

"Sorry, sir."

"Can you shoot?"

"No, sir."

When he was first wounded—the round came through the windshield of the Humvee, and his fingers were sliced through by the shattered glass—Haubert had managed to hold it together. But now he was quaking with fright. Aguero tried to persuade him to go inside and stand watch over the Iraqi family, but Haubert couldn't move.

Guzman came over to tend to Haubert's hand. Aguero caught his eye, nodded toward Chen. Guzman just shook his head. "There's nothing we can do," he said.

Aguero walked over to Chen's body. A small potted plant, droopy and dried out, sat on the western side of the courtyard. The door to the house, battered by his soldiers when they forced their way inside, hung awkwardly from its hinges. Sergeant Chen lay uncovered on a small patch of dirt in the shade, a smear of blood near his mouth.

Shane Aguero fingered the set of rosary beads in his pocket, and knelt next to his gunner. He didn't seem like a real human being anymore, Aguero thought. This wasn't Eddie Chen—this was just a body. Aguero placed his thumb on Chen's forehead, made the sign of the cross, and bowed his head. *I'm sorry, Chen. I'm so sorry.*

But Aguero did not linger. Guzman had brought Chen's body armor and helmet in from the Humvee; it lay beside the body. Aguero grabbed it and went to find Jassim.

"Here, use this," Aguero said, handing Jassim the body armor before returning to the alley. The Iraqi slipped his arms into the heavy vest, relieved to have the protection. He didn't even notice the deep red stains across the vest—he was already covered in Chen's blood anyway.

From the roof, Bourquin saw Jassim putting on Eddie Chen's body armor and helmet and was momentarily outraged. *What the fuck is he doing? One, it's Chen's, the guy's still warm! And two, Jassim's no soldier; he's not even an American.* He'd heard too many horror stories about supposedly trusted interpreters selling you out. But then he remembered the image of Jassim working so hard to keep Chen alive. Truth was, Jassim had done just as much as anyone. He was right there with the soldiers when they kicked in the door of this miserable little house. And hadn't he grabbed Chen's weapon in the Humvee, trying to offer whatever fire support to the Americans that he could?

Hell, Bourquin thought, *if the guys driving the honey wagons are afraid of getting the shit kicked out of them for working with the Americans, how bad must it be for an interpreter?*

As Aguero helped Jassim tighten the bottom of the vest around his slim frame, Bourquin shouted down some good news.

"I can see everything from here," he said. "We have the rooftop secured."

Most of the platoon had now moved up to the roof, firing on whatever target they saw. Trevor Davis hauled an M-240 up the stairs together with all the ammo he had pulled from the disabled vehicles, passing small cloth-covered windows as he climbed. There were two M-240 machine guns now mounted on the roof. But Davis was still without a personal weapon—his M-16 had been disabled by that bullet.

"Go down and get Haubert's weapon," a soldier yelled. "He's not using it."

Davis headed back downstairs and saw Haubert leaning against the wall in shock, eyes bulging, bright white. *He's out of it,* thought Davis. He grabbed the M-16 out of Haubert's bloodied hands. "I'm taking this," he said. Haubert didn't try to stop him. Davis mentally subtracted Haubert from the number of soldiers now in the fight. With Chen dead and Haubert unable to shoot, that left sixteen soldiers, plus Jassim, who had Chen's weapon at the ready.

Three soldiers remained in the alleyway: Swope and Coleman in one Humvee, and gunner James Fisk in the other. Swope's Humvee had the only radios that could still communicate with the TOC. He'd been told by headquarters to abandon the vehicles and get inside the house; it was an order he respectfully chose not to follow.

"I gotta let you know what's happening," he explained. "I gotta be able to talk to you."

Swope could also radio the soldiers on the roof, but they were hoarse from yelling into the Motorolas over the sounds of gunshots and grenades. This was especially true of Bourquin, who kept shouting, "Have you made contact? We need the Quick Reaction Force. Call in the fucking QRF."

For twenty minutes or so, the enemy fire from the streets had been intense but wildly off the mark. But then the tactics changed. Small children, younger than ten, started poking their heads around the side of the building. If a U.S. soldier started to rise from a position on the roof or lean out the door of the Humvee, a child would point at the soldier, tracking every move with a finger. The child's gestures would be followed shortly by shots, aimed right at where the child was pointing.

"Peekers," the soldiers started calling them. "We got a peeker at two o'clock." It was a strategy that Aguero knew well. It had been used in countless conflicts.

But the enemy tactics were not always so clever. Specialist Joshua Rogers spotted someone on the street below coming around the corner with what appeared to be an AK-47. Rogers was momentarily stunned by his lack of guile. *What is this guy doing? Does he not realize he's out in the open?* When the Iraqi steadied himself, took aim, and fired on the platoon, Rogers quickly shot him. *What an idiot,* he thought. Moments later a woman rounded the corner, gathered up the rifle from where it lay next to the dead man, and started firing. Rogers shot her, too.

Aguero saw the sequence. *This is ridiculous,* he thought. He didn't feel bad for the man and woman, he couldn't believe their stupidity. Who the hell would grab a weapon from the same spot where someone had just died?

He saw more movement, and this time his heart fell. A young boy scrambled out of hiding and ran to the middle of the alley, grabbed the AK-47 in his gangly arms, and aimed squarely at the soldiers. He never got a chance to fire. Aguero felt sickened that the child had been placed in that position.

The grenade fire had now become heavy, with one landing behind the concrete wall in the casualty collection point in the courtyard. Haubert, still in shock, was moved inside the house. Sergeant Bourquin ran downstairs and carried Chen's body to a room near the front door. Bourquin spotted a long black burka hanging on a clothesline nearby. Having finally accepted that his friend was dead, he placed it over Eddie Chen's body.

IN THE ALLEYWAY, where Swope, Coleman, and Fisk held a position in the Humvees, the small-arms fire had picked up once again. Swope was communicating with someone on the roof when he heard Coleman yell.

"I'm hit!" he shouted.

"Where?" Swope asked. "Are you bleeding?"

"I'm hit! I'm hit! In the leg!" Coleman repeated.

Swope quickly scanned his gunner's clothing, but saw nothing. He asked again: "Are you bleeding?"

By now Coleman had done a check of his own body. His camouflage uniform was torn, but the bullet had struck the Gerber knife he kept strapped to his right thigh. The five-inch blade was shattered, but it had prevented the bullet from entering Coleman's leg. Now the gunner revised his assessment. "Well, no, I guess I'm not hit!"

"All right, then," Swope said. "Keep firing."

But the shot sparked an idea in Sergeant Fisk, who was in the adjacent Humvee with just an M-16, his .50-cal no longer working. The enemy was starting to come from all sides and all directions, more and more of them. *There are so many shooters,* he thought. Maybe he could take out more of the enemy if he mobilized, moving his vehicle up and down the alleyway, firing—drive-by style—at one side then the other.

"Whaddya think?" he hollered to Sergeant Swope.

"Man, get your dumb ass behind the gun and stay put," Swope said to Fisk. "We're in the best place we can be."

The enemy started hopping from one adjoining rooftop to the next, getting closer and closer to the platoon, lobbing grenades, squeezing out five or six rounds of rifle fire, and then ducking for cover, only to pop up again a few minutes later. This was the hell of urban warfare: The enemy knows the streets and every conceivable place to hide.

Davis was starting to wonder if they would ever get off this roof. The platoon had been under attack for more than thirty minutes and there was no sign of a rescue. Then Sergeant Benjamin Hayhurst—who had been firing from a crouched position near the outer wall of the roof—went down.

"Sergeant D, I'm shot. I'm shot!" He had been hit in the shoulder—it wasn't life-threatening but was bad enough that he couldn't keep firing. Davis told him to lie flat on the roof.

Aguero ran down to see if Swope had heard anything.

"Yeah, sir, I got great news," Swope said sarcastically. "The rescue team is receiving fire over on Route Bravo."

Aguero and Swope had the same thought. Route Bravo was miles from the alley. This assault reached far beyond the alleyway. Forty minutes after the first shot was fired, the platoon now had three wounded and one dead. That left fourteen soldiers and an Iraqi interpreter to face down hundreds if not thousands of armed fighters. Swope stared at Aguero from inside the bullet-pocked Humvee. He looked up to the rooftop, where the light was starting to fade. "It's gonna be a long night, sir."

Chapter 8

★

THE RESCUE: CHARLIE COMPANY

1815 hours

THE SOLDIERS OF CHARLIE COMPANY had been called to the rescue team so quickly that some were caught struggling to zip up camouflage pants or lace calf-high boots as they stampeded toward the motor pool. Others were discarding plastic plates of food as they ran. About half the soldiers had been inside the mess tent for evening chow when word came that First Platoon had been ambushed; the rest of the men had been hanging around outside the tents, still trying to get their bearings after arriving in Iraq only days before.

Clattering vehicles surrounded Captain Troy Denomy as his soldiers pulled on bulky body armor, adjusted Kevlar helmets, and made final checks of their weapons. Denomy would lead the rescue convoy. The men in the pinned-down platoon were from Charlie Company, *his* company. *His* responsibility.

"We gotta go," Denomy shouted. "We gotta *GO!*"

The battalion's Quick Reaction Force—Lieutenant Dan Hines's Third Platoon—was already on its way to Sadr City, speeding out of the gates of Camp War Eagle minutes before everyone else. Denomy's soldiers would follow close on Hines's heels.

Denomy, in the lead, was riding in an M-998 Humvee with add-on armor, but his vehicle had no roof, just a canvas top fastened to the frame. If they were cornered in a serious firefight, Denomy and his crew could be cut to pieces. As the company commander, Denomy would not normally be in such a vulnerable vehicle or in the lead of the convoy, a position that offers less protection in a fight. But for this mission Denomy insisted on being first in line, in a vehicle that would give him the best view possible. He was not thinking about personal risk.

As the last of his soldiers hauled themselves into their vehicles, Denomy gave the signal to move. His driver, Specialist Seth Wiebley, pulled through the gate and turned left. Sitting behind Denomy was his executive officer, Lieutenant Clay Spicer, and Staff Sergeant John Dumdie, a squad leader from the Third Platoon who was there to provide additional combat power. Specialist Leeton Burkholder crouched in the open back of the Humvee, behind an M-240 machine gun bolted to the bed.

Denomy wasn't exactly sure what route Hines had taken, and he hadn't yet located him on the radio. Normally the First Cav entered the city by heading south from Camp War Eagle on a road the U.S. military called Route Aeros. Nobody bothered to learn the Iraqi names of the roads; instead they were overlaid with an alphabetical grid of English-language names (there was Route Aeros, which ran parallel to Route Bravo, followed by Routes Charlie, Delta, and so on). After several miles, patrols heading for the center of Sadr City would make a right turn onto one of the east-west streets (these were generally named after U.S. states

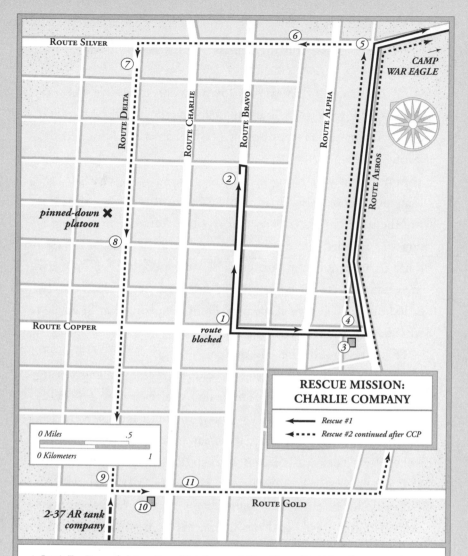

ROUTE SILVER

⑥

⑤

CAMP
WAR EAGLE

⑦

ROUTE DELTA

ROUTE CHARLIE

ROUTE BRAVO

ROUTE ALPHA

ROUTE AEROS

②

**pinned-down ✖
platoon**

⑧

①

④

ROUTE COPPER

**route
blocked**

③

**RESCUE MISSION:
CHARLIE COMPANY**

⟵ Rescue #1

◄∙∙∙∙ Rescue #2 continued after CCP

0 Miles 5

0 Kilometers 1

⑨

⑪

⑩

ROUTE GOLD

**2-37 AR tank
company**

© 2006 Jeffrey L. Ward

1. Captain Troy Denomy finds Route Copper blocked at the intersection with Route Bravo and encounters heavy gunfire. His convoy heads north on Bravo.

2. Because of the large number of wounded soldiers, the convoy turns around to establish a casualty collection point.

3. Denomy and Lieutenant Colonel Gary Volesky secure CCP #1. The wounded are sent back to Camp War Eagle.

4. Sixteen fresh soldiers, led by Staff Sergeant Alfonso Miranda and Staff Sergeant Robert Miltenberger, join the convoy. They try a different route and move north up Route Aeros.

5. The soldiers are hit with heavy fire on Route Silver.

6. Denomy calls for the Bushmaster cannon.

7. Miltenberger and his soldiers sustain heavy fire and numerous injuries.

8. The convoy accidentally passes the pinned-down platoon.

9. The soldiers must change course because the 2-37 AR tank company is attacking up Route Delta.

10. Denomy and Volesky establish a second CCP.

11. The men return to Camp War Eagle.

or precious metals), and then cross Routes Bravo, Charlie, and Delta.

Whatever names they were known by, the roadways were always bustling, with noisy lines of beat-up trucks and overloaded buses belching exhaust into crowds of people who clogged the thoroughfares.

But not today.

Captain Denomy had made only three trips into Sadr City, but from the moment his convoy turned onto Aeros he knew something was wrong. There were no people on the streets, no sign of life in the shops or houses. The only people Denomy saw were grim-faced families in battered cars, and they appeared to be headed out of town, as if fleeing. Denomy glanced at Specialist Seth Wiebley and frowned.

"This is not good," he said quietly.

Wiebley grunted, pushing the vehicle as fast as it would go along the deserted streets. Trailing Denomy were two more Humvees followed by a pair of LMTVs—light medium tactical vehicles, military terminology for what were essentially open-back supply trucks. Each truck was packed with soldiers armed with M-4 or M-16 rifles. Next came two more Humvees; a pair of M-2A3 Bradley fighting vehicles brought up the convoy rear, their steel tracks clanging noisily and raising clouds of dust in their wake. As tracked vehicles, the Bradleys couldn't move as fast as the Humvees, and before long they were trailing far behind.

DENOMY DIDN'T BOTHER to check the side-view mirror; the Bradley crews, he reasoned, could take care of themselves. His eyes were fixed on the road ahead, and he was thinking of Swope's last radio transmission, calmly but urgently emphasizing that his platoon was in trouble and needed to be rescued right away. De-nomy wondered what his company was heading into.

Counting the tanks Lieutenant Colonel Volesky had requested from Martyr's Monument from the south, and the two Bradleys at the end of his convoy, the battalion commander was reasonably comfortable that he had enough armor. And the Charlie Com-pany soldiers certainly didn't lack for motivation—they were go-ing in to rescue their own. So on the face of it, they seemed outfitted to face down a hostile enemy force.

The question Denomy didn't have a handle on was *How many enemy are there?* What was the size of the force they'd encounter? Initially he'd assumed the ambush had been an isolated event. Now he was getting a very different feeling.

Off to Denomy's right, a boy played alone on a sidewalk, a momentarily reassuring sight. Then a woman, covered head to toe in black robes, dashed out from a doorway, scooped the boy in her arms, and quickly disappeared into the house, slamming the door shut behind her.

"The shit is about to hit the fan," Denomy said to his crew.

He picked up his radio and alerted the vehicles in the convoy to prepare for contact. The soldiers in the four Humvees behind him heard his transmission and nervously fingered their wea-pons. But because the LMTVs were designed for transporting soldiers and supplies, not for combat, there was no radio commu-nication to warn those men. And even if there had been—even if the radio message got through to the drivers and commanders in the cabs of the LMTVs—the men in the back would not have received the word.

The soldiers riding in the back had only their own helmets, blast glasses, fire-resistant Kevlar gloves, and Kevlar vests, each outfit-ted on the front and back with ceramic SAPI plates, small-arms protective inserts. A few soldiers had throat protectors snapped to the top of their vests, but not everyone had bothered to wear them. One of the trucks had some extra armor on the side, but the second one was entirely unprotected.

"Route Copper is coming up ahead, sir," Lieutenant Clay Spicer said. Spicer had arrived in Baghdad three weeks earlier, and Denomy made sure he came along on this mission to help him keep his bearings in the still-unfamiliar environment.

At the intersection with Route Copper, Wiebley spun the Humvee hard to the right, tires squealing, and headed west. The plan was to follow Copper into the middle of the city, then turn right on Delta. Shane Aguero's platoon was somewhere up there, a few blocks to the north. Now they were driving into the heart of Sadr City, past nondescript two- and three-story apartment buildings, each one home to dozens of families. When Denomy had passed through this area on earlier visits, it had been mobbed—pedestrians dodging cars and motorbikes, street vendors lining the streets, and children running in every direction. Now nothing moved, save the trash in the breeze and a few mangy animals. A huge, sprawling neighborhood of 2.5 million people had suddenly fallen eerily silent.

Where is everyone?

Denomy watched two men peek out from behind a metal gate and then quickly pull back inside. Up ahead, several cars raced down the street to the west, away from the convoy. Denomy had the radio in his hand, ready to advise the battalion of his progress, when he heard a distinct *POP!* Then another, and another.

None of the men in Denomy's vehicle had ever been shot at before, but they'd been quietly bracing for this since leaving Camp War Eagle.

"Okay, here it comes!" Denomy cried, clutching the radio.

"Lancer Fourteen, this is Comanche Six," Denomy said. "We're on Copper, and we have contact."

UNBEKNOWNST TO TROY DENOMY, Lieutenant Colonel Gary Volesky and his Humvee crew had rolled out of Camp War Eagle just after Denomy's convoy left, and had caught up with the trailing Bradleys. Volesky had also noticed how empty the streets were, and assumed some kind of warning must have gone out to the population to stay indoors. When he heard Denomy report that his vehicle was coming under fire, Volesky leaned forward and peered out his windshield, scanning the rooftops for snipers but finding none. Up ahead, the two Bradleys at the tail end of Denomy's convoy were just making the turn onto Copper. Volesky's driver, Sergeant Michael Adkins—A-Train—followed them.

CRRAAK! CRRAAK! The shooting started immediately and from every direction. *POP! POP! POP!* It was as if someone had signaled: *The trail vehicle has turned onto Route Copper. Commence firing.* At the head of the convoy, Denomy's driver floored the gas pedal, hoping he could drive through the mess. In what seemed like just a few seconds, the gunfire had gone from an occasional shot to a steady barrage.

Denomy did his best to return fire, but the windows on his Humvee opened only partly, so it was difficult to get his M-4 in a good position to fire. And there was little to aim at. Denomy saw an AK-47 slide over the edge of a roof, rattle off a burst of rounds in the general direction of the convoy, then slide back. Through the windshield, Denomy could see bullets—scores of them—peppering the street ahead of his vehicle. *My God,* he thought, *it's like rain pounding a puddle.* Denomy glanced up at the canvas roof on the Humvee, which offered about as much protection as a cheap umbrella. The rounds that were hitting his vehicle could quickly kill him or his gunner or—worse—his driver. They had to keep moving.

"Close your window!" he yelled to Seth Wiebley. "You're the one guy in this vehicle who absolutely can't go down!" Denomy had his M-4 out his window and was shooting at muzzle flashes. It was the best he could do—it was impossible to spot the people on the rooftops who were actually firing at them.

"Over there!" Spicer shouted, pointing. "In the alley!" Denomy turned and saw a dozen men in black uniforms with green scarves on their heads holding automatic weapons. Spicer fired in their direction, but the Humvee was moving so fast he had a hard time getting off a clean shot.

TWO BLOCKS BACK—behind the Bradleys, rumbling down Route Copper—Lieutenant Colonel Volesky had his passenger-side window open partway, leaving just enough room for him to stick his M-4 over the top. He was holding the radio microphone in his right hand, staying in nearly constant touch with Major Alan Streeter at battalion headquarters and with SFC Swope in the alley. Volesky would fire, shout into the radio, and shoot again, holding the weapon out the window with his left hand braced against the door frame. Talking and shooting. Talking and shooting. Though he was holding the gun with only one hand, his fire was steady. The gun's hot brass casings ejected directly into his face, leaving bright red marks on his cheeks before dropping into his lap.

Volesky by now knew that one of his soldiers in the stranded platoon was dead, and at least two were injured. The men were in danger of being overrun by the enemy at any moment, and there was no telling how long their ammunition would hold out. Swope was Volesky's only link to the platoon, and he was sitting, exposed, in the Humvee. Charlie Company would have to fight its way to reach the platoon, and the alley was still at least two miles away. Sadr City, the place Volesky had come here to rebuild, was now enemy territory. The mission in Iraq had suddenly changed.

THE CONVOY OF VEHICLES stretched out in front of Volesky illustrated precisely the imperfect assumptions that had gone into the planning of U.S. military operations in Iraq. The Humvee (high-mobility multipurpose wheeled vehicle) was the U.S. military's standard ground transport, designed for use over all types of roads, in all weather conditions. The lightweight, open-topped variety like the one Captain Denomy was using seemed ideal for getting around a big city like Baghdad, where U.S. forces were expected to be carrying out a wide variety of "civil affairs" and reconstruction missions. The two LMTV trucks that followed Denomy were also effective transport vehicles, rugged and high-performing, and they fit right in with the civilian traffic clogging Baghdad streets.

The two Bradleys directly in front of Volesky, on the other hand, were fearsome killing machines. Heavily armored and highly maneuverable, they were designed to take infantry soldiers into combat and provide the firepower to back them up. The First Cavalry Division was equipped with a vast array of Bradleys and tanks, but the U.S. Army leadership and the Office of the Secretary of Defense at the Pentagon had concluded that a lot of heavy armor would be inappropriate for a "stability" operation like the one being carried out in Iraq. Under army orders, the division brought only a fraction of its standard armor component for the 2004 deployment in Iraq.

The stated mission was to focus on improving the quality of life for the people of Sadr City. To do that, the soldiers would need to interact effectively with the native population. Driving around in Bradleys, the men would have been cut off from civilians; furthermore, the dangerous weaponry of the Bradley, if employed, could inflict heavy damage on the people and the infrastructure of any city. Above all, perhaps, they would have sent signals—both overt and subliminal—of potentially hostile intent. The Bradley had therefore been deemed an inappropriate choice for Sadr City, a bad fit.

But now—fifteen minutes after taking command—so much had changed. A rescue mission like the one Volesky was now directing in these suddenly frightening streets and alleyways was essentially incompatible with the idea of a stability operation. This was urban combat, a scenario envisioned during the original Iraq invasion more than a year earlier, but not since. In this case, extra protection and firepower were urgent necessities. Looking at the column of Humvees and open trucks in front of him, Volesky could think only of how vulnerable his soldiers were. Of the thirty vehicles he had at his disposal at Camp War Eagle that afternoon, only ten were Bradleys. Three were trucks. Seventeen were Humvees, and of those only eight were M-1114s, the fully armored Humvee outfitted with ballistic glass. The rest were M-998s like Captain Denomy's, built for noncombat use, with at most a little armor added on the sides.

And yet there wasn't any question about the right course of action. Volesky had no choice but to proceed with what he had available.

Jerry Swope was on the radio again from the alleyway. With Sergeant Matthew Martinez making such a pounding racket with his M-240 machine gun, Volesky could hear only intermittently. But he knew there was really just one question on Swope's mind: When could he and his fellow soldiers expect the rescue force?

"We're coming up along Copper," Volesky shouted into the radio. "We're on our way!"

But up ahead, Captain Denomy's Humvee had slowed, finding Route Copper completely blocked at the intersection with Route Bravo. A two-foot-tall concrete barrier ran down the middle of Route Bravo, cutting off the cross-traffic on Copper.

In addition, just as they had done to block Aguero's platoon, Mahdi militiamen and their sympathizers in the neighborhood had hauled every obstacle they could find into the intersection, from old rusting freezers and fruit stands from the market to rows of metal spike strips. A tank or a Bradley might be able to plow its way through, but a Humvee had no chance. Denomy told his driver to turn north on Bravo, and he alerted the rest of his convoy to the situation. The stranded platoon was still more than a mile to the west, and Denomy and his driver would now have to find a new way to reach them.

Route Bravo turned out to be one long nightmarish stretch of gunfire and explosions. People were shooting from every rooftop, every alleyway, and every window. RPGs soared over the convoy vehicles, blasting into buildings on the other side of the street. Denomy feared it would be only a matter of time before one hit a Humvee dead-on. Homemade pipe bombs tossed from doorways bounced and skipped across the street and exploded under or around the convoy vehicles. A huge fireball erupted above the convoy from a propane tank set by the side of the road and armed with a fuse. Shrapnel and incoming rounds were soon tearing the canvas top of Denomy's Humvee to shreds, leaving the crew exposed. It was a miracle they weren't dead already.

To make matters worse, the drivers could no longer speed through the attack as they had on Copper. The street dubbed Route Bravo was an open-air market area; "Shit Market," the soldiers had called it, because of the raw sewage that surrounded it. Always congested with tables and vendor stands, the street was further obstructed this Sunday evening with junk strewn to deliberately impede their progress, tree stumps, and discarded furniture, anything that would slow the convoy traffic and leave the vehicles more exposed. This made Denomy's vulnerable M-998 even more dangerous. Within moments, Staff Sergeant Dumdie had been hit in the foot—whether by shrapnel or an incoming round, Dumdie didn't know.

Spicer, sitting next to Dumdie, asked if he could continue to fire his weapon. Through clenched teeth, Dumdie assured him he could and raised his M-4 and resumed shooting. Moments later a bullet tore through the Humvee's tattered canvas top and caught flesh. Spicer screamed, dropped his weapon, and grabbed his leg, now ripped and bloody. Denomy spun in his seat, alarm on his face.

"Are you okay? You okay?" Denomy asked, looking Spicer straight in the eyes. Spicer nodded, grimacing. The captain said nothing more but stared intently at Spicer, and in that moment both men realized the worst was still to come. Without his commander's saying a single word, Spicer realized how critical it was that he hold it together. Spicer and Denomy were the senior officers for Charlie Company. It was up to them to get their troops through this, and they had to depend on each other.

Spicer nodded again and reached down for his rifle.

A few vehicles back, an explosion suddenly stopped one of the Humvees in its tracks. Lieutenant John Gilbreth, Denomy's Second Platoon leader, radioed his company commander for help. Denomy saw a street corner ahead that offered a place to make a quick turnaround, and he told his driver to go back to Gilbreth's Humvee. The Bradleys that were following at the end of the convoy had by then pulled up alongside and provided rudimentary protection to the crew of the disabled Humvee. That's when Denomy was hit. He felt a sharp burn, deep in his shoulder, then another one, this one hotter and wider, ripping into his back. Denomy didn't know whether it was shrapnel, a bullet or both. It didn't really matter.

He steadied himself inside the Humvee. Wiebley blanched at the sight of the bright red spots seeping through Denomy's uniform.

"I'm okay, I'm okay!" Denomy yelled. "Just keep heading south!" The convoy was turning back in the direction from which it had come. Whatever they had learned in training, the idea that anyone could assault through this kind of ambush was absurd.

Spicer ripped open a pressure bandage, pushing on Denomy's wound to stop the bleeding while simultaneously applying pressure to his own leg wound. Denomy tried to raise Volesky, his battalion commander, on the radio.

"Lancer Six, this is Comanche Six," Denomy said. "We have a disabled vehicle and multiple casualties throughout the convoy. We can't go on. I'm gonna need to establish a casualty collection point."

Lieutenant Colonel Volesky, coming up in the rear, had heard Gilbreth's report and seen the convoy turn back on Route Bravo. Now Volesky told his driver to do the same; as the last vehicle in the convoy, they were now in the lead heading south. Over the radio, Volesky told Denomy the convoy should go back to Route Copper and regroup at the corner of Copper and Route Aeros, a spot where the gunfire had been minimal. For the moment, the rescue mission was off. Volesky would have to break the news to Jerry Swope: Charlie Company's first effort to reach the stranded platoon had failed.

The reports reaching Volesky from battalion headquarters were no better. Third Platoon, the battalion's Quick Reaction Force

under the command of Lieutenant Dan Hines, had pressed farther south on Route Aeros to the far corner of Sadr City before
turning west on Route Florida. Hines hoped to come up north
again on Route Delta to reach the stranded platoon, but he had
run into very heavy fire. His vehicle heavily damaged, Hines was
forced to return the way he had come. At Volesky's orders, he settled for a lesser objective: to secure a local government building
and the area around it.

Captain Denomy, the Charlie Company commander, led his
soldiers out of the Sadr City slum the same way they came in, firing all the way. Everyone in the Humvee had been injured in one
way or another with the miraculous exception of Denomy's gunner, Specialist Burkholder, the soldier in the back of the vehicle
who had been the most exposed. Burkholder had spent the entire
time swiveling from right to left behind his M-240, engaging targets on both sides of the street. As they headed back to Camp
War Eagle, Burkholder couldn't wait to jump in another vehicle
and go right back into the fight. Neither could Troy Denomy. But
Denomy was hurt, and so were several of his men. For now, it
would be up to Alpha Company to find the stranded platoon.

Chapter 9

★

THE RESCUE:
ALPHA
COMPANY

1820 hours

ABOUT TEN MINUTES AFTER Captain Troy Denomy led Charlie Company toward Sadr City, Captain George Lewis's Alpha Company had lined up to follow. Lewis stood at the front of the long column, squinting through bursts of dirt as the twenty-one vehicles moved into place in the convoy. The noise was overwhelming: men shouting, gears grinding, the clank of equipment, and the slap of boots on hard sand as soldiers rushed to load rifles, ammo, and communications gear into any vehicle that moved. Captain Lewis moved stiffly among his men, his pale blue eyes scanning rapidly, without expression. He was a small, wiry man, painfully introverted, with a bit of bright red stubble visible around the strap of his helmet.

Lieutenant Colonel Gary Volesky, who was commanding the operation, wanted all the power the battalion could muster, and he wanted it directed immediately toward the platoon of soldiers pinned in the alley.

For a moment, though, George Lewis hesitated. Staff Sergeant Edward Elliott's LMTV, the second vehicle in line, idling directly behind his own unarmored Humvee, was giving Lewis pause. A two-and-a-half-ton cargo truck, this particular LMTV provided no protection whatsoever for the fifteen or sixteen soldiers it would carry. Its thick canvas sides had been rolled up recently to help ease the heat, revealing metal benches along either side of the truck that could be raised or lowered, depending on whether the cargo was men or supplies.

Sergeant Elliott was no more pleased with the vehicle than Lewis was: His second squad of the Third Platoon should have been in a Bradley. But when Elliott arrived at the motor pool, the LMTV was sitting there with a supply clerk, Private Peter Baah, at the wheel. Baah had slept in the vehicle the night before; when he heard that a platoon was in trouble and saw the other vehicles lining up, he just moved in among them. Elliott stared at the truck for a second, but before he could say anything, his soldiers began piling in the back. "Let's go! Let's go!" Fellow soldiers were downrange and in trouble. *They're right,* thought Elliott. *We've gotta go help.*

But Sergeant Elliott's "we" was not meant to include Private Baah, the driver. Elliott wasn't going to let some skinny supply clerk join his rescue team—certainly not as his driver. The sergeant swung open the cab door and grabbed Baah by the sleeve of his uniform.

"Get the fuck out," he said. "Go on! Get moving!"

Baah did as he was ordered—he'd expected it, but it still stung. A native of Ghana, Baah had immigrated to the United States at

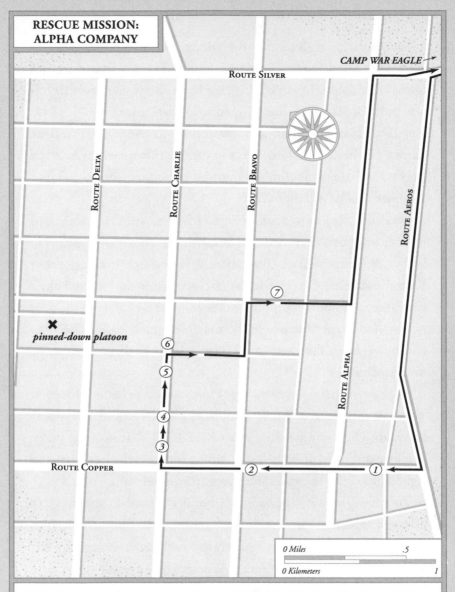

RESCUE MISSION: ALPHA COMPANY

CAMP WAR EAGLE

ROUTE SILVER

ROUTE DELTA

ROUTE CHARLIE

ROUTE BRAVO

ROUTE AEROS

ROUTE ALPHA

✗ *pinned-down platoon*

⑦

⑥

⑤

④

③

ROUTE COPPER ② ①

0 Miles .5

0 Kilometers 1

1. Alpha Company convoy first encounters enemy fire.

2. Specialist Stephen Hiller is able to navigate through concrete barriers that had previously rerouted Charlie Company.

3. Gunfire intensifies, and Route Charlie quickly turns into a major ambush site.

4. Specialist Ahmed Cason is hit.

5. Hiller is hit, and the convoy is forced to stop. Specialist Israel Garza and Specialist Robert Arsiaga are hit.

6. The convoy takes the first possible right and heads back to Camp War Eagle.

7. Captain George Lewis, First Lieutenant Chris Cannon, and Specialist Joel Rabideau are forced to abandon their Humvee when the engine fails. They manage to climb into a Bradley.

© 2006 Jeffrey L. Ward

fifteen, gone to high school in Harlem, and then joined the U.S. Army; yet he and the other clerks were constantly teased for not doing true soldierly work. To Peter Baah, Staff Sergeant Elliott was only the latest in a line of men who had treated him this way. But Baah had a weapon and knew how to use it, and he'd be damned if he wasn't going to help out on this mission. As soon as the staff sergeant climbed into the cab, Baah scrambled into the back, out of Elliott's view.

Specialist Ray Flores sat a couple of seats away. He had been in Iraq only two days and had returned from his first patrol in Sadr City only hours before. Barely seated for evening chow, Flores had heard the call for the rescue mission and moved like a firefighter, dumping his dinner in the trash and retrieving the gear he'd just stowed away inside the maintenance bay, then heading for the vehicles. Like Sergeant Elliott, Flores had been expecting to see a Bradley.

Why are we getting onto that thing? Flores couldn't believe his eyes. Why was his platoon piling into an LMTV? He and the others had trained on the Bradley, not on an LMTV. It seemed crazy. But he climbed in nonetheless, taking a place on the bench on the right side of the vehicle, three seats from the front.

To his right was Specialist Armando Olazaba, and next to Olazaba, squeezed directly behind the cab, was Specialist Robert Arsiaga. Across from Arsiaga, on the bench on the truck's left side, was Specialist Israel Garza, Arsiaga's best friend—they even looked alike, so much so that people often confused them. They both sat with weapons pointed up and propped between their legs, occasionally turning to peer outside the truck or give each other a nod.

Flores still couldn't get over the LMTV. *This is ridiculous.* There was no protection from the outside; sitting on those benches, facing inward, they were in no position to defend themselves;

and if they fired their weapons from this position, they were more likely to kill one another than the enemy—they were facing one another, for Christ's sake! He wondered if he should say something to Elliott. Yet there was so much adrenaline working in the truck, so little thought of anything but Shane Aguero's stranded platoon, that Flores decided to keep quiet.

If Garza and Arsiaga had concerns, they weren't voicing them either. Both were respectful soldiers who'd married young and followed orders without complaint. At twenty-five, Garza was just a year older than Arsiaga but much more mature, and Arsiaga leaned on him for support. Sometimes Arsiaga carried himself like a kid, naïve and guileless. In the LMTV he made no effort to hide his nervousness, telling his fellow soldiers, without hesitation or self-consciousness, that he was scared. He repeatedly took off his ballistic glasses and wiped the lenses, as though he couldn't quite convince himself he was prepared for whatever was coming.

"Aw, come on, you're going to be all right," Specialist Richard Thompson told him. "I'll take care of you." Arsiaga's friend Garza just grinned at him.

Garza and his wife, Guadalupe, already had two young boys. Being away from his boys had made this deployment difficult enough, but Lupe's incessant worrying made it even harder.

"If anything happened to you, I couldn't live," she'd told him before he left. Israel heard those words constantly. He had talked to Lupe on their anniversary a few days earlier; feeling blue about the prospect of a long deployment, he let down his guard a little. "I'm ready to come home now," he told her. Usually he spent so much energy telling her everything was going to be fine; this made her feel closer than ever to him.

Near the left rear of the truck was Sergeant Stevenson Charite, a former Marine and a native of Haiti. When President Bush said the United States was going into Iraq, Charite wanted to be part of it. By then, he was out of the Marine Corps, so he joined the Army. For Charite, the politics didn't matter; he just wanted to serve his country in time of war. Now he sat on a metal seat, clutching his M-16 and the ten magazines of ammunition he'd grabbed, trying to keep himself calm.

As the squad leader, Edward Elliott, a husky African-American, sat in the LMTV passenger seat; he would direct the vehicle into the city. The new driver, replacing Private Baah, was Specialist Travis Walker. Sitting between them in the cab was Sergeant Oracio Pena. Sixteen other soldiers (including, unbeknownst to Elliott, the supply clerk Baah) were now crammed into the back, covered only by the loose layer of canvas above them. Boxes of water bottles and stacks of dark green plastic MRE (meals ready to eat) packages were loaded onto the truck and shoved to the front. Not one of the soldiers had ever seen real combat, including Staff Sergeant Elliott.

As Walker moved the truck forward, Elliott leaned out the cab's passenger window. "Check your weapons!" he shouted. Altogether, they carried two M-249 light machine guns, known as squad automatic weapons (SAWs), two M-203 grenade launchers, and one M-4 or M-16 rifle per man. Something about Elliott's tone surprised Oracio Pena, who had been in the city the day before and had a few rocks hurled his way. He hadn't been expecting anything very different on this mission, but now he looked worriedly at his sergeant. Elliott leaned over and whispered, "This is some serious shit."

Several vehicles behind Sergeant Elliott's LMTV was the M-1114 Humvee commanded by SFC Reginald Butler. Butler was tall and thick-shouldered, with a bearing that commanded respect. That hadn't always been the case. Joining the National Guard after his junior year in a small-town high school in Oklahoma, he had been the only black man in a unit of 120 soldiers, and endured being called "Pudding," "Chocolate," and a few equally cruel nicknames. Butler responded with humor and determination. Reginald Butler was just thirty years old, but he radiated calm and wisdom beyond his years; some of the younger soldiers saw him as a father figure. Like many strong army leaders, he demanded discipline from the young men and rewarded them with absolute loyalty.

No one looked up to Butler more than his gunner, Specialist Ahmed Cason. He was twenty-four and married, with a son and a daughter. Cason and his wife, Allison, hadn't planned to have kids so young; it just worked out that way. And it was no secret that Cason, who loved to party, hadn't taken easily to being a parent. Early in their marriage, Cason constantly prodded Allison to lighten up and enjoy life more; but it was she who finally convinced her husband that being a parent was not about that.

In the months before his deployment, Cason had begun taking his responsibilities more seriously. SFC Butler, who had one failed marriage behind him, helped Cason turn that corner, and Cason was deeply grateful to him. So indebted that shortly before the platoon left Fort Hood for Iraq, Cason awakened Butler in the middle of the night. He told Butler that he wanted to be his gunner—not just another soldier in the platoon, but the one responsible for the safety of the men inside his vehicle, the soldiers who would be at SFC Butler's side through whatever mess they found themselves in.

"I'm not going to Iraq unless I can be in your vehicle," Cason said.

"I'll make sure you're on my truck," his groggy sergeant assured him, intent on getting back to sleep.

"I'm serious," Cason said. "You won't be disappointed."

"Don't worry," Butler said, his promise concluding the conversation. "You'll be with me."

That was just a month before. Since then Butler and Cason, both African-Americans, had developed an easy, sometimes comic rapport—bantering with each other in a way that amused the other soldiers. Cason was always respectful of Butler's rank but felt entirely comfortable around the sergeant.

They were still joking—nervously—as they waited in the column of idling vehicles. The only hint of Butler's anxiety about the mission was the quivering in his legs. As a child he'd worn braces on his inexplicably weak legs. Unable to run, or even to sit with his legs bent, he had been called "Frankenstein" by the other kids. His mother had dragged him to every doctor she could find. Finally his grandfather bought him a tricycle, and Butler rode it everywhere. When he turned five, he took it on himself to shed his braces, put on long pants so his mother wouldn't see, and to the amazement of everyone, took off running. Eventually the cruel teasing stopped; by the time Butler was in high school, he was a track star. In a movie theater years later, he watched a character named Forrest Gump go through the same transformation, and cried quietly.

"Mount up," Butler bellowed. "Let's go!" He climbed into the passenger seat of his M-1114 alongside his driver, Specialist Heriberto Arambula, a Mexican immigrant from Los Angeles. Arambula was close to both Butler and Cason, the gunner. He thought Cason was the strongest guy in the platoon, both physically and mentally, and he idolized Butler for his leadership. Arambula had already been on a few patrols in Sadr City, and he thought it was just about the worst place on earth. The raw sewage ran so deep in some places that it would splash down the turret when the Humvee hit a bump. The first time out, he felt like he was going to puke. Arambula soon got used to the smell but not the boredom. He was itching for action, and he had been disappointed that the few patrols he had been on were all routine.

Sergeant Richard Gonzales sat behind Arambula in the Humvee, and Specialist Sean Crabbe, the medic, was behind Butler. All the men had automatic weapons at their sides, and holstered pistols strapped to their legs or torsos. The communications in the Humvee had yet to be hooked up, so the soldiers carried only handheld radios. Cason slid up through the turret in the center of the Humvee, gripping the M-240 gun—considerably bigger than the SAW M-249s in Sergeant Elliott's LMTV—and began preparing the heavy belts of munitions to "go red" whenever necessary. He stood on the small platform below the turret, centered in the vehicle between the front and back seats and between the passenger and driver sides. A thick strap was attached to each side of the vehicle so Cason could lean on top of it like a swing when he wasn't standing in the turret.

Butler loaded eight magazines of thirty rounds each for his M-16 rifle, which was capable of firing eight hundred rounds per minute. And even though Butler expected this mission to be over quickly, darkness was only an hour or so away, so the men brought along night-vision goggles—a lesson drilled into every American soldier after the disastrous ambush in Somalia's capital, Mogadishu, in 1993. There the soldiers had abandoned the cumbersome night-vision equipment, certain that their routine patrol would be over before daylight ended. Hours later, they were stranded in the dark, taking mounting casualties.

Up at the front of the convoy, Captain Lewis was almost ready to give the signal to move. Like Captain Denomy, Lewis would be leading his company into the city in an unarmored Humvee. But Lewis's vehicle offered even less protection—it didn't even have *doors*. Originally it had been outfitted with canvas doors, to go along with its canvas top. But since the doors provided no protection, they'd been removed on the drive up from Kuwait; the soldiers figured that removing them would make it easier to get in and out with the heavy gear. Lewis's Humvee was the only one in his convoy with no added protection. Its back was open, too, and it had a standard glass windshield, like the one on his '94 Oldsmobile parked in his driveway in Killeen, Texas.

Lewis's decision to ride in the lead vehicle was unusual—just as Charlie Company commander Troy Denomy's choice had been. Yet Lewis knew the city better than the other soldiers, having been one of those who had arrived in the advance unit. He, too, should have been riding in a Bradley for this mission, but the one assigned to him was now being used as a company command post at Camp War Eagle. With a tarp staked outside the hatch, and tracking boards and external speakers set up alongside, it would have taken at least ten minutes extra to break down the gear and get the Bradley ready to roll. Lewis decided there wasn't time. He chose the M-998 Humvee because it was the only available vehicle with two radios. Almost all the others were having communications problems. In this M-998, Lewis could at least stay in close contact with the TOC—critical for the company commander.

Lewis took his seat in the front of the Humvee, next to Specialist Stephen "Dusty" Hiller, who'd been his driver for nine months, since long before the Iraq deployment. Earlier in the day, when Lewis and Hiller had been out on patrol, Hiller was busting to report the good news that his wife, Lesley, had given him the night before: The baby they were expecting was a boy. They already had two daughters at home.

"Finally!" Hiller said to Lewis, in his amiable southern drawl. "I won't have to worry about putting the toilet seat down all the time!"

Lewis had to laugh. In a lot of ways they couldn't have been more different. Lewis, thirty-six, was older than most army captains, and he carried himself quietly, with less than the typical army *hoo-ah;* he grew up in Michigan and Connecticut, about as far north of the Mason-Dixon line as Hiller's Alabama hometown was south of it. Twelve years younger than his commanding officer, Hiller was naturally gregarious and always eager to tell a funny story, and at six-foot-three, he towered over his captain. Lewis had no children and had never been married, but he enjoyed hearing Hiller talk about fatherhood. For the last year Lewis had been seriously involved with a woman named Elvy, who had a six-year-old daughter, Lizzy. She was one of the best things about the relationship, and he had grown close to the little girl.

Sitting directly behind Lewis was Specialist Joel Rabideau; behind Hiller was First Lieutenant Chris Cannon. The gunner, PFC Jerry Bune, was completely exposed in the open bed of the Humvee.

Before giving the order to proceed, Lewis jumped out and took another long look at the convoy. He was still troubled. It was not his own unarmored Humvee that bothered him so much as the LMTV directly behind it. That truck was loaded with soldiers, and nothing shielded them from whatever awaited outside the gate. It just seemed too vulnerable.

So Lewis made one last decision. Instead of having the LMTV directly behind his own unprotected vehicle, he moved one of the Bradleys between his Humvee and Elliott's LMTV, thus providing both soft-sided vehicles with at least some firepower if things got rough.

"All right, let's move!" Lewis, who rarely shouted, forced his voice deeper and louder. He hoped he sounded more confident than he felt.

Specialist Hiller hit the gas. The Alpha Company convoy rolled out the gate.

DUSTY HILLER had been directed to follow a route similar to the one taken by Charlie Company: head south on Route Aeros and then west on Copper. Captain Lewis then intended to turn north on Route Charlie, which would put his convoy parallel to Route Delta, where Shane Aguero's platoon had been ambushed. Lewis's plan was to position his soldiers as close as possible to the pinned-down platoon and then have them dismount and proceed on foot rather than leave them exposed in the back of the truck or in open Humvees.

Immediately upon leaving Camp War Eagle, the Alpha Company soldiers noticed the same exodus of civilian cars that Charlie Company had just seen. Moving down Route Aeros, they were similarly struck by the silence and the emptied streets, and they were just as unnerved by the scene.

BACK IN THE number-six vehicle—SFC Butler's Humvee— it was Ahmed Cason, the gunner, who finally broke the silence.

"Sergeant Butler!" Cason shouted from the turret.

"What?"

"You scared, Sergeant Butler?"

"Hell no, I'm not scared," Butler bellowed. "You scared, Cason?"

Cason smiled, and the other soldiers in the Humvee allowed themselves to laugh. It was Cason and Butler's bravado routine, and it always managed to take the edge off a tense situation. But the men had never been in a situation like this before, and this time the amusement didn't last. It was just too quiet out there.

★   ★   ★

IN THE LEAD HUMVEE, Captain Lewis was eyeing the alley-ways and rooftops, worrying about snipers. Over the radio, he re-minded all his soldiers to lock and load, and to take their weapons off safety. Two miles down Route Aeros, Specialist Hiller made the right turn onto Copper and pressed harder on the gas. The roar of the Humvee engine and the heavy clanking of gears filled the vehicle.

Perhaps a minute later, Lewis heard the distinct sound of an AK-47 rifle somewhere behind him, around the center of his convoy. Seven vehicles back, Sergeant Tim Apple was standing in the gunner's turret of his armored Humvee and thought for sure he'd heard sniper fire. He gripped the machine gun in front of him a little tighter. Again he heard shots, again it was not clear where they were coming from.

A spray of dust caught Sergeant Butler's eye; at about the same time, Specialist Cason heard from his perch up in the turret the sound of gunfire coming from both sides of the street. He could see a few people running between the cinder-block buildings that lined the street. Bright streamers and laundry hung from the sides of dirty buildings, waving with each gust of dry wind. But-ler watched from the passenger seat, sweating nervously under his body armor, his hand on his weapon.

A sharp, sudden burst from Cason's M-240 shook the Hum-vee, a bone-rattling *DDDDRRRRRRR* reverberating through the vehicle and sending hot shell casings flying.

"Cason, what the hell you shooting at?" Butler had heard the gunfire from the AK-47 but couldn't see onto the rooftops through his window and had not spotted anyone with a weapon. He couldn't have Cason firing that big gun indiscriminately in this city center, no matter what they were hearing.

"Guys on the roof," Cason hollered down from the turret. "Shooting at us!" Butler slid down in his seat to get a clearer upward angle through the small window on his right. Sure enough, there they were, on top of the building: heads popping up to take quick shots and then disappearing behind the jagged ledge that ran along the front of the roof. The design of the ledge allowed just enough room for a rifle butt and just enough protection for the trigger puller. Cason, with an unobstructed view, crouched down slightly and fired nonstop. The noise was overwhelming. It was clear Cason was not the only gunner in the convoy firing at rooftops.

FROM HIS MIDDLE SEAT in the LMTV cab near the front of the convoy, Sergeant Oracio Pena saw one man, then two, appear from behind a building, fire weapons, and then disappear. Pena shoved his M-4 out the window, across Sergeant Elliott's chest, and let loose. Pena saw more faces and then, briefly, weapons—a blur of flesh and steel, poking out and quickly pulling back. Wedged next to Pena in the truck cab, Elliott raised his weapon, too, searching for targets. The enemy gunfire was getting louder and more frequent.

And there, inexplicably, in the middle of this mess, with bullets raining on all sides, Elliott spotted a family standing in front of a house, waving at the convoy as it passed. A mom, a dad, and a handful of kids. "What the fuck?!" he exclaimed. *People are shooting out here and you're standing there smiling at me like you're headed for a picnic!*

The convoy kept moving forward. Sergeant Elliott still couldn't tell where the rounds were coming from because he couldn't see anybody. The doors were closed, the windows opaque from the dirt; who knew where the shooters were? He wasn't becoming afraid as much as he was getting angry. With the "stabilizing operation" rhetoric ringing loudly in his head, he was stunned by what he saw: *We're here to help. Why the hell are they shooting at us?* With Travis Walker doing his best to steer the truck through the gunfire and Sergeant Pena firing across Elliott's chest, Elliott was pumping adrenaline but finding it nearly impossible to shoot. Finally he managed to stick his M-4 out the window next to Pena's, and he opened up with a hail of bullets. The two men were wedged together, and Elliott's heavy body armor acted as Pena's elbow rest.

"You're going to make me deaf, man!" Elliott shouted.

"We need to do something, dude!" Pena said.

The solution seemed obvious: Elliott and Pena raised their desert combat boots and kicked out the LMTV windshield with one tremendous blow. Pena continued pounding to clear out all the glass, which shattered and covered the truck seat and dashboard. The soldiers could shoot their weapons through a much wider opening now, but still had to lean out sideways, since their own men were positioned directly in front of them.

As they were leaning through the windshield, their weapons blasting, a streak of black smoke and flame shot right across the front of the truck, knocking Elliott and Pena back into their seats. It was a rocket-propelled grenade, launched from a shoulder-fired weapon, that had sailed miraculously through the gap between their truck and the Bradley ahead of them, missing both vehicles and landing in a nearby pile of dirt without exploding. Elliott shifted his gaze to the right, where the RPG had come from, and he noticed a gate being pulled shut. Sticking his weapon out the window, Elliott fired at the closed gate, hoping to stop anyone behind it from launching more grenades. He would have blown the house to bits if he could have.

Seconds later another RPG exploded on the ground next to the truck, sending the soldiers in the back diving to the floorboards. All they had heard was a powerful *whoosh,* and then they felt the thud. The RPG did not hit the truck squarely, so its impact was partly deflected. Still, a shower of lead and fire poured over the truck. On each side, the soldiers got on their knees, turned to face outward, and started shooting, their weapons propped on the truck sides.

Sergeant Salvador Beltran lifted his squad automatic weapon, set it on top of the truck cab, aimed it generally up at the rooftops, and held down the trigger. Suddenly, through the din of fire, Beltran heard the voice of a child. He looked down to find a boy of about eight running alongside the truck, holding a Coke can in his hand. "Mister! Mister!" he shouted. In one horrifying second, the boy hurled the can at the soldiers in the truck and then ducked. An explosion rocked the truck, sending chunks of shrapnel into Beltran's face and knocking him over. A homemade bomb. The boy continued to chase the truck. Two soldiers, picking themselves up off the truck bed, lowered their rifles at the boy and—fearing another bomb—shot him. Beltran was spitting blood, and his face was badly cut. He leaned against the truck cab for a few moments, looking dazed, thin trails of red streaking his face. After a minute or two, he stood back up, grabbed the SAW, and resumed firing at rooftops and balconies.

SIX VEHICLES BACK, Sergeant Tim Apple was hunched in the gunner's turret of Staff Sergeant Ernesto Hernandez's Humvee, firing at anything he deemed threatening. From time to time, he could make out a single black-clad figure on a rooftop, but there were obviously dozens—or hundreds—more enemy fighters at work. Apple would listen, then fire; look, then fire. He aimed for windows and doors and anything that moved. At twenty-four, he had never been so scared in his life. *I am going to shit my pants!* Soon he was spinning around the turret in a blur, gripping his weapon hard but not bothering to aim, whirling in place, just holding down the trigger and letting it rip. *If there were Depends for young men, I'd like to be wearing them right now,* he thought.

IN THE LEAD VEHICLE, Captain Lewis could hear the gunfire, but most of it was still to his rear. He couldn't stop worrying about the LMTV behind him, wondering what had become of his soldiers stuck back there, entirely exposed. SPC Hiller was getting nervous and disoriented. Coming up on the intersection with Route Bravo, Hiller saw the same concrete barriers that had stopped the Charlie Company convoy not ten minutes before. "Oh crap, sir, what do I do?"

Lewis directed Hiller to an opening he had spotted in the barrier—either an RPG had opened it up, or the militia had decided to move a section—and they pushed on through. A few blocks later, the men reached the intersection with Route Charlie.

"Here, here, turn right," Lewis said.

Hiller's huge hands gripped the wheel tighter, rounding the corner slowly so the line of vehicles behind him could easily follow. As they came around onto Route Charlie, Dusty Hiller and his sergeant were stunned by what they saw down the street: Concrete planters, car parts, refrigerators, metal bed frames all deliberately piled in the street and surrounded by burning trash and tires. It was another deadly junkyard snare. A kill zone. With the turn onto Route Charlie, the gunfire suddenly turned withering, and this time it seemed focused squarely on the unarmored, unprotected Humvee at the front of the convoy.

"Oh crap! Crap!" Hiller moaned, shaking his head. He tried to keep his foot on the gas, dodging or driving over barricades the best he could, while instinctively ducking behind the wheel to avoid the bullets whizzing by his head and making explosive sounds all around him, like corn popping. At Hiller's side, Captain Lewis had been trying to talk on the radio, but once the bullets started hitting his Humvee and ripping holes in the metal, Lewis could no longer manage any communication.

The rest of the long convoy followed Hiller and Elliott onto Route Charlie. Every soldier who looked down the street could see the vehicles being pounded up ahead. Clearly the situation had worsened dramatically. The men had unwittingly driven straight into a three-hundred-yard-long ambush site, with hundreds if not thousands of unseen enemies poised and determined to kill them. In the cab of the LMTV, Sergeant Elliott hadn't believed the shooting could get any louder and heavier, but now it did. Sergeant Beltran was bleeding heavily from his shrapnel wound, the RPG had left a sizable dent in the side of the truck, and Elliott knew the attack was far from over. He kept looking for a target for his rage but was still having trouble making out any of the shooters from inside the cab. He could hear the bullets whistling past his head, but they came from behind walls, or through holes drilled in the concrete blocks or slots in the metal gates. There was no enemy to be found; no target to aim for.

"There! Up there!" Elliott shouted, spotting a flash of fire. It was a mosque, forbidden territory for Americans. The soldiers had been told not to shoot at mosques. But this was the first person Elliott had clearly seen with a weapon, firing at his soldiers from the top of a minaret. Elliott raised his M-4 and squeezed the trigger. He watched the man drop the weapon, teeter for a moment, and then fall dead from the tower.

"Fuck you!" he screamed. He was starting to lose it. "How you gonna be shooting at us now, you sonsabitches!" A second man in the mosque tower raised a weapon, and Elliott took him out as well. He was looking for more, adrenaline surging, daring anyone to fire at him, but also telling himself he might not have much of a chance if they did.

It's not a question of if *I'm gonna get shot,* he thought. *It's more a question of* when.

FROM THE FRONT of the line, Captain George Lewis was hearing a constant *ping, ping, ping* as bullets hit the sides of his Humvee, ripping holes in its soft skin with every impact. Behind the steering wheel, Hiller was mumbling, swerving the vehicle from side to side and bobbing his head up and down as the bullets tore through the canvas roof just inches above him. They had been on Route Charlie for less than two minutes when Lewis glanced at the open back of his Humvee and saw his gunner on fire. PFC Jerry Bune, standing fully exposed behind his weapon, had taken a glancing shot to his chest, and one of the 40mm grenades he had in the ammo-packed vest he wore over his body armor had started to burn. Bune was firing his weapon so intently that he hadn't even noticed he'd been hit, or that little swirls of smoke and flame were rising from his chest. Lewis pointed frantically at the burning vest. Bune finally noticed. He pulled the vest off, nodded to his captain, and went back to firing his gun.

Bune was hit again almost instantly. A bullet tore through his lower leg, shattering bone and ripping flesh. His pants oozed red, and Bune fell back in the Humvee, clutching his leg and writhing in pain. "Oh fuck, oh fuck, fuck, I'm hit! Oh God, I'm hit!" Lewis hollered for Bune to stay low and remain calm, all the while signaling Hiller to continue driving. Bune was in terrible pain, but Lewis doubted the injury was life-threatening. The Alpha convoy was now less than a mile from Shane Aguero's stranded platoon. Captain Lewis was determined not to abort the rescue mission, or even slow it down, to tend to his wounded private.

The next block looked relatively clear, but the gunfire was still deafening. Lewis leaned forward just as two rounds came through the windshield, shattering the glass and lodging slivers in Lewis's neck. He put a hand to his throat but didn't panic; his wounds appeared to be minor. He was growing increasingly concerned, however, about all that was happening to the men in the vehicles behind him. Lewis was looking back at the convoy out the right side of the Humvee when Dusty Hiller suddenly took his foot off the gas, and the M-998 came to a halt.

WITH THE RIGHT TURN onto Route Charlie, the gunfire had grown so intense, so quickly, that the Alpha Company convoy was losing cohesion. The RPG explosions and gunfire were deafening. In SFC Reggie Butler's Humvee, everybody was shooting except for the driver, Specialist Arambula, who was trying to negotiate the barriers in the street and the Bradley in front of him, which had suddenly slowed and then stopped, squarely in a kill zone. Butler couldn't believe it. He grabbed his radio and called First Sergeant Rick Stuckey, who was in a Humvee a few vehicles behind.

"What the hell is going on?" Butler screamed. "Why are we stopping?" Stuckey wasn't even sure what Butler was saying. With the gunfire now coming from all sides, it was almost impossible to hear anything on the radio. Something had apparently happened at the front of the convoy, but no one knew precisely what. Even as he shouted into the radio, Stuckey watched the repeated flash of a muzzle from a nearby rooftop. Then he saw a man with a machine gun grinning widely as he fired down at the convoy.

Up in the turret, Specialist Cason seemed to be shooting in all directions at once, swinging from one side to the other so quickly that he was spinning in the gunner's sling. And then, in an instant, he stopped.

"I'm hit! I'm hit!" he screamed. Butler turned to see Cason grab his side and arch his back away from the gun.

"Oh, my God, it burns, it's burning," he yelled. And then, remarkably, after only a minute or so, Ahmed Cason stopped screaming, straightened up, grabbed the gun, and resumed firing.

Butler was relieved to see his gunner recover so quickly, and immediately went back to firing his own weapon out the window. "You'll be all right," he yelled to Cason between bursts of his M-16. But moments later, Cason's big gun suddenly fell silent, and he dropped down into the Humvee. Specialist Sean Crabbe, the medic, who was sitting behind Butler, moved to Cason's side and gently turned him over. The front of his vest was covered with blood, and when Crabbe lifted it he saw a hole in Cason's abdomen.

"We've got to get him out of here," Crabbe said, applying pressure to the wound.

TWO VEHICLES BACK, Sergeant Tim Apple had gotten a clear view of one Iraqi with a weapon, a man dressed in black crouched on a rooftop, but that hadn't stopped Apple from shooting. He was aiming at doors and windows, stopping only for a few moments from time to time to listen and look, hoping to identify the source of all the gunfire directed toward the soldiers. Suddenly Tim Apple felt something hit him hard and heavy—*like a ton of bricks,* he thought. Then he collapsed onto the Humvee floor.

UP AHEAD, Butler grabbed his radio again to alert Stuckey. "Warrior Nine, this is Red Four!" he said. "I've got a guy hit. Cason, he's hit."

But Stuckey did not respond. The radio just then was buzzing with names, broadcasting a run of bad news.

"BARRERA IS HIT!"

"Apple is down!"

"Ryan is hit!"

Reggie Butler saw one of the Bradleys in front of him move slightly, and he slapped his driver on the arm. "Go now!" he screamed. Arambula squeezed around the Bradley and then floored it. "Take a right!" Butler yelled. "Go! Go!" With the convoy breaking apart, each vehicle was now essentially on its own, and Butler wanted only to get out of the kill zone and back to some point where his buddy Ahmed Cason, whose moans were filling the Humvee, could get medical attention.

Please, please, please, get him back alive.

Chapter 10

★

JUST ANOTHER SUNDAY

9:45 a.m.

From Texas to Alabama

AT THE EXACT MOMENT Allison Cason's twenty-four-year-old husband took a bullet in his abdomen, she was celebrating her grandfather's eighty-first year of life at his home in Tuscaloosa, Alabama. She experienced no sudden feeling of dread, no searing sympathetic pain, no notion that her husband was fighting for breath eight thousand miles away. The young mother was enjoying her last hours of ignorant bliss.

Surrounded by her parents, uncles, aunts, and her two children, Allison was helping with last-minute preparations for the all-day feast. Her mother, a caterer in Birmingham, had already done much of the cooking. Three-year-old Akilaah Cason was dancing around the cake, the kitchen, the yard, bouncing her baby brother, Gabe, on her hip, showing him off to her cousins, and sneaking dollops of frosting for the eight-month-old. Everyone was there.

Everyone, of course, except Ahmed.

Her family asked about him, dutifully, awkwardly—but in truth Allison wished they wouldn't. For one thing, she had precious little information to share—if all had gone according to plan, Ahmed would be in Iraq now, having arrived from Kuwait four or five days earlier. That was all she knew, all she could tell her relatives. She hadn't spoken to her husband in maybe ten days.

It wasn't unusual to go so long without hearing from him—but that didn't mean Allison Cason didn't worry about him more or less all the time.

Allison had never wanted Ahmed to join the army. Never mind that she was carrying his child—Ahmed always did what Ahmed wanted to do. That was just the way he was. Akilaah had been born a month after Ahmed left for basic training. When they got married, a month after that, Allison was eighteen years old, Ahmed was just twenty-one.

The wedding, such as it was, cost forty-two dollars. They were married in a courthouse ceremony in Bessemer, Alabama, a town of thirty thousand that boasts of distinctive outlet shopping and the popular Alabama Adventure amusement park. Allison didn't care about the venue; she was just happy to be getting married. They had met in 1999 while working at Job Corps, a government education and vocational training program. They hit it off immediately, despite Allison's reservations and the stark differences in their personalities. Ahmed was three years older than Allison, but she thought of him as much less mature. Drinking, carousing, having fun, these had been Ahmed Cason's priorities most of the time.

Allison was just the opposite, at least on the outside. She had grown up fast, passed from childhood to motherhood without pause and mostly without regretting that she had missed so much in between. Her perfect posture and pursed lips had often made her seem like the most serious girl in the room. The couple would argue about Ahmed's misplaced priorities, and friends wondered privately if they were suited to each other. But Allison had never let herself worry about that. She loved him. He was her husband, the father of her children, and they'd make it work.

As the wife of a young enlisted soldier—one of the soldiers who had joined the service mostly right out of high school—Allison had a lifestyle very different from that of the officers' wives. The housing for the enlisted soldiers had gradually improved over the years, but it was the raucous neighbors she tried to avoid. Allison thought there was too much drinking, too much fooling around, too many undisciplined children doing whatever they pleased. The best she could say about life on post was that it was convenient— grocery shopping at the post exchange, a pool for the kids—but besides going to church every Sunday, Allison didn't socialize with the other army wives. When Ahmed Cason found out he was going to Iraq, the idea of staying on post became unbearable for her. The couple made a decision: Allison and the kids would move in with her parents in Birmingham.

IN EARLY MARCH 2004, just days before his deployment to Kuwait, Ahmed Cason stunned his wife with eight stark words.

"I'm not going to make it back home."

Allison was already dreading the deployment, which would leave her with two babies and no husband for a year, and now he was telling her he wasn't going to make it out of Iraq alive? She sat there, shocked, staring at her husband. *How could he say that to me?* They'd been assured this wouldn't be a particularly dangerous mission. Did he know something more that he couldn't tell her?

Allison had spoken to him just three times since he'd left, and then only while he was still in Kuwait. She hadn't heard a word from him since his arrival in Iraq four days earlier. Access to e-mail for lower-ranking soldiers was difficult. But in their few minutes on the phone together, Ahmed had seemed different somehow, more focused and motivated. He had sounded enthusiastic about what he would be doing in Iraq, but he was also curious to know every detail about the children and about Allison. She had noticed him making progress as a father and a husband in the months before he left. Allison thought Ahmed finally seemed to understand what it meant to be a man.

But Allison's parents still worried about the couple. On the morning of April 4, before the preparations for her grandfather's birthday party had begun, they'd met privately with Ahmed's uncle Wendell Hunt. He had taken Ahmed in after he moved out of his mother's house during high school. Wendell knew Ahmed's imperfections; but he also believed that his nephew had it in him to do better for himself, and for his family, than he had done so far. That was what Allison's parents and Wendell had discussed over breakfast—how to help "the kids" straighten themselves out. The older relatives planned to push the couple to finish their education and assume more control of their lives as soon as Ahmed returned from Iraq.

By late afternoon, Akilaah and Gabe were getting tired. Allison intended to gather them up soon for the drive home, where bath time and bed awaited. It had been a wonderful day with her family, relaxed and easy. Allison had put thoughts of Iraq out of her head, had managed not to worry for a change. Akilaah jumped into her mother's lap just then and smiled up at her. As Allison

Cason brushed a smudge of frosting from her daughter's face, thoughts of Ahmed suddenly crowded her again. How could they not? The girl was the spitting image of her father.

EIGHT HUNDRED MILES west of Birmingham, outside the army post from which Allison Cason had happily fled, Angie Upton was also celebrating an April 4 birthday: her own. Twenty-eight years old, she was trying very hard not to think, *Almost thirty.* The birthday calls from family and friends had already started coming in, as well as a long line of e-mail greetings. Angie's husband, Trent, had moved the computer station next to the bed before heading to Iraq. If Trent was on instant message, Angie would be able to hear the *ping* of his sign-on and roll off the bed to join him. That morning, curled up in front of the computer in a pair of Trent's boxer shorts and his soft T-shirt from college ROTC days trumpeting "The Mighty Warriors," Angie found a birthday message from her husband. It was still hard for her to believe she could get e-mail from Iraq, but there it was:

> Happy Birthday! I love you. I don't think I'll be able to call today. The phone lines are down again, which really pisses me off because I was making it a point to call you on your birthday. I will call as soon as I can. Love, Trent

Angie was disappointed that she wouldn't get to speak to Trent on her birthday, but having the e-mail waiting for her, and knowing he was just as disappointed, made it easier to take. Angie noticed Trent had written the e-mail hours before, while she had slept. It was odd to wake up and know that her husband's day was already more than half over when hers was just beginning. By now, as the battalion's S-1, responsible for personnel, he would be in the middle of his evening battle update in the headquarters. By the time she met her friends Aimee Randazzo and Gina Denomy for her birthday dinner, Trent would be sound asleep. Angie, Aimee, and Gina's husbands were all young officers in the same battalion—captains, around thirty years old—and they lived together at Camp War Eagle. Troy Denomy was a company commander; Dylan Randazzo was the battalion's intelligence officer; Trent Upton was the personnel officer. The men were close, and so were the wives. The women had developed a tight network of communication, figuring they could gather three times as much information by sharing. If Angie hadn't heard from Trent in a couple of days, she could check in with Gina or Aimee to see if they'd been on the Net with their husbands, and vice versa. It worked well, and it always amused the men that the women were keeping such close track.

The big birthday dinner that Gina and Aimee had planned for Angie meant a night on the town in Killeen, which was just outside the gates of Fort Hood, where Trent and Angie lived. "On the town" tonight meant dinner at the local Bennigan's. Bennigan's and Applebee's were what the chamber of commerce meant when it touted Killeen's "nationally known restaurants." The only thing Killeen *really* was known for nationally was a 1991 mass murder, one of the worst in U.S. history. Twenty-three people had been gunned down by an unemployed musician who drove his truck into the local Luby's cafeteria and opened fire, shouting, "This is what Bell County has done to me!" Survivors of the massacre still huddled in local coffee shops more than a decade later, telling and retelling the grim tale. No army family that had spent time in Killeen had been spared the details.

Unlike Aimee and Gina, Angie did not have kids yet. She was working full-time as a juvenile probation officer at a Killeen women's shelter and rape crisis center. She figured that between her job and the redecorating she wanted to do while Trent was gone, the time would pass fairly quickly. And there were always the "woofers," the three dogs that she and Trent treated like children.

Angie and Trent Upton had met at Ohio State University while Trent was a senior and she was a sophomore. Their first date was in February 1996, and by December Trent had proposed. Like many military couples before them and many since, the Uptons had been married twice—to each other. The first marriage came just before Trent left for a year in Korea. Friends kept telling Angie and Trent to make it legal so they could get paid as a married couple and enjoy other benefits as well, and they followed the advice. While Angie was visiting Trent at basic training on a July weekend in 1997, the two ran off to the courthouse in Fort Benning, Georgia, and exchanged vows. Unlike Allison Cason, however, Angie hadn't been satisfied with just a civil ceremony. Coming from a strict Catholic family, she had always assumed that she'd be married in a church, before friends, family, and God.

Angie told her mother about the marriage after the fact, and the news didn't sit too well with Maria Lopez. "I'm happy for you," she told Angie, "but I'm upset because it's not a marriage in the eyes of the Lord." Angie understood. Her parents had come to the United States from Colombia before she was born, during the 1960s, when the Vietnam War was raging. Angie's father and his brothers had been offered visas and moved north. One month later, the men were all drafted. The Lopez family eventually settled in Ohio, but kept in close touch with relatives in Colombia. That was Angie's mother's biggest concern—the very religious, very traditional Colombians. They would never accept, or even fathom, a courthouse wedding. So, more than a year after their first wedding, Trent and Angie did it again. On September 5, 1998, with Angie in a long white gown, before 150 people crowded into a small church in Newark, Ohio, the couple held hands, looked into each other's eyes, and said, "I do," performing a flawless and beautiful rerun. Except for a few close friends, everyone at the wedding thought they were witnessing the beginning of Angie and Trent's life together. Maria Lopez had made sure of that, warning her daughter not to breathe a word. "Are you kidding me?" she'd said. "All these people are going to come and they're going to find out you're already married? That can't happen!"

In fact Angie's mother was one of the rare military parents let in on the secret of the "first marriage." Almost all Angie and Trent's friends had done it, and almost all had kept it from their parents, even years after the wedding.

Now, mid-morning on April 4, 2004, with no call to look forward to, Angie dove deeper into her e-mail, scrolling through all the messages Trent had sent since leaving for Iraq a little more than two weeks before. The first e-mail was dated March 17, written just minutes after the couple had said goodbye. Trent was still at Fort Hood, waiting to board the plane:

> Hi Schmoo. Sending you this from Abrams Gym while we wait to go to the airfield. I love you. I'm sorry for everything I've failed to do for you while I was here. I want to make it up to you when I get back. Give the woofers a kiss for me.

The words made Angie tear up and return to the warmth of her king-sized bed. Every time she read the message she would get weepy. It had been unlike Trent to be so emotional, she thought, and it signaled to her just how difficult the separation was going to be for both of them.

Across town, Gina Denomy and her newborn son, Merrick, were heading over to Aimee Randazzo's house. Aimee had a young son, Dominic, and she and Gina had become very close.

They each filled in a bit for the other's missing husband. It was different in the military, and few outside their world could understand. Lots of jobs involved travel, but few occupations separated families for an entire year at a time, as this deployment would. Of course, there was one even more fundamental difference: *Other* spouses didn't work in war zones.

LUPE GARZA THOUGHT about her husband, Israel, *all the time.* Thought about him, worried about him, prayed for him. Everyone else seemed to be handling the deployment so well, but Lupe managed to turn the smallest concern into a major crisis, to "what if" herself into a panic, every single day. It was embarrassing, she thought, but she couldn't stop herself. She had read in the *Killeen Daily Herald* about a woman whose husband had been killed in Iraq and how a chaplain informed her just after ringing the doorbell. *If anybody ever comes to my door and tells me my husband died, I will not be able to live.*

Lupe's fears and fantasies drove her family crazy, especially her twenty-five-year-old husband. In the days before he left, there seemed to be nothing Israel Garza could say to Lupe that would make her feel better. On their last day together, they barely spoke. Israel was focused on practical matters, planning for his deployment, and Lupe was nervous. Israel felt he had to prepare himself mentally for the year ahead. He turned to Lupe and said, with little emotion, "I'm ready to go. I'm ready to fight." She hated hearing that.

They had been married three years and had two young children, and when Israel finally boarded the bus that would take him to the airfield, Lupe sobbed as never before. Israel had joined the army so he could provide for his family, and now he was leaving them all behind.

It had now been four days since Lupe and Israel had spoken, but she was still thinking about their last conversation.

"Hey. How ya doin?" the voice on the other end said, when Lupe picked up the phone.

"Sweetie!"

It was an anniversary call—that was the excuse anyway. But Lupe could tell that despite Israel's initial bravado about going to Iraq, he was having as hard a time being apart as she was.

"I'm so tired," Israel said. "I'm ready to go home. Lemme talk to Junior."

Lupe placed the phone next to fourteen-month-old Junior's ear. He made a few grunting sounds, but the boy seemed more interested in teething on the phone than talking into it.

"Now lemme talk to the baby," Israel said. Lupe held the phone up to their infant's mouth. The little one was babbling so much that Lupe could hear Israel laugh on the other end. She gently pulled the phone away from the baby and got on the phone to say good night to her husband.

"I had a dream last night," Israel said.

"A dream?"

"I had a dream that I was hugging Junior so hard and hugging and hugging him and telling him I would be back soon. Then I woke up and realized I was hugging my rucksack.

"I love you all so much," Israel Garza said at the end. "I miss you."

And then he was gone. That was last Wednesday, four days ago. Israel had promised to call again Friday, but the day came and went, and Saturday as well. Now here it was Sunday, and he still hadn't called. All the waiting and the worrying had drained Lupe of energy. She usually spent Sundays at Fort Hood shopping with Israel's sister. But today she wasn't in the mood. She decided to just stay home, watch TV, and look after the children. Maybe Israel would call after all.

LESLEY HILLER and her husband had a deal. He would not let three days go by without a phone call or e-mail. By late afternoon on Palm Sunday it was clear that the three-day limit was going to expire and Dusty Hiller wasn't going to keep his end of the bargain. Lesley stood outside her Killeen home and tried to calm herself.

When Lesley had last spoken to Dusty, the previous Thursday, he'd talked nonstop about the ride in from Kuwait. The couple had grown up together in Alabama, and shared everything with each other. Lesley listened patiently but then could wait no longer. "Dusty, I have some news." Fingering the laminated ultrasound images she had made for her husband, she said with pride and great drama, "It's a boy." Dusty adored his two daughters. But he had made no secret that he longed for a boy.

"It is? It's a boy? Are you sure?" Dusty Hiller was ecstatic, imagining sporting events, fishing, all things male. Then it hit him. It was April 1. April Fools' Day! "Lesley, are you kidding with me?" he asked. Lesley assured her husband that she wouldn't pull such a cruel stunt. But Dusty called back twice in the middle of the night, just to be sure Lesley wasn't joking.

"Why would I lie to you?" she said. Lesley was amused by her husband's skepticism and thrilled by his enthusiasm, but she was exhausted and wanted to go back to sleep. They said good night, and Lesley rolled over.

Three days later, standing in the shade of a small Texas oak, Lesley thought of how much more she had meant to say.

★

THE
PINNED-DOWN
PLATOON

1845 hours

Sadr City

THE SOLDIERS ON THE ROOF saw them first.

At least two hundred Mahdi militiamen and Sadr supporters were coming down the alley en masse from both directions, converging on the house where Shane Aguero's platoon had taken refuge. Some were singing and waving scimitars over their heads like Muslim warriors from another era; many more bore AK-47s, menacingly trained on the U.S. soldiers. Women and children were among them—the children at the very front. Old men carried green banners emblazoned with the name of Moqtada al-Sadr.

In the alleyway, Lieutenant Shane Aguero heard them before he saw them, the chaotic amalgam of chanting and shouting and hundreds of approaching footsteps signaling an unsettling change in enemy tactics. Aguero and his gunner, Sergeant James Fisk, manned one of the two armored Humvees blocking the entrance to the two-story home where the soldiers had taken refuge. Sergeant First Class Jerry Swope and his gunner, Corporal Shane Coleman, were a few feet away in the second Humvee. Both gunners were perched in turrets behind their big .50-caliber guns, staring in disbelief at what was coming at them from either end of the narrow alley. The largest concentration of militia was approaching from Route Delta, toward Swope's Humvee. Aguero jumped out of his own Humvee and moved toward Swope's vehicle, taking cover behind it.

For more than forty-five minutes, they had faced a steady volley of grenades and small-arms fire from rooftop snipers and militiamen dashing quickly from doorways and parked vehicles. Marching an armed crowd down the street toward a secured enemy position was an entirely new tactic—a breathtakingly stupid one, Aguero thought.

"What the fuck?" he shouted up to Coleman. "I guess they want to die!"

The alley, flanked mostly by single-story concrete houses, was roughly ten feet wide, so the crowd could advance only five or six abreast. With a hundred or more people pressing behind them, those in front were marching directly into a line of fire, with no place to hide, no way to turn back. On Aguero's command, Fiske pointed his .50-cal at the crowd approaching from the west, and Coleman aimed his at the mob coming from the direction of Route Delta. Sergeant Eric Bourquin stood in an exposed position alongside the Humvees, ready to fire his M-203 grenade launcher. The rest of the soldiers were hunkered down on the roof of the house with the two M-240s and two M-249s. No one was shooting yet. They knew this kind of firepower could rip through the crowd in seconds.

To Aguero, the most horrifying aspect of what he was watching unfold was that the Mahdi militiamen had put women and children at the front of the advancing horde. Behind them came young men in civilian clothes, many armed with AK-47s, and behind them row after row of Mahdi militiamen, dressed in black, their weapons pointed at the Humvees. Next came the elderly men and women, waving flags and banners and shouting, "Moqtada! Moqtada!"

Jassim, the platoon's Iraqi interpreter, shouted to the crowds, imploring the women and kids at the front, "If you go back, you won't get hurt!"

They didn't listen. The men in civilian clothes began firing on the Humvees, directly over the heads of the children. The militiamen shot at the Americans on the roof. As the firing continued, the mob pressed closer and closer. Aguero and his soldiers were growing increasingly frustrated. They could not fire accurately back at the militiamen without hitting the children in front, but at some point the Americans would have to defend themselves. Aguero calculated that once the crowd approaching from Route Delta got within fifty feet of his platoon, his men would no longer be able to stop them. There would be too many people, too close. Aguero drew an imaginary line in the alley, about fifty yards beyond his current position, and waited. When the front rank of the crowd crossed the line, Aguero started shooting into the crowd. His soldiers, having held their fire until that point, joined in.

Aguero had set his M-4 rifle on a three-round "burst," meaning a single pull of the trigger would fire three rounds. He set his aim at four feet off the ground, trying to avoid the children and hit the militiamen in their upper torsos. Within seconds, he emptied a thirty-round magazine. Aguero hated firing knowing that kids could be hit, and he knew his men felt the same way. *These people are so stupid,* he thought. It was unimaginable to him that someone would intentionally put children in harm's way, and he wished he and his men could be more discriminating. But it was all happening too fast. The gunmen in the crowd kept firing relentlessly, advancing all the while.

The burst setting tended to lift the muzzle of his rifle, sending the rounds too high. The first shot would be accurate, the second would hit about a foot above the aim point, and the third would inevitably miss. So Aguero set his weapon on semiautomatic, dropped the sight level to three feet, and fired off another five or six magazines.

If they don't care about their own children, he told himself, *I don't care either.* Aguero knew he had to protect his platoon.

Jassim, the Iraqi interpreter, and Specialist Carl Wild had taken positions a few feet from Sergeant Fisk's position, and they were now firing on the crowd as well. Jassim was using Sergeant Chen's weapon; Chen lay dead inside. Once the militia started shooting at him and the Americans he was with, the interpreter didn't hesitate to return fire. The gunfire from the platoon was now constant, the soldiers following a well-practiced routine: Look through the gunsight, acquire a target, fire until the target drops. Scan and acquire another target, fire until it drops. Repeat until it's time to reload. Hurry. *Hurry.* The soldiers were now firing in both directions, at the crowd approaching from the west as well as at the people marching in from Route Delta.

The Americans' most damaging fire was coming from the big guns mounted on the Humvees and the machine guns on the rooftop. Each round from a .50-cal could penetrate at least four bodies, and the M-240 was capable of slicing through yards of flesh and bone with a single shot. Sergeant Eric Bourquin launched two grenades, and the fragments ricocheted off walls and through the alleyway at dizzying speed. In little more than thirty seconds, the platoon went through more than three thousand rounds. In barely a minute, the gunfight was over.

Aguero and his men stopped firing and stared, stunned. It was surreal. A tangle of bodies lay in the street, some on top of one another, a cloud of acrid smoke curling over them. Aguero estimated there were at least a hundred dead, including children, stretching back over a distance of about fifty yards. Slowly at first, and then more quickly, townspeople and militiamen began collecting the bodies, dragging them by the legs or under the arms, leaving trails of blood in the street.

The U.S. soldiers kept their weapons ready. If they spotted someone with a gun, they shot him, but if people wandered in unarmed they left them alone. Those were the laws of war. Two ambulances came to carry away some of the dead and wounded. To Aguero and his men, the quick response of medical personnel suggested that officials in the hospitals or local government agencies were complicit in the militia's assault. The sight of the ambulance crews helping the insurgents was infuriating. Here was the platoon, trapped for close to an hour, with one soldier dead and three others wounded, and they couldn't get any help at all. Aguero gripped his weapon tighter.

⎯⎯⎯⎯ ★ ⎯⎯⎯⎯

ALPHA
COMPANY
UNDER
FIRE

⎯⎯⎯⎯⎯⎯

1845 hours

THE DEADLY WHIR OF RPGs, the crack of a rifle shot, the friction from the firing of his own weapon—all these brought Captain George Lewis to a terrible realization: He would never reach Shane Aguero's stranded platoon. And if he didn't find a way out fast, he would soon be watching his own men die one by one.

"There—go!" Lewis shouted to Dusty Hiller, his driver, pointing toward what he thought might be a relatively clear path down Route Charlie for the convoy to follow. It was still a kill zone, but it looked as if enough obstacles had been cleared that at least the vehicles could keep moving. Hiller steered the Humvee in that direction, his big suede boot pressing the accelerator to the floor.

Go, go, go, Lewis thought, repeating the word to himself. Nothing stopping them. *Keep going, yes, yes.* The vehicle kept moving through the gunfire. He looked back at the convoy from the right side of the Humvee, trying to see what was happening to the men in the vehicles behind him, when suddenly his M-998 lurched to a halt.

He glanced forward reflexively, saw nothing blocking the way. "Why the hell are we slowing down?" Lewis shouted. Then he turned to his driver. Dusty Hiller was slumped over the steering wheel.

Oh God, no.

"Sir, sir, he's been shot!" Lieutenant Chris Cannon, sitting in the backseat, was already pulling himself forward to help. But from where Lewis sat, he knew that Hiller was beyond help.

In what seemed like a fraction of a second, Dusty Hiller was dead. One round had entered his neck from above, passed down through the chest cavity. Another had ripped through his side. Blood was collecting on the front of his uniform. He had collapsed the moment he was hit, his foot slipping off the gas pedal. If he'd made any sound, there was too much noise to hear it.

The baby. That was Lewis's first thought: *The baby boy.*

GEORGE LEWIS'S HUMVEE WAS STOPPED, his driver was dead, and PFC Jerry Bune, his wounded gunner, was curled in a fetal position in the back of the Humvee, moaning quietly. Gunfire and explosions continued to rock the vehicle from all sides. The men in the Bradley behind Lewis had moved up on the right side to provide some protection, and the LMTV came up behind it. The Bradley dropped its back ramp so the men from Lewis's vehicle could climb inside. Lewis still saw rounds hitting the dirt as he quickly moved around to the back of his Humvee to coax Bune out.

"I can't, sir," Bune said. "I can't move."

"Come on, Bune!" Lewis, normally soft-spoken, was scream-ing at his gunner. "Get your ass out of there now! Get the fuck out, or we're going to fucking leave you here!" When Bune didn't move, Lewis grabbed him off the back of the Humvee, put his arms around him, and dragged him over to the Bradley.

Lieutenant Cannon, meanwhile, scrambled into the front seat next to Hiller's body and tried to step on the gas to see if he could get the Humvee moving again. But Cannon and Hiller were both big men, and there was no way they both could fit in the driver's seat. Returning to the Humvee, even as shots continued to fly, Captain Lewis told Cannon and Specialist Joel Rabideau, who'd been sitting directly behind Lewis, to pull Hiller into the back. It was impossible. At six-foot-three and well over 240 pounds, Hiller could not be maneuvered. His slumped body slid partway out the door. Lewis agonized over how long this was taking, aware that the rest of the men in his convoy were taking steady fire while their vehicles sat still.

MOST OF THE SIXTEEN SOLDIERS in the back of Sergeant Elliott's LMTV had no idea what was happening. They were shooting in every direction, and explosions were going off all around them. SPC Robert Arsiaga sat scrunched near the cab of the truck, directly across from his friend SPC Israel Garza when, right before Arsiaga's eyes, Garza took a round straight to the gut.

Garza let out a guttural scream and tumbled backward. It was the sound Garza made, at least as much as the sight of the gap-ing entry wound, that flooded Specialist Ray Flores with a brief but undeniable surge of fear.

"I'm dying," Garza wailed. "Oh God, I'm dying!" He started

acting wildly, grabbing at the soldiers around him with blood-soaked hands, falling back on his rear and then struggling to get up.

Flores told everyone to get down, take a knee and keep firing. But the men in the truck were defenseless. "I'm hit! I'm hit!" someone shouted. Almost immediately there followed more cries from several soldiers at once. The militiamen firing at them were getting a clear fix on their targets and growing bolder by the minute. Where faces had appeared only briefly before, the shooters were now taking fixed positions on the rooftops, peering hard down at the convoy, carefully aiming their weapons and firing.

Fish in a barrel, Flores thought. *We're fish in a fucking barrel!* Sixteen men totally exposed in an old bucket of a truck were being shot to pieces, one by one. Men were dropping everywhere. Next to Flores, a deep pink mist spurted from both of Private Michael Pfahler's hands. A bullet had shot a clean hole through one wrist and shattered the bone of the other. The young private began to cry; he fell to the bed of the truck, squeezing the wounds between his knees. Sergeant Stevenson Charite dropped his weapon, grabbed a dressing, and knelt next to Pfahler.

"Charite, what are you doin', man? We're in a kill zone! You can't do first aid yet!"

It was Private Baah, the supply clerk, hollering at Charite. Baah had been firing his weapon nonstop. Charite ignored Baah. Pfahler's wounds were bleeding so heavily that Charite feared the young soldier would be dead in minutes. He was applying pressure to Pfahler's wrists when he saw Robert Arsiaga take a round high on the center of his cheekbone, just below the eye. It left a dime-sized hole; bits of brain and blood flew out from underneath his helmet. His eyes remained open but rolled back in his head. Arsiaga was alive, Baah thought, technically at least. But it was also obvious there was nothing anyone could do.

"Arsiaga!" Baah yelled. "Arsiaga is gone!"

In the middle of the truck, Sergeant Mike Timm felt a thud on his chest, another and another, each one snapping his head back. His body armor saved him, the bullets hitting him squarely in the SAPI plate. Specialist Richard Thompson took a round to the hand, which nearly severed several fingers, but Thompson managed to hold on to his weapon and continue firing and calling out enemy positions. Everyone who could was fighting now, except for one panicked soldier who'd crawled under one of the bench seats and lay there whimpering. The back of the LMTV was now littered with shell casings and filling slowly with blood. The water bottles and brown plastic MRE packages were streaked red. The smell of blood and burned flesh mingled with the stench of gunpowder and explosives.

The moaning and screaming from the back of the truck was nearly as loud as the gunfire. Flores noticed that Private Steven Greenwood had stopped firing. He was just staring at his weapon. "Come on, man," Flores said, urgently but gently. "We need you! I know you're scared, but we're all scared." Then Flores noticed that Greenwood was missing several fingers on his right hand, his shooting hand. He had tried to fire his weapon with his left hand, but he couldn't.

There was so much pain and confusion and gore in the back of the truck that Flores was no longer sure what was happening. When an RPG hit nearby, Flores crouched down as far as he could.

"Are you hit?" another soldier asked.

Shit, Flores thought, noticing the blood now covering his uniform. He assumed it wasn't his: Arsiaga was lying right next to him, still gasping for air, foam and blood caked around his mouth. Hours later, Flores would discover that indeed his own scalp had been split and shrapnel had embedded itself in the flesh of his neck and side: He had, in fact, been hit twice, in the head. But in the moment he hardly noticed; instead he rolled onto his back and started firing straight up at the rooftops.

The truck took a direct hit from yet another RPG, and this one left almost everyone in the vehicle sprayed with blood. Sergeant Salvador Beltran, spitting up bits of tissue, his face pocked with bloody hunks of shrapnel and rock, kept firing.

Private Baah silently recited a prayer, trying desperately to stave off the pain from the shrapnel wound in his thigh—*Yea, though I walk through the valley of the shadow of death I will fear no evil*—all the time firing wildly at the buildings lining the street. *Just keep shooting,* he told himself. Arsiaga had given him that advice when they'd jumped into the truck back at Eagle base. "Don't worry. Anything happens, just keep shooting." Now Arsiaga lay in a pitiful mound next to Baah, his half-open eyes fixed in a death stare.

Then a flash, a high-pitched whir, and Baah saw his own knuckle explode, bones shredded and exposed, as he was knocked back into the bloody heap of wounded soldiers. Sergeant Charite, a massive gunshot wound in his leg, screamed in pain as all of Baah's weight landed on top of him. By now there was no place to lie, because the bed was filled with bleeding and broken soldiers. Private Fabrizzio Panimboza swung his arm around Baah and pulled him down next to himself, trying to get Baah out of the line of fire. Baah covered his head with his hands and kept praying.

SERGEANT EDWARD ELLIOTT and Oracio Pena, manning the front of the LMTV, had no idea how bad things had gotten in back. As soon as the truck had pulled up near Lewis's Humvee, Lewis called to Elliott to help move Hiller's body. Elliott and Pena jumped from the truck, darting through the gunfire, to help Chris Cannon lift Hiller up, equipment and all, and prop him in the Humvee passenger seat. But no sooner had Elliott headed back to his truck than Hiller fell out, headfirst, onto the ground. With no door in the Humvee, there was no way to keep his body upright.

Captain Lewis, meanwhile, saw blood spilling over the left side of the LMTV, right where Garza had been shot. He could see some of the guys were covered with blood and terrified. "How many?" he shouted up to Sergeant Beltran. Before Beltran could answer, Specialist Thompson—still trying to fight despite nearly losing his fingers—started screaming at his company commander.

"What the fuck are you doing, sir?!" he yelled at Lewis. "We gotta get out of here!"

"Yeah, I know," Lewis said.

"Let's go!" Thompson screamed. "We're all gonna die here!"

"Calm down, soldier," Lewis ordered.

Only then did Thompson and the other soldiers in the truck see Hiller, covered in blood and lifeless. Lewis grabbed him under the arms, and Cannon and Rabideau took his ankles, and the three of them carried Hiller over to the nearby Bradley. AK-47 rounds were ricocheting off the pavement all around them. Lewis saw at least two spark right next to his feet. Once Hiller had been loaded into the Bradley, Lewis, Rabideau, and Cannon ran back to their Humvee. Though it had no doors, no top, no armor, the vehicle was still full of weaponry and sensitive equipment, and if they could get it out of there, they were determined to do so. As they climbed in, SFC Reggie Butler's Humvee pulled past them and took off, bumping down the street. No one was in the gun turret. Sergeant Elliott and Specialist Walker also ran back to their vehicle and jumped into the cab.

"You ready to go?" Elliott said to Walker, the driver.

"Roger, Sergeant," Walker said. He stepped on the gas and the truck jerked forward. All four tires had been blown out, and it would have to be driven on the wheel rims. And they weren't out of the fire yet. With the windshield knocked out, the soldiers in the cab could easily be seen, and within moments Elliott took a round in the leg. Walker was hit in the arm a few minutes later, but he kept his grip on the steering wheel and continued driving.

Lieutenant Cannon took Hiller's spot behind the wheel and got the lead Humvee moving again up Route Charlie. Lewis told Cannon to take the first right and go straight back to Camp War Eagle. His plan was to return the wounded to base, get the remaining men into heavier vehicles, and then head back out to continue the rescue mission. Lewis still had some communications capability on an FM frequency with a Bradley farther back in the convoy, and via the Bradley crew he relayed word to the other vehicles in the convoy what he had planned. At Route Bravo, heading back east in their battered and bloodied Humvee, Cannon and Lewis ran into the same trap of obstacles and debris that had blocked the Charlie Company convoy. Lewis told Cannon to turn north, hoping that the farther they drove from the city center, the less gunfire they would face. A Bradley followed close behind, attempting to give Lewis and his crew some protection.

Just ahead, the LMTV staggered back toward the base. By now, only three soldiers in the back of the truck were still capable of firing a weapon. Specialists Ray Flores and Armando Olazaba had both been injured by shrapnel but could still fight, as could Private Fabrizzio Panimboza, who had only been grazed by a bullet.

Lieutenant Cannon took another turn off Route Bravo to get farther away from the kill zone, but then a new nightmare came to Cannon and his men, their engine quit, and the Humvee came to a stop. The gas tank had ruptured; the vehicle was out of fuel. For the second time in a quarter hour, Cannon and the others in the Humvee were exposed and under fire. This time, Captain

Lewis told Cannon and Specialist Rabideau to leave the Humvee and take cover with him in a nearby building. The men did not hesitate. The three soldiers pressed up against the wall of the building as rounds popped all around them. Cannon prepared to kick a door in to get inside. Lewis looked across the intersection and spotted a guy on a rooftop taking aim with an AK-47. Raising his M-16 toward the muzzle flashes, Lewis fired. Just then, the Bradley that had been following his Humvee pulled up next to the building, spitting dirt in all directions, and the ramp dropped. Lewis, Rabideau, and Cannon hurried inside to safety.

Bune was sitting on the left bench, his pant leg cut off and his calf wrapped in bandages. The panic had subsided, and he was now quiet. Sprawled in the middle of the Bradley was Hiller, on his back between the two seats, his eyes partially open. His body armor had been opened, so the full severity of his wounds was visible. Lewis saw him for only a moment before the ramp closed, leaving the vehicle's interior shrouded in darkness. It smelled like a butcher shop, Lewis thought, and he was momentarily overwhelmed, his nostrils involuntarily twitching. Hiller had bled almost dry. Lewis looked down at the laces of his own boot, now soaked red. He heard three or four RPGs go off in quick succession.

The LMTV rocked from side to side on its wheel rims. The soldiers in SFC Reggie Butler's Humvee saw the vehicle as it entered a traffic circle near Route Silver. Blood ran in wide swaths from the rear of the truck, pouring out in such volume that Butler at first thought a water jug had burst. Inside, the wounded lay one on top of another. Of the sixteen men who had left the base in the back of the LMTV, one was dead, another near death, and all but one had suffered shrapnel or gunshot wounds. The one soldier who had escaped unharmed still cowered under the bench, where he had been almost since the shooting started.

Chapter 13

★

CASUALTY

COLLECTION

1845 hours

THE COLLECTION OF HOBBLED Charlie Company vehicles
that made it back to the intersection of routes Aeros and Copper
bore no resemblance to the powerful convoy that had passed
through the gates of Camp War Eagle just half an hour earlier.
Thirty minutes, and the entire lot had been scorched, perforated,
or dented, singed black by homemade bombs and RPGs, riddled
with bullet holes, windshields shattered, tires flat. The last vehicle
to pull up at the intersection was an unarmored LMTV that wob-
bled along on four blown tires, its engine smoking. Even the
mighty Bradley escorting the truck had been scarred by enemy
fire; all the gear strapped to the vehicle's armored sides was lost,
blasted away.

The Charlie Company commander, Captain Troy Denomy,
designated the Aeros–Copper intersection a "casualty collection
point," where he and his officers could take a quick accounting of
their soldiers and transfer the most seriously wounded into one

or two vehicles for dispatch back to the base. Denomy put his ex-ecutive officer, Lieutenant Clay Spicer, in charge of organizing the evacuation, despite the fact that Spicer had a bullet lodged in his calf and needed medical help himself.

The Aeros–Copper intersection lay on the far eastern edge of Sadr City, where hostile fire was less intense. Still, it was a danger-ous location. The trucks and the more vulnerable Humvees were clustered together in the middle of the intersection, the Bradleys parked alongside to shield them from rooftop snipers who were still shooting, still determined to kill Americans. Some of the un-injured soldiers left their vehicles and began taking up positions in doorways and behind walls, their weapons held high, watching for any Iraqis who might have hostile intent.

"Back! Get back! Go inside!" one soldier yelled, gesturing menacingly with his rifle. He had seen an Iraqi man poke his head out the window of his apartment. Every few moments, it seemed, somebody somewhere took a potshot at the small U.S. military encampment in the middle of the road, but as usual it was hard to pinpoint the shooter.

Denomy moved from vehicle to vehicle, checking on his Charlie Company soldiers, his own left arm and shoulder wrapped tightly in a white bandage. He'd been hearing radio reports of casualties all the way through the city, but he was shaken to see for himself how gravely his company had been hit. In the back of one of the Bradleys he found two soldiers with serious leg injuries, including Staff Sergeant Robert Reynolds—"Big Country"—who had been put on a stretcher and laboriously lifted out of one of the LMTVs. At nearly three hundred pounds, Reynolds had been especially dif-ficult to move. As a squad leader in Third Platoon, he had been manning the mounted machine gun in the truck when a high-velocity round tore into his upper thigh, blasting it wide open. Denomy had wanted to take all the heavily armored vehicles back into the city for a second rescue effort, but he didn't have the heart to move Big Country out of the Bradley, and decided to reserve it for evacuating the wounded to the aid station back at Camp War Eagle instead.

THE CASUALTY COLLECTION stop provided Denomy and the other soldiers a brief respite, during which they began to reflect on what they'd just gone through: This had been for almost all of the men the first combat experience of their lives. A few found themselves shaking uncontrollably, even as they vowed to return to the city and resume fighting. Better, they reasoned, to get back before they had more time to think about it. Denomy himself realized two things once he stopped fighting: First, his injured shoulder was throbbing. Second, he seriously had to take a leak. He was wearing a Camelbak, the backpack-like water reservoirs that soldiers often wore in the heat, and while fighting his way up and down Route Bravo he had sucked it dry without even knowing it. His bladder was about to burst, and he had to step behind a Humvee to relieve himself against a tire.

On this far end of Sadr City, the sounds of gunfire were more distant, but they were incessant. Somewhere nearby, Captain Lewis and his Alpha Company soldiers must have been shooting it out with the Mahdi militia forces, but Denomy had no idea where they were. Shortly after leaving the base camp, he and Lewis had switched to different radio frequencies, and amid the chaos of battle and the congestion of the radio communications, they had lost touch with each other.

What Denomy did know was that his First Platoon remained stranded in an alley off Route Delta. All attempts to reach Shane Aguero and his soldiers had failed; no U.S. military unit had advanced within a mile of the building where they had taken refuge.

It was not for lack of trying, though, and Denomy wished there was a way for Aguero and his men to know how determined their brothers were to find them. If only they could see Big Country, the loud and gutsy warrior whose personality matched his out-sized physique. Even as he lay wounded, Reynolds was struggling to rally his buddies to keep fighting. When Denomy had checked on him in the Bradley, Reynolds grabbed him by the arm to tell him something. Denomy thought he knew what Reynolds wanted to say.

"Don't worry," Denomy told him. "We're going back to kill every goddamn one of those sonsabitches."

IN THE CENTER of the intersection, Lieutenant Colonel Volesky sat in his Humvee with the door ajar and one foot on the ground, intense but in control. He was on the radio urgently devising a new rescue plan with his battalion officers back at the Tactical Operations Center, when up ahead he spotted Lieutenant John Gilbreth, the Second Platoon commander who had been forced to abandon his disabled Humvee under fire on Route Bravo.

"Hey, John."

"Colonel Volesky, sir," Gilbreth said, obviously surprised. "What are you doing here?" In the heat and confusion of the Sadr City fighting, neither Denomy nor Gilbreth knew Volesky had been following them, even though they had been in regular radio communication. Nor had they realized he was parked virtually next to them at the casualty collection point.

"I followed up behind you," Volesky said. "Where's your company commander?"

"He's around here somewhere. I'll find him." Moments later, Denomy came running up to Volesky's Humvee.

"Troy, how are you? What happened?" Volesky asked, gesturing at the bandage on Denomy's arm. There was a stillness about his demeanor that was reassuring. The world was going to hell all around them, yet Gary Volesky seemed calm, focused on the situation at hand.

"I got shot," Denomy replied.

"Are you all right?" Volesky asked. He paused to get a read on Denomy—not just his wound but his mental state; Volesky knew how grave the situation was. What he wanted to know now was how his men were bearing up.

"Yes, sir, I'm okay," Denomy said.

Volesky nodded. "Great. Okay, then. As soon as you get your guys patched up, let's get going. We have to try something different."

Denomy dropped to his knee behind the Humvee door, shielding himself from possible sniper fire, and gave Volesky a quick summary of his casualty situation and the status of his vehicles. Volesky's new plan was to head out again with the Charlie Company convoy, but this time to use a different route into the city. The convoy would go back north on Aeros to the far northeast corner, then turn west on Route Silver, along the northern edge of Sadr City, proceed to Route Delta, and then attack south down that street until reaching the alley where Aguero's platoon was located. This new route would minimize the convoy's exposure, because Route Silver was bordered on its northern side by a canal, rather than the three- and four-story concrete buildings that had proved so dangerous in the city center. Two Bradleys would lead that arm of the rescue mission.

After conferring with Volesky, Denomy dashed back to reassemble his remaining soldiers—meaning anyone who could still fight, despite the agony of small wounds. Lieutenant Spicer was leading a Bradley and an LMTV, both vehicles were filled with seriously wounded soldiers, back to the first aid station at Camp War

Eagle. The rest of Charlie Company would accompany Denomy on the new rescue mission. Denomy could barely hold his weapon, but he would direct the Charlie Company soldiers on the mission, with a total of seven men now squeezed inside his battered, open-topped Humvee. His driver, Specialist Seth Wiebley, and Staff Sergeant John Dumdie had both been wounded during the Route Bravo run, but they insisted on staying alongside Denomy and riding in the open back of the Humvee with Specialist Leeton Burkholder, the gunner who had miraculously avoided injury during the first trip.

There were significant additions to Denomy's unit: Fifteen fresh soldiers from Alpha Company, riding in an unarmored LMTV, pulled in behind Denomy's convoy and followed it into the city. These soldiers, led by Staff Sergeant Alfonso Miranda and Staff Sergeant Robert Miltenberger, hadn't yet seen any combat. They had been the last to leave Camp War Eagle when the rescue convoys were first organized, and they had fallen far behind the rest of their company. Their truck reached the Aeros–Copper intersection just as the first vehicles from Captain Denomy's convoy were returning from their run down Route Bravo, and Miranda and Miltenberger decided to stop to help Charlie Company set up its casualty collection point. Miltenberger was stunned by the injuries he saw when the truck pulled in.

What went on out there?

But he had to put that out of his mind—the situation was bad, no doubt about it, but Shane Aguero's platoon was in trouble, needed help, and to Miltenberger and his men, that was all that mattered. The good news was that, by joining Denomy's convoy, he would gain the much-needed firepower from the Bradleys and Humvees.

Once the casualty collection operation was complete, Miltenberger and Miranda loaded up to follow Volesky and Denomy back into the city. As they were getting ready to roll, Volesky's Humvee pulled forward. He leaned out the window and called to anyone in earshot:

"Are we all ready? Our boys are out there!"

Someone—Volesky wasn't sure who—yelled out a response.

"We're just waiting for you, sir."

Chapter 14

★

BEDLAM

1900 hours

FROM THE DOORWAY of the small aid station at Camp War Eagle, Captain David Mathias had a sweeping vista of bedlam. And it was coming straight at him—blackened Humvees careening through the gates on rubberless rims. Trailing far behind, a blackened LMTV, blood covering the sides, with soldiers screaming for help—or just plain screaming.

Oh my word, Mathias thought. *This is unreal.* A deeply religious young man, the pediatrician who had never treated a traumatic injury was now watching a tidal wave of bloodied Alpha Company soldiers coming his way—some carried or dragged on makeshift litters, some staggering and limping, clutching the few of their buddies who could still walk.

Mathias swallowed hard. "Over here!" he shouted. "Bring them over here!" PFC Jerry Bune, Captain Lewis's gunner, had been shot in the leg. He was grimacing, his arms wrapped around the necks of the soldiers who carried him, a trail of blood marking the path below. Mathias directed them to a metal table and immediately got to work, giving Bune an IV to get fluids and painkillers into his body. He dressed the wounds and moved to the next injury. The medics followed him, shearing off uniforms and gear; the soldiers' weapons were collected outside, a pile of black steel that would grow and grow as the evening progressed. Mathias jammed his hands into bloody pants, over shoulders, and around backs, checking for additional wounds that might be hidden from view.

Move. Move. Keep moving.

They kept coming. Soon it was clear that there wasn't enough room in the aid station for all the wounded. The hardest hit were carried inside. The rest were laid outside on the ground.

Mathias was plugging holes as fast as possible, doing everything he could. The aid station wasn't set up for surgery—it lacked the equipment and had no blood supply, which made even removing a bullet a perilous procedure. For now Mathias needed to stop blood loss, secure airways, and dress shattered limbs. The most seriously injured men would have to be medevaced to the combat support hospital in Baghdad's Green Zone.

The only good luck of the night was that there were almost thirty doctors, medics, and physician's assistants at the aid station— far more than normal. The outgoing medical unit from the Second Armored Cavalry Regiment had yet to leave, so the outgoing and incoming teams were working together. But even with the extra hands, Mathias worried that the torrent of casualties would overwhelm them.

CHAPLAIN RAMON PENA followed a group of medics as they hustled back to the vehicles for a second load of wounded soldiers.

"Can you breathe?" he asked the first man he saw. "Can you walk?" He was improvising. He'd worked as a hospital chaplain before, but this was far more devastating than anything he'd ever witnessed. This was war.

"We need help!" screamed Staff Sergeant David Ryan. He'd been running alongside his Humvee, guiding the driver through the gates of Camp War Eagle to the aid station. Ryan could use his right eye, but his left eye was pulp. A chunk of shrapnel had opened a blinding gash, leaving chunks of tissue hanging down his cheek, drenching the eyeball in blood. Seemingly unfazed, he began lifting his buddies out of the vehicle.

Pena hurried to Ryan as soon as he saw how seriously he was hurt. It wasn't just the eye; Ryan had chunks of rock and shrapnel lodged in his lips, his nose, his forehead. Pena took him by the arm.

"You need to come with me," he said.

Ryan resisted. "I'm trying to help these guys!" he screamed. "Leave me the fuck alone."

Ryan had no idea he was so badly injured. He could think only of his buddies. Pena assured him that his fellow soldiers were in good hands, and persuaded him to sit down. A moment later, two medics were leaning over Ryan, pulling off his body armor to search for additional wounds.

"Are you okay?" the medics asked calmly. They didn't want him to sense how badly he was injured. But Ryan caught passing soldiers gaping at him with open mouths.

"Quit staring and go help out!" he yelled. He was starting to shiver. The brutal desert heat had eased, replaced by an evening chill. The dirt David Ryan sat on was cool to the touch now. He looked up into the moonlit sky. Ryan had always wanted to fly planes, and he had started drawing them as a child, dreaming of the day he'd take the controls himself. However, his grades kept him grounded, and instead of a career in the U.S. Air Force, Ryan had joined the Army, and now he lay bleeding in a Sadr City aid station surrounded by infantrymen in the same sorry shape.

PENA HEARD the soldiers calling for him. "Chaplain, please help me." Some begged him not to leave their sides, scared to be left alone; others moaned for their buddies. Pena offered comfort and prayer. He tried to reach everyone.

"You're going to be okay," he said over and over.

One soldier with minor injuries became terrified when he saw the black cross on Pena's uniform as he approached. "Don't worry," Pena assured him. "You're not going to die. I'm just here to see if you're okay."

WITH A BULLET lodged near his spine, Sergeant Tim Apple was delirious during the ride back to Camp War Eagle. He'd been shot while manning the gun in Staff Sergeant Ernesto Hernandez's Humvee.

"Don't die, Sergeant Apple!" his buddies screamed at him, but that only scared him more. He thought, *Am I going to die?* Apple felt the sting, the burning in his back. Oh yeah, it burned. *But is it going to kill me?*

He heard screaming in the aid station. He saw chaos all around him, soldiers lying on the ground and medics running past. Someone leaned close and whispered, "You're going to be okay."

He wasn't so sure.

FAR BEHIND THE FIRST GROUP of Humvees, the Alpha Company LMTV limped into camp. From the back of the truck came a horrible cacophony of wailing and moaning. There was blood everywhere. The soldiers were covered in it. The plastic-wrapped MREs and the quart-sized water bottles were sliding around in the streams of blood between the men.

"We've got a soldier in serious trouble!" someone hollered to the head doctor, Lieutenant Colonel Robert Gerhardt.

Gerhardt had just arrived. He threw off his helmet, dropped his weapon, and grabbed his medical gear. The soldier was Specialist Israel Garza, who'd been lifted from the back of the LMTV with his abdomen blown out. Gerhardt had treated trauma before as a firefighter and an army emergency room doctor, but it was nothing like this.

Vomit, brown and bloody, erupted from Garza, drenching Gerhardt as he moved closer to examine him. Gerhardt didn't flinch. He turned Garza's head to clear the vomit then struggled to open up the airway. The soldier wasn't making a sound. Gerhardt grabbed a thick clear plastic tube and pushed it past the soldier's tongue and into his swollen throat. It didn't work. He tried again and again. Gerhardt knew he was running out of time. He put his fingers on the soft patch of skin below the Adam's apple and, with a small surgical knife, made a quick incision, half an inch wide, half an inch deep, into the brittle pink cartilage of Garza's windpipe. Then he spread open the bloody hole with his fingers and inserted the plastic tracheostomy tube. The airway opened. The tracheostomy was complete. The medics started an IV, and Gerhardt moved on.

Dr. Mathias bent close to Specialist Sergio Estrella. His shirt had been torn open, and Mathias could see a small gaping wound in the chest. A wheezing sound came from the hole, which meant air was escaping from the chest cavity. But Estrella was fully conscious. Mathias called out for help. "He has a sucking chest wound!"

This is bad, Mathias thought.

Just then, Estrella perked up. "A sucking chest wound? I do?" he whispered. "Really? I've heard about those." Estrella's curiosity—excitement, almost—defused Mathias's anxiety a little. He smiled and continued working feverishly to seal the wound.

Captain Trent Upton was doing his best to keep track of the nightmarish number of casualties. *Gunshot wound to the leg. Gunshot wound to the head. RPG shrapnel to the shoulder.* Upton's job was to tally the injuries like an accountant, but he was badly shaken. He knew some of the soldiers by name, others only by the small metal dog tags dangling around their necks or tied to their belt loops or bootlaces.

Upton was beginning to worry about the fading light. There was no electricity outside the aid station, so he ordered that all available Humvees, even the ones shot up in the battle, be moved to the immediate perimeter of the aid station. Beams from the muddied headlights sent a grainy glow across the soldiers lying in the dirt. Then Upton spotted a soldier lying outside the aid station, close to the wall. He didn't know who it was, only that the soldier was dead. And big. And white. His uniform top and T-shirt had been pulled up over his face, and his chest was smeared with blood.

"Chaplain Pena!" Upton shouted.

The chaplain made his way past the stretcher, through the men sprawled on the ground and the others stumbling around aimlessly. He and Upton exchanged a grim look and then peered down at the body.

"Okay," Upton finally whispered, rolling down the uniform top that was covering the face, until the name tape was visible. *Hiller.*

Trent Upton had never seen a dead body before, and here was a soldier he'd *known.* Hiller's eyes were slightly open—opaque—his lips parted and slack. A father and husband, with a pregnant wife waiting at home. Upton and Pena crouched on either side of him. Pena lifted Hiller's fingers and whispered a prayer, while Upton bowed his head. Then Pena covered the body with a flowery, fuzzy blanket, an Iraqi blanket. He took one final look at Hiller's face and wished he hadn't. The image seared itself into his mind— ghoulish, large, and haunting.

Then Pena moved away. There were other soldiers who needed comfort.

IN THE FRONT of the aid station, Colonel Robert Abrams stared in disbelief at the men lying before him. He'd gunned his Humvee, watching the streaks of tracer fire over Sadr City while he drove the four miles from brigade headquarters to Camp War Eagle. The ride had taken fifteen minutes. Though he'd received radio updates, Abrams was not prepared for what met him inside the gates.

The first thing he saw was the Alpha Company LMTV, all shot to hell, blood pouring off its left side. Nearby, naked and bloody soldiers lay moaning in the sand, their uniforms cut off and thrown in a growing pile. Abrams thought it looked like a slaughterhouse. Green plastic wrappers from field dressings were strewn everywhere, bloody footprints ground into them. Next to the station lay a pile of discarded M-16s and M-4s, the guns piled like a giant steel haystack. Abrams was horrified. *A soldier doesn't willingly abandon his weapon,* he thought. And then: *I couldn't possibly have this many wounded soldiers.*

Then he saw "Big Country"—Sergeant Robert Reynolds— lying on a litter.

"Big Country?" Abrams crouched beside him.

"Yes, sir," Reynolds said. "Shit. Fucking A. *Mother fucking A.*"

Abrams stared at him. One of his best squad leaders, so massive that his M-4 looked like a toothpick in his arms, his head shaved high and tight, Reynolds now lay on the ground with a wound that had blown out most of his inner thigh. That's when it hit Colonel Abrams—that his men were really *at war*.

Robert Abrams grew up around war but he had never lost anyone in combat. His father, Creighton Abrams, had commanded U.S. military forces in Vietnam between 1968 and 1972, when he became the army chief of staff. Robert "Abe" Abrams was the youngest of six Abrams children, but the only one to have shared a remarkable summer with his father in the Vietnam war zone— when he was only eight years old. In 1969, his two older brothers, already serving as army officers, by then were doing tours of duty in Vietnam. Abe was living in Thailand with his mother. When Julia Abrams was called back to the United States to spend a few months helping her daughter and daughter-in-law with newborns, she made what must have seemed to her friends an astonishing move: She sent young Robert to live with his father in Saigon.

The youngest Abrams was given a special camouflage suit— "jungle stripes"—with his name tag sewn above the pocket, just like what the soldiers wore. He spent his days with his father's security personnel, riding around in jeeps and firing his .22 rifle on the range. In the evenings there was almost always time for father and son to have dinner together. Abrams loved hearing his father's stories and over time would appreciate more and more the efforts his father made to maintain a bond with his son. It was an unforgettable summer; afterward there was never any doubt that Robert Abrams would follow his father and brothers into the army.

Abrams noticed Trent Upton walking forward through the light of the Humvees. He didn't look good. Upton approached him and began to speak rapidly, eyes burning and fists clenched. Abrams understood well the difference between a military aid station and a civilian hospital. While both may see horrific injuries, for the men in this aid station, the soldiers they were treating could also be close friends, dinner mates, poker buddies.

Abrams knew that Upton was trying to contend with that terrible strain now—he could see it in the young man's face. Upton looked the way Abrams felt in his own sore heart.

My friends are dying—I have to try to save them.

Fighting his own emotions, Abrams snapped at Upton, "Do you have an accurate count?" He wanted to be sure every soldier's wounds and treatment plans were carefully documented.

"No, sir. Not yet, sir."

"Get one."

"Yes, sir."

Upton had been working since the first soldiers arrived at the aid station, but the confusion and the scores of casualties were nearly impossible to tally. Two Black Hawk helicopters with a team of doctors had finally landed about two hundred yards from the aid station, and now they were waiting to ferry the critically wounded to Baghdad. Upton turned and hurried inside.

Specialist Ahmed Cason was in serious trouble. His eyes were open and he was awake, but he wasn't talking. The Alpha Company gunner had gone down early in the battle. His veins were shriveled, and his dark black skin had turned a milky brown. Doc Gerhardt had been trying to find a vein, but now he gave up and jammed a needle deep into the muscle to get whatever fluids and antibiotics he could into Cason's body. Then he signaled to Upton to get Cason to the helicopters.

Cason was swaddled in blankets and a sleeping bag, loaded onto a litter, and carried to the choppers in a swirl of darkening dust. Upton ran alongside him, clutching Cason's hand. "How ya doin'?" he asked. "Hang in there." Cason smiled weakly. He said nothing. As Upton let go of Cason's hand to load him into the helicopter, the wounded soldier lifted his left thumb. He was telling Upton he'd be okay.

Specialist Israel Garza wasn't as lucky. Abrams had gone out to the landing zone and was watching the medics load him into a helicopter. Garza was naked, a space blanket tucked loosely around him, the deep red of his abdominal wound stark against his ashen body. The doctors had done emergency CPR even as they transported him to the chopper, and it continued once he was inside. But it was too late. Abrams could see that he wasn't going to make it. Garza, like most of the soldiers from the 2-5 Cav, had been in Iraq only four days.

Sergeant Oracio Pena, one of the Alpha Company gunners (no relation to Chaplain Pena), had returned to Camp War Eagle in the safety of a Bradley. After his company was assaulted, he'd jumped out of the LMTV to help load Hiller, Bune, and some of the other injured soldiers into the Bradley, and then he had stayed with them. Now, watching the carnage outside the aid station, Oracio Pena realized how much hell the soldiers in the LMTV had gone through after he'd left them. Baah. Charite. Thompson. Elliott. Nearly all nineteen men who had been in the LMTV lay bleeding and groaning around him. Some made no sound at all.

One of them was Specialist Robert Arsiaga. He'd been shot in the head, and Pena walked by several times without recognizing him. Sergeant Flores tugged him on the sleeve and pointed.

"Arsiaga is dead," he said.

"No, he's not," Pena said. *Maybe,* he thought, *if I argue with Flores, it won't be true.* Arsiaga had been his friend, closer to him than the other soldiers. Now Tracy, Arsiaga's wife of only five months, was a widow. Pena was seized with guilt and rage. He howled at the sky, picking up whatever he could get his hands on—discarded bottles, shredded uniforms—and throwing them wildly.

"I can't believe this!" he screamed. "I can't believe I'm the only one who didn't get hit!"

He knelt in the dirt at the side of the aid station and pounded on the wall, sobbing. Upton and Staff Sergeant Keith Harris rushed up to him. Harris grabbed his shoulders and shook him.

"Hey, big sergeant, you gotta hang in there and be tough for your soldiers." Harris knew a panicked, hysterical sergeant wasn't going to do anyone any good.

Pena stood slowly and tried to pull himself together. *The rest of his men,* he had to check on the rest of his men. During the farewell ceremony at Fort Hood, the mother of one of his soldiers had made a request he had not forgotten.

"Please bring my baby home," she'd said.

Captain Jeff Oliver had been at the brigade headquarters operations center in Baghdad with Colonel Abrams when he saw a small red square with a K in the middle pop up on a digital screen in front of him. Oliver, a physician, knew what that meant. *A soldier is dying.* Oliver was still sweating from a trip to the gym. He grabbed his bags and headed to Camp War Eagle.

Twenty minutes later, he was standing outside the aid station, stunned by the volume of casualties. The cries of anguish, the awful musky smell. The first person Oliver saw was Doc Gerhardt. Beads of perspiration blended sickeningly with the blood and vomit staining the camouflage of his uniform. They'd completed an emergency medicine fellowship together in 2000, and decided then that they made perfect partners. They could read each other's hand signals and eye movements. Now, four years later, the two men grabbed each other in a tight embrace.

"It's good to see you, brother."

"Good to see you, too."

There was no time to talk. They split up, moving from one casualty to the next.

"Don't help me, help my buddy," a wounded soldier would say. The words nearly brought Gerhardt to tears.

"He's all right," the doctor would say in response. "He wants us to take care of you."

Meanwhile, Upton was walking and writing, jotting down the names of soldiers who had been medevaced. A doctor called out to him.

"Can you get me another field dressing?"

Upton found one. The doctor asked him to open it and wait there a moment. The wounded soldier, Specialist Jeffrey Jahelka, had a large white gauze dressing on the left side of his neck, but no other visible trauma. He was smiling strangely and jabbering nonsense. Upton figured the morphine had kicked in. He talked to Jahelka, watching as the doctor peeled back the dressing on his neck.

Oh shit! Upton said to himself. He looked away so Jahelka wouldn't see his horror. The soldier had a deep wound from the back of his hairline to his jawbone. His throat lay open, revealing a mass of tendons and tissue pulsing inside. A wave of nausea gripped Upton, but he forced it back. As the doctor replaced the dressing, Upton turned to Jahelka and smiled.

"I'll check on you again later," he said.

Leaning against the wall of the aid station, Upton saw Sergeant Joshua Daniels and PFC Duncan Koebrick sitting together, shivering. Their boots were off and their uniform tops were spread open—a sign that they'd already been checked for serious wounds. But something looked wrong. They seemed to be in shock. Upton squatted beside them and asked if they were okay.

Both men had taken multiple rounds to the chest, every round deflected by their ceramic SAPI plates, the small-arms protective inserts that slip inside Kevlar vests. These plates had provided lifesaving protection from high-velocity bullets. Daniels had been hit three or four times, Koebrick at least twice. The impact force had left deep bruises, but the men were alive, and they couldn't believe it. They stared blankly ahead, talking rapidly.

"We got shot. The SAPI saved my life, sir. The SAPI saved my life."

Upton grabbed a nearby sleeping bag, wrapped it snugly around the soldiers, and told them to hang in there.

Half an hour after the first wave of casualties, the aid station seemed to settle into organized chaos. More than two dozen soldiers still lay on the ground, while the more seriously injured men had been medevaced to Baghdad. Gerhardt was exhausted. He'd lost track of the number of soldiers he'd treated, and he'd pronounced Hiller killed in action—his first-ever KIA. Worse, the gunfire from the city had grown louder and more frequent, and there was still no word about the ambushed platoon.

Could there be more on the way? Gerhardt wondered.

Just then, a soldier rushed in to announce he'd heard of a possible attack on Camp War Eagle itself. Mobs of people from Sadr City might try to break through the gates, the soldier shouted. *Probably just a rumor,* Gerhardt thought. *But still.*

Another soldier grabbed a helmet and threw it to Gerhardt.

"Here, Doc, put this on."

Gerhardt caught the helmet, the blast goggles still attached. He'd tossed his own aside when he first got to the aid station.

"This isn't my helmet."

"Don't worry, Doc, just put it on."

Gerhardt put on the helmet and went back to work. It was only later, much later, that he took off the helmet and looked at the name on the front. *Shit,* he thought. *Which soldier was this?* It was a name he didn't recognize. *I hope he's okay.*

★

Chapter 15

CHARLIE
COMPANY:
RULES OF
ENGAGEMENT

1900 hours

IT WASN'T A BULLET or an RPG that brought Captain Troy Denomy's Humvee to a near halt, but a blanket of raw sewage so thick that the driver, SPC Seth Wiebley, suddenly couldn't see through the windshield.

"Holy shit!" Wiebley yelled. The irony of his expletive was lost on the young soldier. Wiebley had swerved around a concrete barrier in the road and driven straight through a pool of human waste that splattered across much of the chassis. A collective retch came from the soldiers as the full stink of the mixture filled the vehicle. But Wiebley kept plowing through the brown muck, peering low through a small section of filmy glass, trying to follow the Humvee in front of him. His wipers had been blown off during his last run into the city, but he didn't dare stop to clean the windshield.

Route Silver had proved to be just as dangerous as the streets to the south. As soon as the convoy turned off Route Aeros, the buildings on the left erupted with small-arms fire and rocket-propelled grenades, every bit as intense as what Charlie Company had seen on Route Bravo twenty minutes earlier. Most of the RPGs were poorly aimed, their grenades exploding on the trash-strewn lots on the right side of the road. But sooner or later, one was sure to hit its mark.

Denomy, the Charlie Company commander, was now certain of the nature and scale of what they were up against: an organized, premeditated attack, involving hundreds—*thousands*, perhaps—of heavily armed Mahdi militiamen and Sadr supporters. This wasn't the kind of conventional battle the United States fought during the 1991 Gulf War, or even the 2003 march to Baghdad. The American forces that had so swiftly defeated Saddam Hussein's regular army were ill prepared to fight the urban, guerrilla-style warfare now unfolding before their eyes.

What had been conceived as a peacekeeping mission had changed utterly, in a matter of minutes. Vehicles that had been appropriate for their mission earlier that day were overmatched just two hours later. What Denomy's company faced now was a new kind of war, the front lines blurred or gone altogether. The makeshift barricades and coordinated ambushes made it clear: Moqtada al-Sadr and his Mahdi Army were determined to halt further U.S. penetration into their territory—and to kill as many Americans as possible.

Denomy believed that if the situation didn't improve soon, it might be too late to save Aguero's platoon. Denomy decided it was time to take the fight up a notch. He radioed ahead to the commander of the lead Bradley.

"White Four, this is Comanche Six," he said. "Go ahead and engage with the twenty-five-millimeter." The Bradley's 25-millimeter M-242 Bushmaster cannon could fire two hundred high-explosive rounds a minute, piercing armor or anything else in its way.

"Kill every target you identify," Denomy said coolly.

Denomy could see hundreds of militiamen moving through the buildings and crossing rooftops. He felt that unless he used all the weaponry at his disposal—including the cannon—he and his men would be at a distinct tactical disadvantage. If he worried about the decision because of the collateral damage it could cause, he didn't have to worry long: Just as Denomy was telling his Bradley crew to use the 25mm, he got a call from Volesky, his battalion commander, from the vehicle immediately ahead of him in the convoy, also under intense fire.

"Comanche Six, you can go ahead and start shooting the twenty-five," Volesky shouted.

"Yes, sir," Denomy responded. "I already gave the order."

Within moments, the scene on Route Silver took on a new, deadlier dimension. The Bushmaster cannon fire began obliterating its targets; the most deafening explosions along Route Silver were now coming from the Bradley guns, not from the militia's primitive rocket launchers and improvised pipe bombs. Even while clambering over barriers at twenty miles an hour, the 25's targeting mechanism stayed stable and accurate. The cannon blasted through three-foot-thick masonry walls, leaving gaping, smoking holes in the sides of buildings and spraying a powdery white mist over the bloodied, black-clad Mahdi fighters.

Despite the awesome display of firepower, the militiamen were slow to get the message, or perhaps they were determined to fight, no matter what the odds. A battered car pulled alongside the convoy, its gunmen firing their AK-47s while hanging out the windows. The gunner in the turret of the lead Bradley swiveled quickly, fixed the car in his sights, and fired three times, blasting the car and sending the flesh and bones of its occupants spraying across the street. Moments later, the gas tank blew up, the explosion lifting the burning hulk of a car two feet off the ground.

At the corner of Route Delta, the two Bradleys leading the convoy made a left and headed south. Charlie Company was now only a mile or so north of the alley where Lieutenant Aguero's platoon was stranded, but the stretch ahead was as dangerous as anything the soldiers had yet encountered. Militiamen were everywhere, and the going would be slow. The soldiers had to wind their way through the now familiar labyrinths of concrete barriers, burning trash, rubble, and junk heaps, all the while dealing with the torrent of gunfire coming from both sides of the street.

Volesky's driver, Sergeant "A-Train" Adkins, was trying to navigate the obstacles, but his Humvee couldn't force its way through the barricades the way the tracked Bradleys could. Dodging a rubble pile, Adkins realized he'd swerved the wrong way and was now on a collision course with a barrier directly in front of him.

"Take the sidewalk!" Volesky yelled.

Adkins jerked the wheel to the right and jumped the curb. "Hang on!" The Humvee rammed straight into a refrigerator, sending it clattering and rolling down the sidewalk. Adkins plowed ahead.

The truly expert driving, however, was being done by Seth Wiebley, in Troy Denomy's Humvee, the vehicle behind Volesky's. Wiebley could barely see through his feces-smeared windshield. He was navigating by gut as much as by sight, trying only to follow the path of the Humvee in front of him. Several times Wiebley had to barrel through hurdles of junk, having seen them too late to swerve around them. The explosions around the convoy were constant—from RPGs, pipe bombs, hand grenades, and improvised explosive devices wired to propane tanks for maximum firepower. Denomy, trying to communicate by radio with his stranded platoon, couldn't hear over the noise.

"Hold your fire!" he screamed, pointing at the radio. "Hold your fire! I can't hear!"

The soldiers pulled their weapons inside the Humvee and raised the windows. Sergeant First Class Swope, transmitting from his bullet-riddled Humvee in the alleyway, was repeating the grid coordinates for his location. Denomy had to ask for the coordinates a second time—while he was firing his weapon, he'd lost the scrap of paper he had written them on before.

Two vehicles behind Denomy lumbered the big unarmored LMTV, commanded by staff sergeants Alfonso Miranda and Robert Miltenberger. Twelve soldiers carrying only their personal weapons lay fully exposed to the fire around them. The truck couldn't maneuver like the three Humvees in front of it. As the convoy neared Route Delta, the LMTV was trailing by a dangerous distance, with virtually no protection from the Bradleys up ahead. Beaten back by the Bradleys, the militiamen recognized the LMTV as a highly vulnerable target and a chance to regain the offensive. They turned their firepower on the men crouching inside. By the time the truck was a few blocks down Delta, not fifteen minutes after the drive began, the radiator had been shot and all four tires blown. It was teetering along on its wheel rims, lurching from side to side at a terrifyingly slow speed.

In back, Staff Sergeant Miltenberger was doing his best to maintain shooting discipline among his soldiers, who were lined up on opposite sides of the truck, facing out, with only a thin metal ledge on the sides of the truck protecting them. Some of the men watched the rooftops. Others focused on window and ground level, searching for snipers on either side of the street. Each man was to stay focused on his particular assignment, and ignore everything else. But when the firing erupted on both sides, the soldiers instinctively began turning to see what was happening behind them.

"Cover your sector!" Miltenberger shouted. "Stagger your fire!"

Miltenberger was keeping his own weapon trained at ground level, watching the alleys and doorways in front of him as the truck rolled slowly past. At thirty-eight, Miltenberger was nearly twice the age of many of the other soldiers in the truck, though he didn't look it. The only thing that gave him away were the dark circles and fine lines framing his pale blue eyes.

Taciturn, sometimes cranky, Miltenberger was well regarded by the young men he commanded, rather like an eccentric old uncle. But if it came down to choosing the soldier to stand next to you in battle, Robert Miltenberger wouldn't likely be first choice. He was capable and dependable, but his men knew that he didn't want to be there. Not in that truck, not in Iraq, not even in the army. He'd have gotten out months before, if not for the "stop loss" policy in his contract, which requires service members to extend their volunteer contract if their unit is deployed. Miltenberger had been set to retire just before the soldiers of the First Cav were told they'd be heading for Iraq. Like it or not, he had to go.

He'd never been a gung-ho soldier and he hadn't been promoted in years. Most soldiers his age had moved beyond staff sergeant a decade before. But Miltenberger didn't care much about status or career. The army offered steady work and a camaraderie unmatched in the civilian workforce. He'd seen the world, provided a decent home in Louisiana for his wife, Belinda, and their two children, and managed to stay out of trouble. For a guy with few childhood advantages, he felt he'd done okay. He was quietly dependable, scrupulously honest, and fair with the enlisted men he commanded. He didn't keep his boots well polished or go out of his way to impress his superiors, but those things didn't matter to him.

On the surface, the call to help the stranded platoon didn't seem to matter to him either. When the order came Sunday evening to assemble for the rescue mission, Miltenberger was eating dinner in the chow hall. When the other soldiers leaped up and ran out the door, he stayed to finish his food. He wanted to join the rescue, too, but he feared this might be his last meal. He'd never seen combat, and he had a feeling the worst would happen. He wasn't scared; he was simply a pessimist. His father, a soldier in Vietnam, had told him stories about the hellish realities of war. Miltenberger figured it was just his luck to make it to the end of his army career and get himself killed.

He pulled on his battle gear and headed out to the convoy. But something changed when he saw the soldiers jumping into the truck. As the sound of gunfire rang out in the city, Miltenberger forgot about himself; now his only thought was for his young soldiers. He walked around the front of the LMTV and stopped. Given his seniority, he could ride in the cab. Instead, he told Staff Sergeant Miranda to climb in front. Miltenberger would ride with his soldiers in the back.

THE LMTV HADN'T gone fifty yards down Route Delta before the first of Miltenberger's men was hit. Twenty-two-year-old Private First Class Luke Fournier, in the seat opposite Miltenberger, suddenly stopped firing his weapon and stood up, as if in a daze. Fournier was a Humvee gunner, but in the haste of the rescue mission he had hopped on the LMTV. As soon as the truck left the gate, he knew he was in trouble. In the blur of noise and chaos and gunfire, he could see rounds easily penetrating the ledge on the side of the truck. Lifting a hand to his left side, Fournier felt a wet, warm spot and saw blood.

"I think I've been shot," he said.

Someone yelled, "Get down!" Fournier dropped back onto the truck's bench. He lay wedged between the others, staring at the sky, trying to catch his breath. Miltenberger, who had been trained as a combat lifesaver, reached over to check him out and saw blood oozing through the sleeve of Fournier's uniform.

"It's just your arm," he said. "You're good. Keep firing." Fournier made a feeble attempt to raise his weapon.

"I can't," he gasped. "I can't."

"All right. Then just stay still." Miltenberger looked up and saw an Iraqi man with an AK-47 lean out of a doorway up the street, lining up a shot at the Humvee ahead. Miltenberger swung his M-16 around and fired five quick rounds. The man fell back, his head bouncing on the sidewalk. Another group of armed men lurked nearby. Miltenberger told the soldier manning the truck's M-249 light machine gun to watch the alleyways. He turned back to Fournier, who was struggling for breath. Wheezing and sucking, fighting to keep air in his lungs. *It's my arm,* he thought. *Just my arm.* And then from deep within came a horrible hack. A stew of blood and tissue coughed up and splattered on the soldiers around him.

Miltenberger moved quickly now, sliding his hand under Fournier's Kevlar vest and feeling for the frothy moisture that would identify the wound beneath. There was a hole in his chest. He grabbed a bandage from Fournier's combat kit and put it in Fournier's hand, guiding it to the small opening. Fournier's eyes fluttered open as he drifted in and out of consciousness.

"You've got a sucking chest wound," Miltenberger said over the gunfire. "I've got to stop the air from going in there, or you'll fill up your lungs with blood." On the first attempt, however,

Miltenberger inadvertently pushed Fournier's finger into the wound.

"Knife!" he yelled. "I need a knife!"

He cut Fournier's uniform top and ripped it open, and then applied a plastic-covered pressure bandage to the wound. He didn't want to remove Fournier's Kevlar vest for fear he might get hit again, but the vest was keeping him from tying the bandage in place. Instead, Miltenberger piled some gear underneath Fournier and rolled him over onto it, so that his own weight would keep pressure on the dressing and maintain a seal on the wound.

Just as he was finishing with Fournier, another soldier in the back of the truck let out a scream. Specialist Rasheed Causey, who'd been sitting farther back on the same side of the truck as Miltenberger, was holding his leg, as a dark red stain spread through his pants. Miltenberger scrambled over and, with the same knife he'd used on Fournier's uniform, slit open Causey's pants. Blood was spurting from a wound on his inner thigh, a sign that the bullet had likely severed an artery. As the truck swerved and bounced down the street, Miltenberger fashioned a tourniquet and tied it around Causey's upper leg.

"Now hold that there!" he shouted.

Miltenberger crept back to his own position and resumed shooting, if only to drive the Sadr City fighters back into their doorways. By now, the truck was barely crawling along on four flattened tires, making the soldiers more vulnerable to enemy fire. Within moments, four more men were shot, each one collapsing onto the truck bed and hollering in pain as other wounded soldiers fell on top of them.

CRAAKKK. Sergeant Brandon Schuler was struck in the leg and, like Causey, needed a tourniquet. Corporal Allan Alexander took a bullet in his right biceps. Sergeant George Barbary was hit in the ankle, and Private First Class Brian Emmett was shot in both legs. Miltenberger laid down his weapon again to attend to the wounded. Still worried that Fournier's chest wound might re-open, he slipped his hand into Fournier's vest once more and held the pressure bandage down as tight as he could, all the while continuing to yell out fire commands to the few soldiers still able to shoot.

It was now around 1900. The sun was beginning to set behind Sadr City, casting dark shadows over the street. Smoke from the burning trash and explosions made it difficult to shoot. Private First Class Tomas Young, sitting next to Miltenberger, hadn't yet fired his weapon. It was as if he couldn't identify any targets—it was all happening so fast. He watched as Miltenberger shifted from one injured soldier to the next, helping Fournier, helping the other guys, knowing they were all so terribly exposed, knowing he needed to do more, too.

That's when Tomas Young was hit: a sharp thump in his chest. Young's whole body went numb. His weapon slid out of his hands. He tried to reach for it, but his arms wouldn't move. He tried again, but he couldn't make his arms or his fingers or his legs respond.

"I can't move," he whispered. "Help me."

With one hand on Fournier's chest wound, Miltenberger used the other to search up and down Young's body. He found nothing. Then he reached inside Young's Kevlar vest and felt a wet spot near the edge of his body armor. Grabbing a bandage, he shoved it against the wound and braced his knee hard against Young's back to keep up the pressure. Young was growing increasingly frightened.

"I can't move!" he yelled. "I'm paralyzed."

"No, you're not. You'll be fine! " Miltenberger yelled, though he knew it wasn't true. "You got all these guys lying on top of you, that's all." Stooping low, with a knee on Young's back and a hand on Fournier's chest wound, bullets whistling overhead, amid the anguished wails of his wounded soldiers, Robert Miltenberger was beginning to despair.

"Hey!" he hollered to Staff Sergeant Miranda, the truck commander, and the driver, Specialist Regan Packwood. "This is crazy! We need to turn around! Hey!" But turning wasn't an option. The LMTV had no radio. If they backtracked, they'd be isolated in Sadr City with no protection from the Bradleys. They had to keep moving forward.

UNAWARE OF THE CARNAGE just two vehicles back, Denomy and his crew were dealing with their own problems. For the second time in thirty minutes, they were under heavy fire. Other than Wiebley, Denomy's driver—whose visibility remained almost completely obscured by the disgusting mess on his windshield— everyone in the Humvee had his weapon out and was firing as fast as he could. In the open rear bed of the Humvee, Specialist Leeton Burkholder, Sergeant Mathen Givens, and Sergeant Aaron Fowler were standing with their backs to one another, firing steadily in separate directions, keeping the enemy gunmen at bay. But they couldn't do much about the roadside bombs and other explosive devices that kept coming their way. One of these went off, hitting Staff Sergeant John Dumdie.

"Aaahhhaaahhh! My leg! MY LEG!" he screamed.

Denomy knew it was serious: Dumdie was one of his toughest soldiers; he'd already been wounded in the foot. At Dumdie's side, Sergeant Joseph Thompson saw that one of Dumdie's lower leg bones was now poking through the skin. Dumdie kept screaming, but there was nothing Thompson could do for him.

"Sergeant!" Denomy shouted. "Just deal with it! Hold the screaming! I can't hear the radios!" Denomy was responsible for directing every vehicle in his convoy, from the Bradleys up front to the Humvees and trucks behind. He had to maintain some level of calm, and he had to maintain communications.

Denomy caught a glimpse of something outside his window that left him momentarily frozen. A boy of about twelve, in blue pants and a multicolored T-shirt, lay dead in the street next to an AK-47. He'd fallen on his knees, his body twisted backward, his eyes closed. Denomy was a new father. The sight horrified him, a sickening image that would later remind him of all that was wrong in Iraq. Suddenly, Specialist Wiebley jerked the Humvee to the left, bouncing over something so big and heavy that everyone in the vehicle was thrown off balance. The Humvee slammed to a stop, its engine racing. Both front wheels were off the ground, and the vehicle couldn't move. Wiebley threw the transmission into reverse and jammed it back into drive, trying to find traction, but the Humvee merely rocked on whatever was under it. Wiebley switched gears and floored the gas, but the vehicle wouldn't budge. Denomy radioed the Bradleys to return and help free the Humvee, but their antennas had been blasted off, and communication was intermittent at best. The Bradleys rumbled on. Meanwhile the snipers on either side of the street could see that a canvas-topped Humvee had stalled. Denomy realized they were about to be picked off one by one. He didn't panic. Instead, in the clearest and calmest voice he could summon, Denomy turned to his driver and said, "If you don't get us off this fucking obstacle, we're all going to die here."

Moments later, the fully armored Humvee trailing them in the convoy came up and rammed Denomy's vehicle hard from behind, freeing its wheels and pitching it forward. The force of the impact caught Denomy's gunner by surprise, and he flew backward out of the Humvee, landing against the vehicle behind him. Shaken but still able to fight, the gunner, Leeton Burkholder, climbed quickly back into his Humvee, picked up his weapon, and resumed shooting. Wiebley pulled forward, but he was determined not to get caught in that situation again. He wouldn't drive another yard, he decided, without clearing the windshield, no matter how many bullets were flying around them. Wiebley hit the brakes, grabbed a rag from underneath the seat, reached for the door handle, and, with the hint of a smile, looked over at Denomy.

"Well, here goes nothing," he said.

"Wiebley, what the hell are you doing?" Denomy shouted. But Seth Wiebley had opened his door and was sliding outside. He wiped his portion of the windshield a couple of times, opening a clear patch, tossed the rag to the street, and jumped back inside, slamming the door behind him.

"All right!" he shouted, amazed he hadn't been shot. Wiebley floored the gas pedal, and the Humvee lurched forward on its flattened tires. Denomy tried again to reach the Bradleys up ahead. According to the grid coordinates Swope had given him, the stranded platoon was now just a few blocks away.

Chapter 16

★

THE

ALLEYWAY

1910 hours

THE SILENCE IN THE ALLEY where Shane Aguero and his platoon remained trapped didn't last long. As the last bodies of the hundreds of dead Sadr supporters were being picked up, the grenades began again, lobbed steadily from behind buildings or across rooftops. Lieutenant Aguero, standing outside his Humvee and keeping an eye on the people down the alleyway, heard a *clunnkk* to his right. He looked over just in time to see a small black object hit a nearby wall.

"What the hell—"

The grenade exploded, throwing Aguero into the side of Sergeant Jerry Swope's vehicle. The left side of Aguero's body was punctured with shrapnel; small chunks of metal lodged in his ear, elbow, buttocks, thigh, calf, and foot, and blood soaked through his uniform from head to toe. Aguero grabbed the passenger-side door and looked up at Swope and his gunner, Shane Coleman.

Are you okay?! Swope screamed at Aguero.

Aguero could read Swope's lips, but he couldn't hear. His hand moved instinctively to his ear. The blast had left him deaf. At least temporarily.

"I'm all right," Aguero yelled to Swope. "It's okay."

He staggered to the driver's side of his Humvee and climbed in, refusing help. "Leave me alone," he said. "I'll be fine."

Aguero radioed the soldiers on the roof to see how the ammunition was holding out. He couldn't hear their response, but moments later he spotted Specialist Jonathan Riddell racing toward Swope's Humvee. He crawled in back and grabbed an armload of ammunition, then turned and headed back upstairs. The platoon was going through rounds quickly.

As soon as Riddell was inside, Aguero heard a volley of small-arms fire much louder than before; he soon saw why. Groups of snipers were now hopping from roof to roof along the interconnected buildings. Every few seconds someone popped out, squeezed off five or six rounds, and disappeared for a minute, only to emerge a little closer to the Americans.

Down in the alleyway, Shane Coleman was having trouble spotting the snipers. Wherever they were, they were too close to the soldiers on the roof, and he could not use the .50-caliber in his Humvee because of the risk of shooting his own men. But the Humvee was getting pounded. Though the ballistic glass was almost impenetrable, a constant barrage of AK-47 rounds would cause it to crack. Soon fragments began breaking away, covering Swope's lap and body armor as he hunched behind his radio in the passenger seat. Yet Jerry Swope was so focused on staying in touch with the other soldiers and the battalion officers coordinating the rescue that the gunfire didn't really faze him. He calmly took his cardboard-mounted map and shoved it against the windshield to stop the spray of glass.

The rooftop assaults were growing more and more dangerous. Battalion HQ had received aviation support in the form of two heavily armed OH-58 Kiowa reconnaissance helicopters. Their job would be to take out the snipers and guide the rescue convoy to the site. It was an obviously dangerous environment for a helicopter. The Kiowa is smaller and more maneuverable than a Black Hawk, but no one wanted a repeat of the Mogadishu "Black Hawk Down" scenario, in which Somali militiamen shot down several helicopters with rocket-propelled grenades. The Kiowa crews wanted more than grid coordinates; they wanted to "get eyes on" the stranded platoon before flying too close.

Where are they?

The dozens of tiny alleyways running in every direction off Route Delta, combined with the chaos of the activity below— fires, smoke, explosions, swirling dust—made the house where the platoon was stranded indistinguishable from the next. Swope managed to get through to the Kiowa crews, trying to guide them to his location. "Our guys are the only ones up on the rooftop not running anywhere," he told them.

But then the helicopters passed right overheard without spotting the soldiers. Sergeant Bourquin, who had been running between the Humvees and the house since Aguero's injury, grabbed a smoke grenade and lobbed it about twenty feet across the roof, trying to signal their location. A dense cloud of white smoke rose in the air and hovered for more than two minutes.

"Do you see us?" Swope shouted into the radio. When he got no reply, he realized that there was already so much smoke in the sky from the weapons and burning debris that it was like throwing a match into a flaming house and expecting someone to find it. No wonder the helicopters couldn't spot them.

"I'll try a red one, sir!" Bourquin said. He grabbed his M-203 grenade launcher in the alleyway. But that didn't work either.

There was no cloud of red smoke, just a short puff low on the walls of the roadway before it vaporized in the breeze.

Aguero, still bleeding inside the Humvee, rummaged around for anything that could be used as a signal. Swope and the gunners were doing the same. "Here, sir!" Coleman hollered. He'd found a VS-17 signal board—a twenty-by-seventy-two-inch orange-and-pink panel for signaling helicopters—in the back. Ignoring his injuries, Aguero grabbed the panel and started toward the house and up the stairs. Hobbling badly, he made it about halfway up before he realized he couldn't go any farther.

"Sergeant Robinson!" he yelled. Darcy Robinson poked his head around the corner of the stairwell from his position on the roof. "Here's a VS-17 panel. Set this up!"

Aguero threw the panel up to Robinson and began picking his way back down the stairs. In the distance they could hear a Kiowa moving in their direction. Robinson spread the panel on the rooftop, hoping the bright orange and pink colors would help the pilot and crew pinpoint their location.

"Can they see it?" Aguero shouted over his handheld Motorola. He held the radio close to his right ear. He still couldn't hear with the left.

Negative. The Kiowa crew explained that many of the houses had Iraqi prayer mats and bedrolls spread out across the roofs. From the crew's perspective, the rooftops were a sea of brightly colored fabrics; the VS-17 panel blended so perfectly in size and color that it didn't stand out.

Aguero staggered back down to the Humvee. A fresh wave of Iraqis—children in front, militiamen behind—began advancing again from both ends, firing down the narrow alley as before, with no cover or escape route. Again the soldiers opened up the .50-cals, M-240s, and M-249s. This second attack was over as quickly and brutally as the first. Bursts from the big guns ripped through the crowd, leaving another bloody mass of casualties.

The mass frontal assaults had achieved almost nothing—and at enormous cost to the Iraqis—except that they had left the American platoon dangerously low on ammunition. To make matters worse, sunset approached. Aguero knew his men were more vulnerable now than ever—it was critical that the Kiowas locate their position.

"You guys gotta think of something else," Aguero yelled into his Motorola.

Up on the roof, Bourquin grabbed Robinson by the arm of his camouflage uniform and told him to stand still. Then he took a knife and started slicing Robinson's sleeve.

"What the hell are you doing that for?" Robinson yelled.

Bourquin laughed. "You'll see, you'll see. I have a plan!" Once he'd sheered off Robinson's sleeves, he cut off his own and put them in a pile on the roof. With snipers everywhere, he started gathering up all the combustible material he could find. Robinson realized what Bourquin was up to and started doing the same; meanwhile, Bourquin crouched low and pulled out a lighter. Sleeves, twigs, papers, and scraps of material all went up in flame.

"Sir, sir, we got our signal up!" he radioed to Aguero.

"Well, what is it?"

"Our sleeves! They're on fire!"

Bourquin knew that the OH-58 had a heat-seeking device. The rooftop fire would guide them home.

Swope passed the information to the helicopters. "We're the ones who have a bonfire!" For the next ten minutes, the soldiers kept feeding the fire, running inside the house to collect whatever flammable materials they could get their hands on.

"Hey, they got us! They can see you!" Swope shouted. The

helicopter crew had confirmed they saw the fire. The gunfire was too heavy for them to be able to land, but at least now they could pass along Aguero's precise location to Captain Troy Denomy and his Charlie Company convoy.

A few minutes later they heard firing nearby.

"Shhh. Shut up. Hear that?" asked Staff Sergeant Trevor Davis. The sounds were unmistakable: the Bradleys' 25mm guns ripping through nearby buildings. Davis was ecstatic. Help was literally just around the corner.

On the rooftop, the men finally allowed themselves to believe that their nightmare was coming to a close.

Davis tried his small Motorola, having had sporadic luck calling the battalion headquarters. He managed to raise First Sergeant Casey Carson back at the TOC.

"We have four wounded and one dead. We're still taking heavy fire." He said the platoon was "going black," meaning the soldiers were running critically short on ammunition. But the Bradleys were on the way: Peering over the side of the roof, Davis could see them at the front of a long line of vehicles coming toward the alley from Route Delta.

"We should be rescued shortly," he told Carson.

Then he nearly dropped the radio.

"Shit!" he screamed. "They rolled right by us!" They all watched, stunned, as Captain Troy Denomy and the Bradleys roared down Route Delta without even slowing at the entrance to the alley.

"You passed us! Turn around!" Swope screamed into the radio. "Stop! Stop!" But the Bradley drivers leading the Charlie Company convoy didn't seem to have a clue where they were.

In the alleyway, Aguero's spirits sank as he watched the last of the rescue vehicles disappear in a curtain of dust. Blood was still running from his left ear. Small chunks of metal were lodged in his elbow, buttocks, thigh, calf, and foot; splotches of blood soaked his uniform from head to toe. Aguero looked up at a small patch of darkening blue sky and noticed a little bird passing overhead. A few wispy clouds were turning gray in the setting sun. Aguero thought of the warning his wife, Amber, had given him before he left for Iraq.

"In every war," she had said, "there is always a platoon that gets pinned down. Don't let it be your platoon."

Watching the black smoke rising over the abandoned Humvees on Route Delta and the dust from the passing convoy drift away, Aguero felt a pang of terror. *She's right,* he thought. *We are going to die in this shitty little alleyway.*

But when he turned to see Swope huddled behind the radio and heard Coleman behind the .50-cal, cursing at the Mahdi militiamen, Aguero felt his resolve harden.

Fuck that, he thought. *I love you, Amber. I'm coming home.*

Chapter 17

★

DARKNESS

FALLS

1920 hours

FROM HIS POSITION near the front of the Charlie Company convoy now moving down Route Delta, Lieutenant Colonel Gary Volesky fought to keep his frustration and worry under control. Volesky had assumed responsibility for Sadr City less than two hours earlier, and now he faced the prospect of losing an entire platoon on the first night of his command. Lieutenant Shane Aguero and his men were holed up in a house on one of the alleyways to the right of Route Delta, but in the smoky twilight all the alleys looked the same. The Charlie Company convoy made its way, block by block, passing shuttered shops and apartment houses and shadowy government buildings—all potential havens for Mahdi militiamen. What few street signs existed were written in Arabic and corresponded not at all to the assigned route names found on the American maps. And virtually none of his soldiers had been in Sadr City long enough to recognize landmarks that might have helped them find their way to the ambushed platoon.

TANK COMPANY, SUCCESSFUL RESCUE

ROUTE SILVER   *CAMP WAR EAGLE* →

④

ROUTE DELTA

ROUTE CHARLIE

ROUTE BRAVO

ROUTE AEROS

③
②

✗
*pinned-down
platoon*

ROUTE ALPHA

ROUTE COPPER

0 Miles   .5

0 Kilometers   1

①

1. Seven tanks attack up Route Delta. Sergeant Michael Mitchell is hit shortly after they leave their headquarters at Martyr's Monument.

2. The convoy passes the alley and Aguero's platoon. They continue driving up Delta until Aguero flags them down.

3. The pinned-down platoon loads into the tanks and their two functioning Humvees.

4. Swope notices the second Humvee has fallen behind. After learning that it's lodged on a concrete block, he flags down a tank to ram the Humvee off the barrier. The convoy proceeds to Camp War Eagle.

© 2006 Jeffrey L. Ward

Volesky peered through the ballistic glass of his armored Humvee, watching for snipers and for any sign of his stranded soldiers. It would be dark soon, and Aguero's men were dangerously low on ammunition. So were his own gunners in the Charlie Company convoy.

Ahead, flames and thick smoke billowed from two blackened vehicles, wedged end to end on the opposite side of the street. As they drew nearer, Volesky saw they were the remains of two U.S. military Humvees. *Aguero's,* he thought. *The platoon has to be just around the corner!*

But the two Bradleys leading the convoy barreled past the burning Humvees. Volesky couldn't believe they weren't slowing down.

"Comanche Six!" he screamed into the radio. "We're passing the platoon! They're right here! What the hell are the Bradleys doing?!"

Without the Bradleys, there would be no rescue. They were the firepower needed to fight the way in, and back out—and they'd also provide transport for the soldiers whose Humvees had been destroyed.

"I can't get hold of them!" Denomy replied over the radio. "They're not answering. I think their antennas must have gotten blown off. Either that or they can't hear me because of the gunfire."

Volesky and Denomy could speak with each other and with the Tactical Operations Center at Camp War Eagle, but not always with other units. The battalion officers at the TOC, Major Alan Streeter and Major Martin Dannat, played a critical role, relaying information to and from Sergeant Swope to try to coordinate the rescue convoys. But there was too much traffic on the frequency. Everyone was talking at once. Vehicle commanders were reporting casualties, and the platoon itself was calling in grid coordinates. Above all, the constant explosions and nonstop shooting made it almost impossible to hear the calls.

So Volesky and Denomy couldn't get through to the Bradleys, and they couldn't hear Jerry Swope calling them in desperation as the convoy sped past. Back at the TOC, however, they could hear Swope loud and clear.

"I can see you!" Swope screamed. "You're going right by us!" By the time the TOC relayed the message to the convoy, the Bradleys were gone.

Volesky was determined to maintain a positive frame of mind: At least they knew where Aguero's platoon was now. But he wasn't sure what to do next. Denomy was reporting casualties among his men, including John Dumdie, in Denomy's vehicle, writhing in pain from a compound leg fracture. And there was the ammunition shortage. Volesky figured that during the three-mile run down Route Delta, the Bradleys had fired about five hundred high-explosive 25mm rounds. Denomy's M-240 gunner had run out of rounds and was using only his M-16. Charlie Company was fast losing its fighting strength.

And then came another potentially deadly complication. The 2-5 Cav battalion operations officer, Major Alan Streeter, radioed from the TOC that the tank company from 2-37 AR (Second Battalion, Thirty-seventh Armored Regiment) at the south end of Sadr City was en route to Aguero's location. They were attacking up Route Delta, the same thoroughfare Charlie Company was moving down. To have Bradleys and tanks heading toward one another, with big guns blazing, was a disaster waiting to happen. Charlie Company had to get off the street immediately.

Denomy radioed Volesky that he urgently needed to establish a new casualty collection point and arrange for the evacuation of his injured soldiers. At this point nobody knew just how bad things were back in Miltenberger's LMTV.

Volesky directed Denomy to establish the casualty collection point just east of Route Delta and to arrange his Bradleys in a blocking position there to defend the approaching tank column against a possible attack on its flank. Denomy finally got word to the lead Bradley driver to make a left turn on Route Gold, a major east-west thoroughfare on the south side of Sadr City, in an area where the gunfire was said to be considerably less intense than it had been in the northern sections. Just as he had done about an hour earlier at the intersection of routes Aeros and Copper, Denomy arranged his three Bradleys and his armored Humvees in a protective ring, leaving a relatively secure area in the center where the soft-skinned vehicles could park. There the wounded soldiers could be prepared for transport back to the base aid station.

When the LMTV truck commanded by staff sergeants Miranda and Miltenberger finally pulled into the ring, Denomy heard loud groans coming from the back and hurried over. Miranda jumped out of the cab, blood streaming from a gunshot wound on his shoulder.

"Sir," he said, "I got a truckload of wounded soldiers here. I gotta get them back."

Denomy looked over the side of the truck. He was horrified. Miltenberger had one hand pressed against one soldier's chest wound and a knee bearing down on the red-stained chest of another. Two other soldiers lay against the side of the truck with blood-soaked pant legs and tourniquets strapped around their thighs. Others were cradling their wounded arms or shoulders or sides, crying and swaying. Denomy could see that they had to get back to Camp War Eagle right away.

"Can you find the base on your own?" Denomy asked. Miranda, the driver, nodded. Well south of the firefight now, Denomy volunteered his own Humvee to guide the LMTV back to Eagle base. The Humvee had four flat tires, and fluid was leaking from nearly every compartment, but vehicles were in short supply. Denomy saw no other way to do it. When he returned to tell them Miranda would be leading an evacuation, Fowler and Burkholder were slouched in the back with Sergeant Givens, who'd managed to come through the fighting unscathed. They were taking their first cigarette break since the fight began.

"Wanna see our wounds, sir?" Burkholder said, rolling up his sleeve.

"What happened?" Denomy deadpanned.

"The motherfuckers shot us, sir," Fowler answered with a grin, as if it were something that happened every day.

For all their wisecracking, Fowler and Burkholder had serious injuries that required prompt treatment. Fowler had been shot twice in his legs, and Burkholder's arm was wounded. Neither had stopped shooting throughout the fight.

"You're gonna get evacuated," Denomy said.

They checked their weapons and ammo supply to make sure they could protect themselves on the ride back to base. Miranda took Denomy's place in the commander's seat, and the battered Humvee headed west down Route Gold. The LMTV rattled along behind.

Denomy, without a vehicle and still bleeding from his own wounds, told one of his Bradley drivers to save him a seat. He went next to consult with his battalion commander. Volesky was on the radio, getting an update on the movement of the 2-37 AR tanks headed up Delta.

"You know, you should just head back to the base," Volesky told Denomy. "The tanks are going to be passing by any minute, and there's nothing more for you to do here."

"Sir, if it's okay, how about I stay until my platoon is rescued," he said. "I want to confirm that the tanks are there and my platoon is safe."

"Understood," Volesky said, knowing he would have done the

same in Denomy's position. Volesky raised a hand, turned, and headed back to the TOC.

STAFF SERGEANT Robert Miltenberger was so busy administering first aid in the back of the LMTV that he barely looked up to see where the truck was heading. PFC Luke Fournier kept blacking out, his eyes rolling backward, his face ashen. Miltenberger leaned heavily his chest wound and yelled at him to stay awake, all the while holding his knee against the wound between Tomas Young's shoulder blades. The others weren't much better off, and they were starting to panic.

"Tell my brother I love him," someone said to Miltenberger.

"Please hurry," another soldier cried.

The only two other uninjured soldiers in the bay pointed their weapons outward, watching for snipers and RPGs. It was almost pitch black now, and for once, no one was shooting at the truck. After a few minutes of quiet, Miltenberger ordered the two soldiers to turn their attention to their wounded comrades.

"Start bandaging these guys!" he hollered. "Why you pulling security? We've got lives to save!"

THE TRUCK was barely moving now. Belches of steam were coming from the radiator, and there was a constant sputter from the engine. Up ahead in Denomy's Humvee, Staff Sergeant Miranda kept stopping, opening his door, and peering back to make sure the truck was still following. As the two vehicles neared the northern end of Route Aeros, about a mile from the front gate of Camp War Eagle, Miltenberger's vehicle suddenly stopped. Fifty yards ahead, Staff Sergeant Miranda noticed the truck had halted, and told his Humvee driver to stop and wait for it to catch up. Miranda assumed the truck was permanently disabled, so he called the base and requested vehicles to pick up the casualties and bring them in. Miranda himself had already lost a lot of blood. He was too weak and woozy to walk back to the truck himself.

THE SIGHT of a stalled truck full of wounded U.S. soldiers in the falling darkness brought scores of curious Iraqis out of their apartments. No one seemed to show outward hostility in this part of the city, but Miltenberger was nervous about his soldiers' being exposed. More important, his wounded soldiers were in no shape to wait indefinitely for another U.S. military vehicle to come along and rescue them. With no radio communication between his truck and Miranda's Humvee fifty yards up ahead, Miltenberger had no way of knowing whether or when anyone would come to his aid. With this many soldiers near death, he couldn't wait. Miltenberger spotted a beat-up white pickup truck coming down the road. He motioned to one of his uninjured soldiers, Specialist Robert Chivas.

"Go get me that truck!" he yelled.

Chivas jumped in front of the pickup and pointed his weapon at the Iraqi driver, making it clear he should get out with his hands up. At the same time, Corporal Allan Alexander, though weakened by the loss of blood from a gunshot wound in his arm, leaned over the side of the LMTV with his M-16 pointed at the Iraqis gathering along the street, muttering to himself as much as to them, "If anyone does something foolish, they die."

With the Iraqi pickup driver under guard, Chivas and another soldier lifted Luke Fournier into the back, while a third soldier maintained pressure on Fournier's chest wound. Specialist Loren

Haller, meanwhile, was out in the street with a flashlight. He stopped a blue van and ordered the driver to pull alongside the truck.

The last few minutes had seemed to bring a resurgence of civilian traffic, at least on this street at the eastern side of the city. And the attitude of the civilians here was vastly different. The van driver cooperated. Together with another Iraqi civilian, he helped the Americans move their injured into his vehicle. Four men put their arms under Young's paralyzed body and gently hoisted him into the van. Sergeant George Barbary, a gunshot wound in his ankle, hobbled into the cab of the pickup, where he could keep an eye on the driver, while two other injured soldiers found places in the back with Fournier. Miltenberger showed them how to keep pressure on the soldier's chest wound. Specialists Rasheed Causey and Brandon Schuler, both with tourniquets on their legs, climbed gingerly into the van, as did Corporal Allan Alexander. Chivas took a seat next to the van driver, in order to guide him to the base.

Almost all the soldiers had serious gunshot wounds. Almost all had lost a lot of blood. Some were slipping into shock. They had no radio communication, it was dark, and everyone was scared. Miltenberger, one of the few men still thinking clearly, was not quite ready to let the vehicles leave. If an Iraqi pickup truck and a van were to come roaring up to the front gate of Camp War Eagle, it was likely someone might shoot at them. He wanted a U.S. military vehicle to escort the Iraqi vehicles if possible, and he dashed into the street with his flashlight to try to flag one down. After a minute or two, a lone Humvee came bumping slowly down the road, riding on four flat tires and with both headlights shot out. Miltenberger stood in the middle of the road, waving frantically. To his astonishment, it was Gary Volesky's Humvee.

The battalion commander—*his* battalion commander—was returning to base.

"What's going on?" Volesky asked.

"Sir, I need somebody to lead these vehicles back," Miltenberger said, gesturing with a hand covered in Tomas Young's blood. His once sandy-colored desert camouflage uniform looked like it had been painted red.

"We've got all our casualties here, sir," he said, the words tumbling out of his mouth. "Our truck broke down. Can you take them, sir?"

"Well, I can't go very fast," Volesky said, "but get 'em ready. Let's go. Now." His driver pressed on, and Miltenberger dashed back to the two vehicles and signaled them to take off behind the Humvee for the final leg of their journey back to base.

About three hundred yards from the front gate, the little convoy met three U.S. armored vehicles coming down the road. Forgetting that Volesky was up ahead—or perhaps no longer seeing him in the darkness—some of the soldiers in the van panicked. Corporal Allan Alexander slid open the side door of the van and stumbled out, waving his one good arm.

"We're Americans! We're Americans!" he shouted.

Miltenberger had stayed behind, along with four other uninjured soldiers: Staff Sergeant Kevin Denson, Sergeant Esmerijildo Acevedo, Specialist Regan Packwood (the LMTV driver), and Specialist Loren Haller (the gunner). Miltenberger and the four men did not want to abandon the LMTV, with the M-249 squad automatic weapon mounted in the cab turret, the ammunition beneath it, and other sensitive items that might fall into the wrong hands. Miltenberger wanted to wait until a Bradley or a tank came along that could tow the LMTV back to the base. But the men were in an extremely vulnerable position and they needed to move somewhere to set up a defense. Miltenberger and Denson spotted a small school building on the west side of the road, surrounded by a stone wall. The five soldiers climbed the wall and took up positions on the other side.

The Iraqi schoolmaster and his family lived on the premises, and the sudden appearance in his courtyard of five heavily armed American soldiers, their hands and uniforms covered with blood, threw them into a panic. The schoolmaster emerged from his house, trembling, and in halting English asked what the soldiers wanted.

"Sir, we mean you no harm," Miltenberger said. "If you could just open the front gate for us, that's all we need."

The schoolmaster couldn't see Miltenberger's face in the darkness, nor did he understand what he'd said, but the tone of his voice was so humble, so unthreatening, that the schoolmaster seemed instantly relieved. After a few more words and gestures, he understood what the soldiers wanted and unlocked the gate. Miltenberger and the other men waited there until they saw two Bradleys coming up Route Aeros, and they ran out to stop them. The Bradleys were Denomy's, carrying Charlie Company soldiers back to base. Specialists Packwood and Haller tied a cargo strap from one of the Bradleys to the front of the LMTV, and the Bradley towed the truck back to Camp War Eagle. Two of Miltenberger's men climbed into the Bradley; he and two other soldiers rode on top.

Miltenberger sat quietly, listening to the gunfire inside the city. He was badly shaken, his bloody hands gripping his knees close to his body. Once inside the front gate, he slid to the ground and ran to the aid station to see whether his men had made it back alive.

Chapter 18

★

RESCUE:

THE

CRUSADERS

1930 hours

JUST PAST SUNSET, a nearly full moon rose east of Sadr City. In the narrow alley where Lieutenant Shane Aguero and his soldiers waited, the moon's dim glow was enough to enhance the power of the soldiers' night-vision goggles, amplifying the existing light several thousand times. The devices looked more like small binoculars snapped onto the front of the helmets than goggles, but they made it possible for the soldiers to see almost everything in the alleyway—albeit with a blurry green hue—as they could before the sun went down.

Which, unfortunately, light or no light, still wasn't much. Moqtada al-Sadr's Mahdi militiamen had kept the Americans pinned down for nearly two hours now, their peekaboo tactics producing enough lucky shots that the eighteen-man platoon, along with the Iraqi interpreter, now had six wounded and one dead, Sergeant Chen, whose body was beginning to stiffen under the black burka.

Then, after dark, one of those enemy rounds found the helmet of Lieutenant Shane Aguero.

Aguero and Sergeant First Class Jerry Swope had been in the alley when they saw the Bradleys pass their location. "You're going right past us!" Swope screamed into the radio. The platoon was already in critical need of ammunition; now, as the Bradleys passed by, his men began to face the very real possibility that they might be stuck there all night. Aguero went inside to check on his wounded and to do what he could to be sure that, despite this setback, everyone remained focused on maintaining their defensive posture.

Swope, too, was determined not to give up hope. His armored Humvee had taken an extraordinary amount of fire, but Swope stayed on the radios, his map board still covering his shattered windshield. He was focused on only one thing: rescue.

Inside, the men began ferrying the dwindling ammunition between the Humvees and the roof, signs of fatigue and plunging morale growing more evident with each trip. The Iraqi family that lived in the house had been moved to a back room, the children playing quietly, while one of the soldiers stood guard.

Aguero, already bloodied by a grenade, stepped back into the alleyway and walked toward Swope's Humvee. As Swope watched, the lieutenant's head jerked horribly, sending him stumbling. Swope knew instantly that Aguero had been hit.

"Lieutenant!" Swope yelled. "Are you all right?"

Aguero fell against the Humvee, his head throbbing. He grabbed his helmet, hands gingerly exploring his aching skull, expecting to feel blood and brains. His fingers came away clean.

Am I hallucinating? What just happened?

He ran his hand along the top of his helmet. There it was. A massive dent in the Kevlar where the round had struck.

Aguero opened the door of the Humvee and sat down to steady himself. There wasn't a doubt in his mind: If not for that helmet, he'd have been a dead man. This realization triggered another: The shooter was going to pay.

"That guy has gotta go," he said.

Sergeant James Fisk had already spotted the man. He pointed down the alleyway to a building about a hundred feet away, where the militiamen had set up an RPK, a Soviet machine gun similar to an AK-47. Tracers were flying off the walls, arcing into brilliant white sparks, then bouncing down the alley.

"Over there," he said.

As Fisk took aim with the .50-cal, Aguero radioed his soldiers behind the M-240 on the roof to do the same. Fisk slowly inhaled as he watched the corner for movement, turning his weapon ever so slightly to the left. When his lungs were full, he stopped and waited. A muzzle flash. Then another.

He wasn't certain whether the M-240 or his .50-cal fired first—all he knew was that the corner of the building, down low where the shooter lay, exploded from the brief, deadly firepower of the big guns. Hunks of concrete vaporized. The RPK fell silent.

One down, Shane Aguero thought. *Hundreds to go.*

SWOPE CONTINUED WORKING the radios. After the initial disappointment about the Charlie Company Bradleys, the TOC gave him some reassuring news. A tank platoon from the Crusaders—Charlie Company, Second Battalion, Thirty-seventh Armored Regiment—was on its way. The 2-37 AR, part of the First Armored Division, had been operating in Sadr City for the last eleven months; Captain John Moore's company's tour in Iraq had literally been in its last minutes when it received the call for assistance from Volesky's TOC. If anyone knew those city streets well enough to find the platoon, it was the C/2-37 AR.

What the TOC hadn't told Swope was that just ten minutes after leaving their base at the Martyr's Monument, one of the C/2-37 AR soldiers from the Crusader Blue platoon had been killed.

Twenty-five-year-old tank mechanic Sergeant Michael Mitchell was among those men scheduled to leave Iraq the very next day; his bags were already packed. He'd be getting married in four months. A handsome Californian who kept himself in extraordinarily good shape, Mitchell had gone for a final run that morning around the perimeter of his forward operating base. But when he heard that a platoon had been ambushed, Mitchell volunteered to ride as a tank loader behind an M-240 machine gun. He had qualified in tank gunnery skills testing and knew how to fire a machine gun. His assignment in the loader's hatch left him fully exposed. As soon as the tanks rolled up Route Delta, RPGs began flying in their direction; small-arms rounds richocheted off the sides of the vehicles. But it wasn't an unseen enemy who took Mitchell's life. A lone gunman dressed in an Iraqi police uniform ran up to the side of the tank, raised his weapon, and shot Mitchell through the right eye. He never had a chance to respond. He died instantly.

WITHIN THIRTY MINUTES, seven of the enormous M-1A2 tanks were roaring up Delta from the southwest. Captain John Moore, the commander of 2-37's C Company, led the charge. Moore was an intense commander, a physically imposing, nononsense leader. At first, the captain considered circumventing the city, heading up Route Aeros to Silver and then down on

Delta. But he didn't want to risk driving by the stranded platoon. From the open hatch on the right side of the turret, a .50-caliber weapon gripped in his hands, Moore led his tankers into the fray.

"Holy fuck," Moore heard one of his soldiers yell when he saw what lay ahead. Route Delta was on fire. While the tanks had been regrouping, fresh heaps of metal and trash had been piled at nearly every intersection and set alight. Hundreds of people were massing along the streets. Some fled as the tanks approached, but the assault from AK-47s and RPGs remained ferocious. The tankers were fighting block by block through a swath of territory that had, in a matter of hours, become completely unlike anything the tank platoon had seen during its deployment. The once friendly residents had suddenly turned on the American troops.

Tanks had long been a familiar sight to the people of Sadr City, and certainly to the Mahdi militia. Saddam Hussein had purposefully designed this slum with broad streets, using tanks to intimidate the local Shiite community whenever he felt they were getting out of line. But the residents were keen observers. They had picked up important lessons about the vulnerabilities of armored vehicles. They knew, for example, that two of the four crew members were almost always exposed in the hatches. A well-aimed round, like the one that hit Michael Mitchell, or the shrapnel from improvised bombs could kill or maim a soldier. The turret holding the big gun didn't turn well in close quarters, making it easier for the militia to attack and run. And if a rocket-propelled grenade struck just the right spot, even a tank could be stopped in its tracks.

The gunner in one of the lead tanks, Staff Sergeant Henry Eldridge, stood behind the M-240 coaxial machine gun, aiming from inside the turret.

"We've got guys out there building barricades," Eldridge yelled to his tank commander, Lieutenant David Fittro. He'd spotted two Iraqi men about a hundred feet ahead of him setting a large heap of debris on fire. He asked for permission to "take 'em out." Fittro gave the okay, and Eldridge squeezed the trigger, watching as the two men collapsed on the pile of trash. He'd never fired at a human being—in fact, he had barely fired his weapon at all. Eldridge, whose grandfather was the first African-American integrated into the Mississippi National Guard, couldn't believe this was the same road he'd been down a hundred times in the past year. During his long deployment, he had not seen a single violent incident. Now his tank platoon was at the center of a maelstrom.

The tank kept rolling, crushing the junk in the street that had brought the Alpha Company Humvees to a halt. Stoves, air conditioners, market stands, dead animals: The seventy-ton vehicles flattened them all.

"Stay to the right, the right!" Captain Moore radioed to Fittro's driver, Specialist Erik Albertson. Moore instructed his own driver, Specialist Jason Rakes, to keep to the left. That put four tanks in the southbound lanes of the road and Fittro's three-tank column in the northbound lanes. They were all heading north. Moore wanted the columns staggered with a good distance between each, so the tankers wouldn't accidentally fire at one another.

"Look right! Look right!" Albertson yelled when he saw something suspicious on his screens. Tank drivers are in a reclined position inside the turret, but with their video monitors and periscopes, they have a better overall view of what's outside than any other crew member. Fittro and Eldridge took their cues from Albertson. A self-assured nineteen-year-old North Dakota native, Eric Albertson had figured out a way to use his own weapon from inside the tank. He had removed two of the periscopes so that he could fire his pistol through the holes. If anyone dangerous got close, Albertson would blast them. He didn't want there to be another Michael Mitchell.

"Over there! Sniper!"

"Third floor!" a spotter yelled. "Second window!"

"Identified!"

"Fire!"

The .50-cal swung and fired at the center window in a three-story building where a muzzle had appeared, the impact shaking loose doors and windows on the floors above and below. An RPG shot in front of Fittro's tank. Eldridge and Fittro quickly identified the source: a group of Mahdi Army with RPGs, standing beneath the giant mural of Moqtada al-Sadr about two hundred meters away. Moore authorized his men to fire the main gun. Eldridge opened up with "the beast"—the main gun, loaded with a 120mm high-explosive round, wide as a salad plate and with the power to crumble entire walls. The tank rocked backward from its blast, jolting the soldiers inside. The building where the Mahdi Army had been standing erupted in fire and smoke, and the tanks kept advancing along Route Delta.

Up ahead, at the side of a building, an older Iraqi man stood as if dumbstruck in the midst of the flaming clamor. At first Albertson felt sorry for the guy.

"Dumbass, get the hell out of here," Albertson yelled, though no one could hear him above all the gunfire.

The man just stared. As they got closer, Albertson saw that it wasn't a case of shell shock: He was helping the militia at a nearby marketplace, signaling the location of the tanks and indicating when they were about to pass in front of the market. Fittro spotted the man, too, and aimed the .50-cal right at him. He was blasted backward, dead in seconds.

After the tanks passed a police station, the northbound lanes became so strewn with obstacles that they were no longer passable, even for tanks. The three tanks that barreled forward in those lanes were forced into the southbound lanes. Even that became tricky, so they started to drive partially on the sidewalk, crushing piles of animal carcasses and scrap appliances. As Albertson's tank rumbled past the remains of an outdoor market, the main gun turret twisted to the side, snagging a kiosk that was dangling now from the gun barrel.

"Red Four, this is Red One," Sergeant Virgil Franklin radioed to Albertson, in the tank just ahead of him. "You have a market stand stuck on your gun tube."

Albertson couldn't see it from his video monitors, but he rotated the gun barrel until the kiosk fell off, and then he ran over it. The thought made him smile. *Not bad for a nineteen-year-old tank driver,* he thought.

But his sense of satisfaction was fleeting. He now faced the most difficult roadblock yet—a rusted metal staircase that must have taken fifty Mahdi militiamen to carry. He didn't know what to do. Albertson needed guidance, but his commander, Lieutenant Fittro, was busy firing at targets. *Fuck, fuck. What do I do?* He slowed the tank considerably and then changed his mind and slammed on the gas. The tank lurched and rocked. Then it rose nearly straight up before plummeting down on the other side and over the stairs.

"Holy hell," he mumbled to himself, startled a little by his own nerve, and relieved that the tank hadn't flipped over backward.

The obstacles and withering gunfire cost the convoy considerable time. Between the shooting and near-constant stopping, it had taken ninety minutes for the tanks to travel two and a half miles up Route Delta. Now it was dark and the tanks were low on ammunition. The platoon sergeant had passed them grid coordinates, so they knew they were close. But the flaming junk heaps and enemy fire from all sides made it hard to see, and alleys seemed to shoot off in every direction. As the tanks proceeded along Delta,

Lieutenant Fittro spotted a large piece of junk smoldering in the road. This was no market stand. It was an abandoned Humvee.

"Stop! Stop!" Fittro screamed. "Stop! They must be around the corner!" But no one could hear over the noise in the turret, and the tank barreled past the turn.

TWO HUNDRED FEET down the alley, from inside his bullet-riddled Humvee, Sergeant Swope could not believe what he was seeing. *Not again!* He'd heard the unmistakable thud of tank fire as the seven M-1A2s made their way up Delta. And now he and the other soldiers in Aguero's platoon watched, dumbstruck, as the tanks rolled right past.

"Look left! Look left!" Swope screamed into the radio. "We're down here. Stop! Stop!" Sergeant Eric Bourquin grabbed a smoke grenade and hurled it toward Route Delta before it occurred to him that the convoy might think it was an enemy attack and return fire. But the tankers didn't even see it. Swope kept yelling into his radio for them to stop, to no avail.

Aguero leaped from his Humvee and took off running toward the passing vehicles. "FUCKIN' STOP!" he screamed, waving desperately at the tankers with a small flashlight. If the tankers could see the light, the Mahdi militiamen could, too, but Aguero figured this was the platoon's last chance. He had to stop those tanks, whatever the risk. Several of his men likewise pulled out their flashlights.

Captain Moore's tank was just clearing the intersection when he spotted something out of the corner of his eye and jerked his head to the left. He saw lights, half a dozen small beams waving frantically from the narrow roadway. *Flashlights,* he realized.

It has to be them!

The screeching grind of brakes from the tanks nearly drowned out the rattle of machine guns. As quickly as possible—and tanks don't stop quickly—Moore repositioned the massive vehicles to block the alleyway from enemy fire. He ordered his crews to stay inside. Removing his tank helmet, which was attached by cable to a radio, he jumped into the middle of the street. Almost immediately he realized his mistake—he'd stepped into enemy fire without any kind of Kevlar head protection. *Shit!* Just as dangerous, he realized, was the possibility that one of the stranded soldiers might fire on him, thinking he was a militiaman dashing down the alley in the dark.

"There's an American coming toward you!" he shouted. "I'm an American!" That's when he saw another soldier—Shane Aguero—limping in his direction in a bloody, dirty uniform.

"You okay?" Moore asked as he introduced himself. The two soldiers—one a tanker, one an infantryman—were in different army divisions and had never met. Aguero waved off Moore's concern and got down to business.

"Okay," he said. "Here's what I got: one dead, six wounded, thirteen not wounded, two armored Humvees that will probably still work. How do you want us to set up in your vehicles? We obviously can't all fit in mine."

"Put the wounded up on the lead tanks," Moore said. "As we roll in, they can be the first ones off." Moore told Aguero there would be four tanks in the lead, followed by Aguero's two Humvees, with the three remaining tanks following in the rear.

Aguero had Swope call up to the roof to tell the soldiers to gather the weapons and hurry down to the alley. Swope, trying to figure out the best way to get his soldiers and equipment down to the relative safety of the tanks waiting on Route Delta, decided to pack the Humvees with the wounded for the short ride. The rest of the men crept the two hundred feet down the alleyway to the tanks, hounded by gunfire.

Sergeant Chen's body was laid carefully on the hood of the lead Humvee. There was no other way to transport him. The burka had been left behind, and the body was uncovered now. A few of the soldiers averted their eyes. But Specialist Justin Bellamy laid his upper body on top of Chen's body to make certain he wouldn't fall off. No one made a sound as the caravan of battered soldiers made their way beneath the moon and the tracer fire that shot across it. Bits of bloodied fabric littered the roadway. A shoe, torn in half, had been kicked to the side. At the end of the alley, through the green hue of their night-vision goggles, the men saw the tanks that would take them to safety.

"Sergeant D, put five guys in each Humvee," Swope told Staff Sergeant Trevor Davis as they approached the tanks. Davis grabbed Specialists Carl Wild and Jonathan Denny. Clearly, even after two hours spent pinned down in the alleyway, the young men were frightened by the thought of getting into the Humvee and out on the streets again. Both vehicles had flattened tires, busted windshields, and more bullet holes than anyone cared to count.

"It's gonna be okay," Davis assured them. "It's almost over."

SFC Swope stopped when he reached the tanks. He wanted a head count to make certain no one was left behind. The platoon counted off: seventeen soldiers, plus one killed, and one interpreter. One man short, Swope thought. He and Aguero knew the platoon had left that morning with twenty men. The soldiers counted off again. There was still a missing soldier.

"Well, what the fuck?" Aguero said. "Where's the last guy?"

Moore, who was leading the tanks, headed over to the group.

"We need to go," Moore told Aguero. "We're getting shot at."

Aguero took a long drag on a cigarette, the first one he had really enjoyed all night. "We're not going anywhere until I account for my soldier."

Moore didn't want to leave anyone behind either, but the men couldn't stand in the street all night. "You've got ten minutes to get this shit straight, or I'm leaving," Moore snapped. The tank commander couldn't believe that after a whole night in the alleyway the platoon leaders couldn't find all their men. He thought that Aguero and Swope had forgotten to count Chen, though they insisted thcy had. When Swope lit his own cigarette, Moore lost it. He grabbed Swope by the body armor.

"This is your job!" he shouted, pulling Swope's face close. "Get a count of your guys and let's get the hell out of here. Goddamn it! Get this straight!"

Moore, who towered over Swope, seemed unimpressed that Swope had spent the entire evening under intense fire, calmly providing the grid coordinates that were key to getting the platoon rescued. Now with his face just inches from Moore's, Swope said, just as coolly, "Yes, sir."

In another minute, the mystery was solved.

"Sergeant Swope," a soldier shouted. "York got the runs today, so he didn't come back out." Swope and Aguero smiled. *Ah yes. Mookie's revenge.* Sergeant Joshua York hadn't made it out of the latrine in time to join the platoon for the ill-fated afternoon sewage run. York was the one who normally kept track of the men in his vehicle, and no one else had remembered to report his absence. That took care of the missing soldier.

"Let's get mounted!" Swope shouted, pointing up to Moore's tank. The men passed Chen's body up to a tanker crouching on top, who grabbed the dead soldier under the arms. Aguero, Davis, and two others crowded on top of the tank near Chen. There was no room for them inside.

Sergeant Bourquin, Specialist Jonathan Riddell, and Specialist Justin Bellamy climbed up on the second tank. Davis and Bourquin, both infantrymen, had never ridden atop a tank before. Now they were sitting in the turret beds on top of their respective tanks— a small carved-out area about two feet wide—their backs up against the turret stand. *This is so cool,* they thought. Never mind the gunfire that was coming at them—this was the platoon's taxi ride home. Bourquin figured he'd made it to nightfall in the alley; he would surely make it back to base on top of a tank. He grabbed his weapon and started returning fire.

On the lead tank, Moore popped his head out of the hatch and handed a pack of ammunition up to Aguero and his men. The bigger guns on the tank, the .50-cal and the M-240B coaxial machine gun, were out of ammo. Moore sat high in the hatch on the right side of the tank, firing the only weapon he had left: his M-4.

Despite its heavy armor, the tank provided little protection for the men on top. The wounded curled up to make themselves a smaller target. The others scanned for the enemy through night-vision goggles.

"One o'clock!" Davis shouted, pointing to a building off to his right. Both Davis and Sergeant Darcy Robinson fired at one of the windows. The sniper kept shooting as the tank rolled to a stop. The turret turned slowly, and the barrel of the main 120mm gun rose. In an instant, the sniper, the window, and a big chunk of the building disappeared.

The convoy picked up speed once it turned right onto Route Silver. With a canal backed by an open field to the north, the gunfire now came only from the south, where a row of houses and shops lined the street. Sporadic fire popped here and there, but with little more than a mile to go before the gates of Camp War Eagle, the soldiers were finally starting to believe they might make it. Swope, riding in the first Humvee, trailing the first four tanks, stared at the dark clouds of dust spitting from the tracked vehicles. *This is good,* he thought. *This is very good.*

"Comanche Red Four," came a voice over the radio. "I think I've lost a wheel."

It was the driver of the Humvee right behind Swope. At least the Humvee was *supposed* to be right behind Swope. But the second Humvee, and the three tanks following it, had stopped at least three hundred yards back. Swope was flabbergasted. *What else can go wrong?* He stopped his vehicle, hopped out, and looked around. His own Humvee was in such bad shape that he knew he couldn't drive back and pick up the others and still make it to safety. But they were so close to Camp War Eagle now; Swope spotted a Humvee that had just pulled out of the gate, and flagged it down and headed back to help his stranded driver.

Swope saw the problem right away. It wasn't the wheel that had stopped the Humvee but a concrete block underneath. The Humvee was high-centered on the slab and going nowhere. Swope hooked a tow strap between his Humvee and the immobilized one. *Pop!* The strap broke before Swope's Humvee even started moving. He'd had it. He ran back to the tanks idling behind the Humvees and hollered up to the tank commander.

"Can you push the Humvee with your tank? Just run into it and push it."

He loaded up all the remaining soldiers onto the tanks and then got back into the passenger seat of the stalled Humvee. "Let's go! Let's go!" he shouted. A powerful thrust from the tank's engine, and the Humvee was free. The tank pushed the Humvee the last mile to the base.

BECAUSE RADIO COMMUNICATIONS still weren't working between the Humvees and the lead tanks, the first part of the convoy had continued toward Camp War Eagle, unaware that the trailing vehicles had fallen behind. Moore stopped his tanks at the casualty collection point just inside the gates of the forward operating base, jumped down from the turret, and helped unload the wounded. Chen's body was lifted off the tank and placed on a litter.

So this is how it is, Shane Aguero thought, watching as Chen was carried away. *You leave in the morning, alive and singing country music, and you return twelve hours later, lifeless and cold.*

Aguero had had no idea his Humvees had dropped out of the column. Barely able to walk himself, Aguero was beginning to grasp the full horror of what his men had been through. He looked around for Swope. Then he realized his two Humvees were missing. He ran up to a soldier, a stranger.

"Where the fuck are my two Humvees?" he screamed.

Aguero was frantic. Covered with blood, hobbling, he grabbed Robinson, Davis, and Bellamy, and the four men headed toward the front gate, ready to walk back to the city if that's what it took to find Swope and the others. Four crazed soldiers, ranting and cursing. A staff sergeant on guard stopped them at the gate.

"Where the fuck do you think you're going?" the sergeant said. Aguero told him loudly that his two Humvees weren't back yet, and they were going to get them. The sergeant assured them that Swope and the three tanks had passed through the other gate just moments before.

Aguero turned then and stumbled back toward the aid station, satisfied with the answer. Now that all his men were accounted for, his own injuries caught up with him. Aguero found he could hardly walk. Davis and Robinson had to hold him up. *Amber,* he thought. He wanted to call his wife, but suddenly he couldn't focus. He saw soldiers huddled together throughout the camp, swearing and sobbing. He was safe, and most of his men were okay. Something *else* must have gone terribly wrong.

Just then, Sergeant First Class Reginald Butler from Alpha Company walked past. Aguero grabbed his shoulder.

"How did you guys do out there?" Aguero asked.

"Bad." As poorly as Aguero felt, Butler looked even worse—not physically wounded so much as shell-shocked.

"I lost one," Aguero said, still trying to figure out what was going on. "Did you have anyone hurt?"

"Forty-seven," Butler said.

Aguero figured he must have misheard. He asked Butler to repeat himself.

"Forty-seven," Butler said again. "That I know about right now." He turned and walked away.

Aguero felt his legs start to give. He tightened his grip on the shoulders of Davis and Robinson, who led him to the aid station. He still wasn't quite sure he understood. *Forty-seven? Is that what he said?* Shane Aguero lowered his head. His body was shaking in disbelief.

It would be a very long time before he could tell Amber the news.

★

Chapter 19

THE

CALL

Noon

Fort Hood

IT WAS NOON on Sunday when Connie Abrams got home from brunch with Casey Sanders and Kelly Lesperance. Her dress and shoes felt just tight enough from brunch that she wanted to get them off. As soon as she walked in the front door she noticed the light on the answering machine signaling two messages. They were both from Lieutenant Colonel Dave Thompson, the executive officer for her husband Abe's brigade in Iraq. She hit *Play* as she kicked off her shoes.

"Connie, I'll call you back," the first message said. The second wasn't much longer. "Connie, I need to get hold of Dexter Jordan." *Click.*

Something wasn't right. Dexter Jordan was the rear detachment commander (RDC) for the brigade, Colonel Abrams's liaison between the soldiers in Iraq and their wives, family, and friends back at Fort Hood. He was the key man for getting equipment or re-

sources over to Iraq and for coordinating the handling of family issues through Family Readiness Group (FRG) leaders like Connie
Abrams. But he took his Sundays seriously. Dexter Jordan would
almost certainly be at church. And Dave Thompson would know.

So what the heck is going on?

Connie put out some games for her son Robbie and went to
her bedroom. She'd call Dave as soon as she changed clothes. But
then the phone rang.

"Connie, I can't get hold of Captain Jordan." It was Dave
Thompon.

"I'll try him," Connie said. "What do you need?"

There was a brief pause.

"The 2-5 Cav has been in a huge battle, Connie," he said. "We
have three KIAs and over thirty wounded."

Connie could barely process the words. Killed in action? *What*
action? They had just gotten there. And this was a peacekeeping
mission! For a moment she was speechless. Then it occurred to her:
Abe had promised to call her personally if something bad happened. Not Dave, or anyone else—Abe himself. Why hadn't he—

"Is Abe okay?" Connie asked suddenly. "Is Abe injured, Dave?
Is he *dead*?"

"I wouldn't do that to you, Connie," Thompson nearly shouted.
"He's just very busy. But I need to get hold of Captain Jordan."

"Okay, okay," Connie said, her heart racing.

Promising to help, she hung up and tried Dexter Jordan's cell
phone. Voice mail. She tried again. Voice mail. She left several
messages, trying not to sound too frantic. But she couldn't stop
thinking about it. *Three dead? Thirty wounded?* And Thompson's re-
assurance hadn't convinced her: She knew full well that Abe
would've ordered Thompson not to tell her even if he had been
hurt.

And if it *wasn't* Abe who was hurt or dead, then who?

Connie started pacing between the bedroom and the kitchen. Why wasn't the phone ringing? When would Dexter Jordan return her calls? He'd be the one to compile the list of casualties in Iraq and send out the military notification teams to tell the families their soldier was wounded, or dead. Then Connie and the other FRG leaders could assemble their teams of women to offer whatever support and resources the grieving families might need. But right now, Connie couldn't even get a grip on *herself*.

When Rod Leary pulled into the driveway, Connie welcomed the help he might provide. Leary was one of the male spouses at Fort Hood—his wife was one of the few women who were deployed to Iraq; the Learys' son Nelson was coming over to play. Connie walked quickly outside and explained to Rod that she couldn't take Nelson for the afternoon, and that she would need someone to look after her own son. "I can't tell you anything right now," she said, "but can you take Robbie today?"

The expression on her face sent a clear message to Rod Leary.

"He'll spend the night," Leary said. "Don't worry about it. You can pick him up before school tomorrow."

Connie hustled Robbie off with a kiss, trying to look as calm as possible. As soon as she walked back inside, the phone rang. It was Dexter Jordan. He had already been in touch with Lieutenant Colonel Thompson in Baghdad, and he repeated what Connie had just been told by Thompson.

"Right now we have three KIAs and over thirty wounded," he said.

ORIGINALLY FROM ATLANTA, Dexter Jordan moved to Fort Hood with his wife in 2001. He was a seasoned company commander by the time the First Cavalry Division received its Iraq deployment orders, and he was eager to see his first war zone.

Then Colonel Abrams asked Jordan to have lunch with him, something that had never happened before. "I need a good rear detachment commander," Abrams said. Jordan immediately offered to find him one.

"No," Abrams replied. "I'd like *you* to be the rear detachment commander." Jordan mumbled an awkward thank you, trying to disguise his disappointment. Abrams understood: Officers as capable as Jordan didn't see RDC as a plum post—while his battalion buddies headed off to war, Jordan would be staying behind with the families. But Abrams knew from experience how critical it was to have an outstanding RDC, someone capable of operating with no guidance or oversight to resolve problems quickly. From Abrams's perspective it was every bit as important as a battlefront posting—he wanted a solid, capable officer helping the families navigate the important and sometimes thorny issues of day-to-day life that had to be contended with stateside.

But nothing quite prepared Jordan for Robert Abrams's call on this Sunday morning with the news that three brigade soldiers had been killed. Because the families had yet to be notified, Abrams could share only the barest details: that a platoon had been ambushed and that rescue forces had also come under fire; that Sergeant Yihjyh Chen, who had been part of the ambushed platoon, was dead, as were Specialists Stephen Hiller and Israel Arsiaga, two Alpha Company soldiers who'd been part of the subsequent rescue effort.

Jordan rushed back to his office and started pulling personnel files, searching for the next of kin for each of the dead soldiers. Once he found them, the casualty notification officers could be dispatched. Only then could he share the names with Connie Abrams and the other FRG leaders.

He knew from talking to Colonel Abrams that the FRG leaders weren't related to any of the dead soldiers, but he had no idea who else was injured or how seriously. And what about the care teams, the wives who'd be dispatched to help the families of the dead and wounded? Jordan feared one of those wives might learn she had a spouse who was injured or dead.

After she spoke with Dexter Jordan, Connie called LeAnn Volesky, the FRG leader whose husband, Gary, was the 2-5 Cav battalion commander.

"What are you doing?" Connie asked.

"Just sitting here with Alex," LeAnn said.

Connie wasted no time. "I just got a call from Dave Thompson," she said.

LeAnn could tell immediately from the strain in Connie's voice that something terrible had happened.

"Oh, my God. What's the matter?"

Her voice shaking, Connie told LeAnn about the three dead soldiers and the dozens who had been hurt. LeAnn was stunned, and terrified.

"Is one of them Gary?" she asked.

"I don't know. I just don't know." But the answer had to be *no,* Connie said to LeAnn: Thompson would have cautioned Connie not to talk to LeAnn right away if he knew Gary had been hurt. LeAnn pondered this, and decided Connie was probably right. If Gary was dead, she realized, she'd be sitting with a casualty notification officer right now. Her doorbell would have rung. That was how these things happened. The doorbell rings and your life changes forever.

After all these years, LeAnn had never had a death in any of Gary's units. She'd helped many families in many ways—depression, isolation, substance abuse, deaths in the family, financial issues—but she had never dealt with anything like this. She didn't want it to be Gary, of course, but she didn't want it to be anybody else either. And there was no getting around one essential fact: Three men from the First Cav were dead. For three families—three of *her* families—nothing would ever be the same again.

For now all they could do was wait. Connie had driven to LeAnn's house as soon as they hung up. For the next hour she and Connie Abrams stared at the phones, at their watches, at the TV. They got up and just as quickly sat down again. LeAnn started to say something, then stopped herself. She didn't want to be rude.

"You're not going to sit here all day with me, are you?" she finally asked.

"Do you not want me to?" Connie said.

"Not that I don't appreciate it," LeAnn said, "but I need to get busy. I can't just sit here."

Back at home, Connie couldn't sit still either. The phone wasn't ringing, the TV wasn't giving her any news, and there was nothing she could do to calm down. She paced and sipped coffee. Several cups. She chewed her fingernails. A nail would snap between her teeth and she'd move on to the next one. Connie had never bitten her nails before. Now she couldn't stop.

Finally she got in her car and drove to brigade headquarters, the place where families usually waited to welcome soldiers home. She didn't want to be alone. Maybe she could make herself useful.

Inside, she found Dexter Jordan digging through a morass of incomplete or outdated paperwork. In theory, every soldier in the military is responsible for regularly updating his emergency contact names and numbers. Abrams's troops were supposed to have done this before deployment. Jordan quickly saw that not everyone had followed instructions. Generally, the married soldiers had updated their contacts, but many of the single soldiers hadn't bothered. Jordan traced a trail of outdated numbers for one of the dead soldiers, Eddie Chen, and as he began collecting the names of the wounded, he found that many of their contact numbers were wrong as well.

While Jordan worked to track down family members and Connie tried to construct a family support plan, the calls kept coming in from Baghdad. The tally of wounded was growing, and now the number of dead had risen to four. *Four.* And from what they could tell, the battle in Sadr City wasn't over yet.

They yearned for news. People were constantly switching the TV from CNN to MSNBC to Fox and back again, looking for anything on Iraq. Finally, a report came on about Sadr City, and everyone froze. CNN anchor Catherine Calloway's voice was suddenly the only one in the room, blaring from the TV screen.

"A senior coalition official tells CNN an ambush in a Shiite neighborhood in Baghdad left four U.S. soldiers dead and at least forty wounded. The official says the army regained control of five stations that a militia loyal to a radical Shiite cleric had taken over."

She went on.

"And John Wayne is helping deliver the mail. Not the Pony Express, it's not coming back. The late actor's likeness appears on a new postage stamp unveiled this weekend."

Oh *please,* Connie thought. She needed to hear more about the soldiers, not about John Wayne! *Back to Iraq, back to Iraq, come on . . .* She was desperate to hear anything. Finally the anchor continued:

"Let's go right to CNN's Jim Clancy. He's joining us from Baghdad with the latest on all the violence that has occurred there today. Jim, what can you tell us?"

"Catherine, as you said, a bloody day, and of the most concern, this new front that may be opening up with the Shia Muslim militant leader Moqtada al-Sadr.

"Now, as you noted, four Americans lost their lives, forty others wounded in an ambush in Sadr City.

"The numbers are very sketchy today, Catherine, but the concern is that a new front is opening up with the Shiites, the sixty percent majority in this country who up until now have been patient, perhaps opposed to the occupation, but happy with the overthrow of Saddam Hussein and largely backing the U.S. effort. If this is a new front, it could be a serious development."

At that point the broadcast turned to other topics. Well, having some news was better than having none, Connie thought. But seeing it on the news only increased the pressure on Jordan to get the notification teams to the families. Connie called LeAnn and told her they should begin calling the care teams, put people in place to go visit the spouses after notification. She didn't know who the KIAs were or when she would find out, but she wanted to let the teams know that they needed to prepare. She wanted to be ready.

Two of the FRG leaders, Aimee Randazzo and Gina Denomy, were preparing to meet Angie Upton for an early birthday dinner in Killeen. As Aimee backed down the short driveway, her mom— visiting from out of town—came running out of the house.

"LeAnn Volesky is on the phone," she called.

Aimee took the cordless phone. Gina watched her. She didn't say much, just an occasional "Uh-huh" or "Okay." She looked at her watch, then glanced at Gina. Aimee had tears in her eyes.

A FEW MILES AWAY, Angie Upton was pulling into the parking lot of the local Bennigan's restaurant. The news was on her car radio, not that she was paying much attention—but then a few words stopped her cold: "Sadr City" and something about a battle. She turned up the volume and waited. A few minutes later, the details were repeated: a major battle in Sadr City, militiamen attacking U.S. troops, many casualties. *Oh my God.* Angie shut the engine off and raced into the restaurant to tell Gina and Aimee, but there was no sign of them. She checked the time. Gina and Aimee were twenty minutes late, and Aimee was never late— *especially* not on Angie's birthday. Something had to be wrong.

Then her cell phone rang. It was Aimee.

"Angie, I know it's your birthday," Aimee said, "but something has come up, and we can't come. I'm so sorry. I'll call you later." Angie had heard the news on the radio and was afraid to ask anything more. Maybe it was a good sign that Aimee and Gina couldn't come. Since Aimee had to visit the families of the wounded and dead, that must mean that Trent was okay. Angie got some food to go and headed back out to the car, the foam container squeaking as she walked.

Before LeAnn called Aimee Randazzo, she had been told that none of the KIAs had a rank of captain or above. That ruled out Gary, most of his headquarters staff, and all of his company commanders. Aimee's husband, Dylan; Gina Denomy's husband, Troy; and Angie Upton's husband, Trent, were all alive. LeAnn had told Aimee and Gina immediately. But she couldn't tell Angie yet, because she wasn't an FRG leader.

Despite the relief that their husbands were alive, Gina, LeAnn, and Aimee were still in shock, and feeling terrible for the families who would be receiving the news. The 2-5 Cav had been gone only a few weeks. Sending their husbands off had been difficult, but it had never really occurred to them that they'd be in the middle of a battle—a deadly battle—two weeks later.

LeAnn was cleaning the house, vacuuming, sweeping, wiping down countertops—anything to stay busy. Nearly seven hundred soldiers were in the 2-5 Cav, and four of them were dead. Somebody had lost a son, a father, a brother. *Please don't let it be ___*, she would think, and the face of a soldier she knew would pop into her head. *Please don't let it be one of the company commanders. Please don't let it be the husband of someone on the care team. Please don't let it be the father of anyone in Alex's class.*

LeAnn's phone rang again. Now it was Dexter Jordan's boss, Colonel Robert Forrester, asking LeAnn to read off the names of her care team members. He wanted to make sure none of them were related to the KIAs. She recited the list.

"Nope," Forrester said. "Nope. Nope." There were more than a dozen names of care team members, each of them no relation. When they'd made it through the list, LeAnn let out a big sigh, unaware she'd been holding her breath. But again she felt only momentary relief: Her good fortune meant someone else would not be so lucky. Maybe she didn't know the people well, but they were her kin, in a way, and she was devastated by the thought of what they were about to go through.

At brigade headquarters, Jordan was still scrambling. He'd found an address for Lesley Hiller, Dusty Hiller's wife, near Fort Hood. Chen's family, however, was unreachable. There was a number listed for his parents in Guam, but it was out of service. Jordan tried to call Chen's brother, but that was proving difficult as well. He began to worry about time. Army policy dictated that death notifications had to be made before ten p.m. and after six a.m. It was considered more humane than waking someone with devastating news. How could a military family ever sleep if they thought they might be awoken with tragedy in the middle of the night? With four KIAs and more than thirty wounded, Jordan knew he needed to get the army notification officers moving. He was becoming exasperated. So many of the contact numbers had turned out to be wrong.

As the names of casualties came in, Jordan grouped them by severity: not seriously injured (NSI), seriously injured (SI), or very seriously injured (VSI). They would contact the families of the VSI soldiers first, along with the KIAs. As soon as they found the families of the KIAs, Jordan would start gathering all the data on each injured soldier—estimated return time, to what hospital, and when the army would fly relatives to meet him.

ANGIE UPTON ARRIVED HOME and again she slipped into the comfort of one of Trent's old T-shirts. She wiped her tears with the shirt's frayed edge. At the computer, she searched for news and read e-mail. She had to e-mail Trent, she thought, though she knew it was probably pointless. As battalion personnel officer, he was no doubt busy tracking all the unit casualties. He'd have no time to respond. Still, Angie Upton could hope. After all, it was her birthday.

> What is going on there? Sadr City is all over the news. I pray that you are ok. I know the odds are small that you are among those who are hurt, but I still worry. Fox News said it happened earlier today but that you guys have established security again in the city. I hope you are ok. I know you won't be able to check your email for a while now, but it makes me feel better to write to you anyway. It makes me feel that you are ok.
>   I love you,
>   Angie

At brigade headquarters, Captain Jordan's assistant cupped his hand over the telephone receiver.

"Sir," he whispered, "we've located two of the families."

Jordan paused for only a moment. He took down the information and immediately relayed it to the notification teams. Israel Garza had died on the chopper, en route from the aid station to the hospital, from the bullets that ripped through his chest and abdomen. Garza's wife and their babies lived in San Antonio, but it had taken hours and a long series of phone calls to track her down. She'd been there in Killeen, just outside Fort Hood, staying with her sister-in-law the whole time, as it turned out. Stephen Hiller's wife was nearby as well.

Jordan called LeAnn Volesky. "LeAnn, you need to get your care teams ready. Notification teams are being dispatched to the families of two of the KIAs within the hour." Jordan told LeAnn he would give her the names as soon as the notification officers left the home.

LeAnn started shaking. Her eyes clouded with tears. "How far away are they?" she asked.

"Half a mile away, LeAnn. Half a mile away."

Chapter 20

★

BACK TO

BASE

1945 hours

Sadr City

"WHAT A FUCKED-UP PLACE," someone said. "As far as I'm concerned, all Iraqis can go to hell."

Troy Denomy and eight of his men rode in the steel troop compartment of the M-2A3 Bradley that carried them, at long last, back to Camp War Eagle. They were jammed so tightly that they had to sit in one another's laps, the barrels of their M-16s and M-4s stuck into their backs and legs, sometimes pointing at their chests, as they jockeyed for space. Inside the Bradley it was dark, it reeked of sweat, gunpowder, and blood, and the men were starting to vent.

Denomy couldn't blame them. They'd come with good intentions, and look what had happened—Aguero and his men ambushed while escorting a sewage truck; the militia so intent on killing them that they had placed women and children in the battle zone. Denomy saw that his soldiers might begin to view the people of Sadr City as the enemy. But he also knew the soldiers couldn't defeat an insurgency if they thought all Iraqis were the enemy.

"You gotta remember these people are scared, really scared," he said. "There are a lot of good people here, but they've been through a lot."

Sergeant John Wanczowski, one of the Bradley crew members, chimed in, "Yeah, man, not all Iraqis are bad. This is just something that's going to happen sometimes."

He was right, but neither he nor any of the other men was under any illusions now. Moqtada al-Sadr's Mahdi militia was determined to take control of this part of Baghdad—in fact, while Denomy had been battling to get to Aguero, the militia had overrun all the Iraqi police stations in Sadr City. Now the 2-5 Cav soldiers would have to take them back. The thought of how much hard work still lay ahead of his soldiers, and what they had already been through, left Denomy exhausted and disturbed.

IT WAS THAT NEXT PHASE of the operation—taking back the police stations—that Gary Volesky and his brigade commander, Colonel Robert Abrams, were contending with now, back at the TOC. Abrams had walked over from the aid station after watching the first wave of wounded soldiers arrive. It had been a rough night already, and it was a long way from being done. When he looked up and saw Volesky, he strode over and put his muscular arm around Volesky's thin frame.

"Where do we stand, Gary?" Abrams asked. Though Abrams's command still hadn't officially begun, he was the senior First Cav Division officer on the scene, and those were his soldiers out there. He had to look no further than the red welts on Volesky's face—from the hot shell casings expelled as he fired his weapon—to

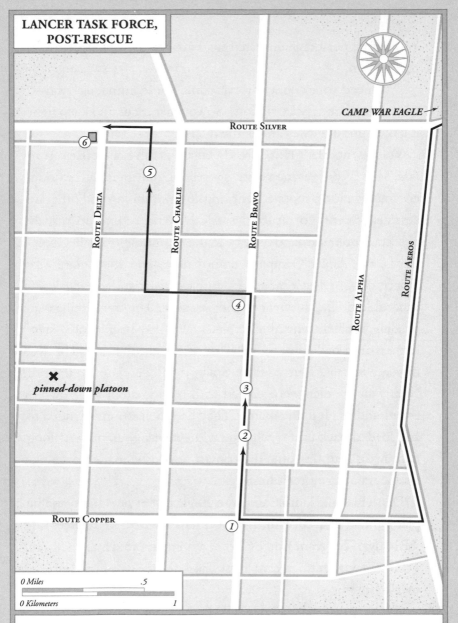

LANCER TASK FORCE, POST-RESCUE

CAMP WAR EAGLE →

ROUTE SILVER

6

5

ROUTE DELTA

ROUTE CHARLIE

ROUTE BRAVO

ROUTE ALPHA

ROUTE AEROS

4

✖ pinned-down platoon

3

2

ROUTE COPPER

1

| 0 Miles | .5 |
| 0 Kilometers | 1 |

1. The convoy turns north on Route Bravo so the Bradleys can clear the obstacles and go after Mahdi insurgents.

2. Soon after turning onto Bravo, the soldiers are ambushed.

3. Specialist Casey Sheehan is hit.

4. The Bravo Company convoy uses side streets to reach a CCP at Delta and Silver.

5. Corporal Forest Jostes is hit.

6. The soldiers reach the CCP.

© 2006 Jeffrey L. Ward

know how personally invested his battalion commander was in the mission.

"We need to account for everyone," he continued. "And we have to seize the police stations. So you just focus and keep fighting the fight. I'll take care of the dust-off."

Volesky nodded. He'd already begun a full-scale effort to retake Sadr City—getting vehicles repaired, outfitted with working communications, supplied with ample ammunition and other necessities; clearing obstructed roadways; and setting up casualty collection points around the city. In the meantime, Captain George Lewis, the Alpha Company commander, and Lieutenant Clay Spicer, the Charlie Company executive officer, and virtually every other able-bodied survivor of the past several hours' fighting were heading back out into the battle. Lewis had been nearly killed himself, and had witnessed the horrifying death of his Humvee driver, Specialist Dusty Hiller. Spicer had been shot in the calf. Nearly all the men were stained with blood, either their own or their buddies'. It didn't matter. They had their wounds tended to, and loaded back up for what they knew was going to be a long, hard night. But this time the convoy would be made up only of Bradleys and armored Humvees.

Denomy pulled into Camp War Eagle just after Aguero and his platoon had arrived with their two tank-escorted Humvees and the body of Sergeant Eddie Chen. Denomy spotted Staff Sergeant Trevor Davis and Sergeant First Class Jerry Swope, and walked over to them.

"Sir, let's go back!" Davis yelled. He'd strained his voice from yelling in the alley, and he spoke with a kind of guttural screech, his adrenaline still surging. "I'm ready! I wanna go kill those fuckers!"

He held up his bloodied fingers, mangled by an AK-47 round. For the first time in his life, Davis had shot a man. He'd watched him die. Now he was in a kind of frenzy. "Let's go back, sir!" he pleaded. "Right now!"

Swope was not nearly as animated. He stood somberly next to Davis and said, simply, "Chen is dead, sir."

"I know," Denomy said.

"Why did it take so long to get us out?" Swope asked. He'd kept radio contact with the rescue units while sitting alone in his Humvee, and he still didn't have a full picture of what had gone wrong. "We were there for hours."

Denomy explained that at least four convoys had rushed out to get them, and that all had suffered serious casualties in the effort. "I'll give you the whole story later," Denomy said. For now, though, Denomy needed Swope to assemble his soldiers in the mess hall. The top priority was to get a full and immediate accounting of everyone in the company.

They'd already began congregating in small groups—some around the gate, some around the motor pool, some around the aid station. Many soldiers knew what had happened only in their own units; they were anxious to learn what their buddies in other units had gone through.

But what little news Staff Sergeant Joshua Rountree had already heard filled him with dread. Rountree, who'd been on one of the Charlie Company Bradleys in Sadr City, knew only that one of Aguero's soldiers had been killed. Now, watching the soldiers head toward the dining hall, Rountree paced alongside his Bradley, sucking on the thick wad of tobacco he kept tucked in his cheek, spitting the juice into the dirt. He had a bad feeling.

Rountree was Eddie Chen's roommate, his best friend. Back in Texas, they had partied together every weekend. He kidded Chen mercilessly about his awful Asian cooking and his ridiculous Chinese-accented country-western singing. They'd celebrated together when Chen got his U.S. citizenship, one of the proudest days of Chen's life.

He hadn't seen Chen since the platoon returned, and he didn't want to know why. So he stayed off by himself. Specialist Justin Bellamy, a gunner who'd been in the alley with Aguero's platoon, had been waiting at the mess hall for Rountree. When Rountree didn't show up, Bellamy stepped outside, saw him standing alone, and started the long walk toward Chen's buddy.

Rountree took one look at Bellamy's anguished face, and he knew.

"It was Chen," Bellamy said.

Joshua Rountree sank to his knees, sobbing so hard that he struggled to breathe. Bellamy dropped beside him and wrapped his arms around Rountree's shoulders.

TROY DENOMY LEFT Davis and Swope and headed straight for the TOC. He wanted an update on his Third Platoon, under Lieutenant Dan Hines, which was still out in the city. He hadn't heard from them in three hours. Hines had checked in with the TOC from time to time, but Denomy was uneasy not knowing exactly where he was.

As Denomy walked in, Abrams looked up, the concern evident on his face.

"Hey, look, Troy," Abrams said. "Everything's gonna be okay." He put an arm around Denomy, just as he had done with Volesky a few minutes before. "But you have to get yourself over to the aid station right away and have them look at that shoulder. Your company needs you now more than ever, and you gotta be there for them."

When he got there, Denomy couldn't believe the number of wounded men. Bloody boots and body armor lay in abandoned piles, and the heap of weapons had grown so high it looked like a bonfire waiting to be lit. He looked around for his men. Big Country Reynolds had been taken by helicopter to the combat support hospital in the Green Zone, along with Sergeant Aaron Fowler. Fowler's two gunshot wounds in his legs had proven more serious than he'd let on at the "blocking position" less than an hour earlier. And it was clear from the mood inside that other units had lost men, lots of them.

A medic examined Denomy's wounds, one on his upper arm and one on the back of his shoulder. He'd barely noticed the back wound, though it was the larger and more serious of the injuries. One of the doctors feared the shrapnel might have penetrated his lungs. While Denomy let the medics examine and bandage him, the realities of the night began to sink in. He thought about Chen's death and the other seriously injured men. The doctor's concern about his own wounds rattled him, and now he thought of Gina and their son, Merrick. He'd almost died. They'd almost lost *him*. He'd almost lost them.

Walking slowly back to the dining hall in the moonlight, Denomy wondered what he should say to the men. He was struggling to keep his emotions under control. He couldn't let his soldiers see him this way. It would shake their confidence. They were certainly as rattled as he was, and they'd need him to be strong. If he was calm, they'd be calm, too. One thing he knew for sure: The fight was just beginning.

I just have to look everybody in the eyes and say, It's going to be okay, and we're going to get through it. And when we have time to talk about what happened to us, we will. Now is not that time.

After he strode into the dining hall, trying not to wince from the sting of his own wounds, Denomy went around the room, giving a reassuring hug to those who looked the most stricken. Some were crying. Others smoked cigarettes or fitfully drank coffee. A few were watching the reports about Sadr City on CNN. Denomy walked over and turned the television off. He needed everyone's attention. One by one, the Charlie Company platoon leaders accounted for their soldiers. About a dozen were wounded, but mildly enough that they could return to duty. Thirteen more had gone by helicopter to the combat support hospital so far. And Chen, as Denomy knew, had been killed in action. And that was just from Charlie Company. Third Platoon soldiers from Charlie Company were still out in the city. The rest of the Charlie Company soldiers—about eighty—were there in the mess hall. The kitchen staff had set out bottles of water and plates of bruised apples, but no one was touching them.

Denomy took a seat up front; Aguero pulled up a chair alongside him. Aguero was still suffering from the deafening grenade blast, and blood had now scabbed around his ear. He wanted to smoke, but his hands were shaking so badly he couldn't get the cigarette into his mouth. He told Denomy he thought the rescue mission had taken too long. Denomy, worried that the other soldiers might start to think they'd somehow failed their mission, stood and addressed the room.

"It's important," Denomy said, addressing Aguero and his men especially, "to understand what this company and the battalion as a whole went through in their efforts to reach you." He explained that the gunfire and assaults in the alley had been just a small part of a much larger uprising. Battalion leadership had estimated that two or three hundred Mahdi militiamen had positioned themselves along each of the major streets in Sadr City. There had been no escaping the ambushes. He told them about the huge number of casualties the militia had taken that day. The soldiers in the alley, he said, weren't the only ones to suffer. He wanted the First Platoon to understand why they'd had to wait so long, but he was also telling his other soldiers that their performance had been nothing short of heroic. They'd fought against overwhelming odds. Despite the chaos of a surprise attack, there'd been no incidents of friendly fire—that in itself was impressive. But he also made clear that Sadr City was now a war zone. They would have to put the Mahdi Army in its place and reestablish order.

"For now, we're going to have to all put what happened today behind us," he continued, "because we have a lot of work to do. Every soldier in this room has to be ready to go back and put himself in harm's way again and again, and to stay there until we've won this fight."

Denomy asked for a moment of silence for the day's casualties. Everyone bowed his head. There was absolute stillness.

When the moment was over, Denomy explained how they'd prepare for the next round of battle. They should all check their first aid dressings, combat lifesaver kits, water supplies, and their MREs. Vehicles would need to be repaired, weapons cleaned and maintained. Most important, the soldiers would need to replenish their ammunition. Stocks of ammo had been brought into the mess hall, and Denomy specified how many rounds each soldier should take.

He sensed that the more he could focus the soldiers on concrete tasks and the work in front of them, the less time they would have to reflect on their fears and the pain of their losses. They were all on edge, of course, though each man showed it differently. Some retreated into themselves, hanging back from conversation, while others stormed and swore. At one point, soldiers from another unit came in, making it obvious they wanted a portion of the mess hall for themselves. When one of the cooks emerged from the kitchen and suggested it was time for the Charlie Company soldiers to clear out, Staff Sergeant Trevor Davis lashed out.

"If you ain't bleeding, get the hell outta here!" he roared.

After the meeting, Denomy went back to the TOC for an update. Battalion units had been in fresh contact with Mahdi militiamen at a variety of locations around the city, and additional casualties were reported. Lieutenant Dan Hines's Third Platoon, whose activities and whereabouts had been such a concern to Denomy, had in the preceding hours retaken the seized Al-Thawra Iraqi police station on the south side of Sadr City and was defending against any attempt by the Mahdi Army to retake it. Captain George Lewis and his Alpha Company soldiers had seized the Al-Rafidan police station in the north of Sadr City and were holding it for the night.

No 2-5 Cav unit had suffered losses comparable to Lewis's Alpha Company—and Lewis's own injuries were growing increasingly painful—but he refused to relent. At the Al-Rafidan police station, Lewis ran into a soldier from another unit, a friend of Specialist Hiller's, who'd just heard that Hiller had been shot. When the soldier asked how his friend was doing, Lewis shook his head and turned away.

Chapter 21

★

WORLDS
APART

2100 hours

Iraq, Illinois, California

IN THE DARKNESS OF THE ALLEY where Shane Aguero and his men had spent two hours waiting for rescue, wild dogs now pawed through the detritus of the firefight. Trash, bloody clothing, and shell casings littered the dirt road; pockmarks from the machine guns and small-arms fire scarred buildings on either side. In the house where the platoon had taken refuge, the family was restoring order, picking through the mess left behind, working by the soft light of a single table lamp to scrub away the bloodstains left by Eddie Chen's body. A faint orange glow hung over the city from the rubbish fires and burning vehicles, and the crack of bullets could be heard in the distance. The rescue was over, but the fighting still raged throughout Sadr City.

In the three hours since he'd taken command of Sadr City, Gary Volesky had called every available unit into action, and they'd all been battered by gunfire and grenades. At least fifty from his battalion were wounded, and four—Chen, Hiller, Arsiaga, and Garza—were confirmed dead. In addition, the C/2-37 tank platoon that had gone in to help with the rescue had lost one of its men, Michael Mitchell. With long hours of fighting still ahead, Volesky sent word that he wanted more casualty collection points set up on the Sadr City perimeter, with military ambulances standing by. He sent additional combat teams into the city to clear streets of obstacles so military vehicles could move more freely. Along with his 2-5 Cav soldiers, Volesky ordered other units assigned to his command to help, including Bravo Company of 1-12 Cav (First Battalion, Twelfth Cavalry Regiment), under the command of Captain Doug Chapman, and Charlie Battery from 1-82 FA (First Battalion, Eighty-second Field Artillery Regiment), commanded by Captain Brian Herzik, to help. All of these units, along with the 2-5 Cav, made up Volesky's larger "Task Force Lancer."

MAHDI MILITIAMEN along Route Bravo were shooting at every U.S. military vehicle in sight. Chapman's Bravo Company was to clear out the market area on Route Bravo, while Herzik's Charlie Battery was assigned to secure a casualty collection point along Route Silver. From Herzik's position, soldiers wounded in the fight could be evacuated to Camp War Eagle. Herzik was an artillery officer who had little experience leading infantry, and he had zero experience leading patrols in Sadr City. Volesky told Chapman to take the lead.

Herzik needed a few soldiers who were good with weapons but also trained to treat battlefield injuries. One who came forward immediately was Specialist Casey Sheehan, a mechanic who'd taken a combat lifesaving course. At heart, Sheehan—a soft-spoken former altar boy, eight months into his second enlistment—was a humanitarian. A mission like this, with the chance to help or rescue the wounded, was a perfect fit. While many of the younger soldiers who had gone out on combat missions that day had worked themselves into a kind of battle frenzy, thumping their chests and whooping the 2-5 Cavalry battle cry as the vehicles drove out toward the gate, Sheehan had watched quietly, almost unnoticed by the other soldiers, fingering one of the dozen rosaries he'd brought to Iraq. In an army filled with bravado, Casey Sheehan stood out as modest and warmhearted, almost a loner.

Husky, with broad cheeks and a placid, pleasant expression, Sheehan seemed incapable of threatening anyone. He could spend hours under the hood of a Humvee without saying a word; it seemed the place he was happiest.

Few troopers in the First Cavalry Division were more devout. On Sunday mornings back in his Fort Hood barracks, Sheehan had been the one to rise early and head off to the post chapel, Bible in hand, greeting fellow soldiers as they stumbled down the hall toward the bathroom, fighting hangovers from their Saturday-night partying. He'd asked to be made a chaplain's assistant when he first enlisted, but no positions had been available.

Now Casey Sheehan's mission was to assist with the evacuation of injured soldiers from Sadr City. "Tonight," one of his officers said, "everyone is an infantryman."

Sheehan donned his Kevlar and his night-vision goggles and grabbed his M-16.

Herzik mustered all the vehicles he could find—just two cargo Humvees and the supply sergeant's LMTV. All three were unarmored. The two LMTV trucks that had ventured into the city earlier that evening had already been badly shot up; both had returned to the base full of dead and wounded soldiers. But in the fog of events and with the Tactical Operations Center barely able to monitor all that was happening, Captain Herzik did not realize the risk he was taking by bringing yet another unarmored truck into the city. He had a mission to carry out, and he felt he had little choice but to go with the vehicles available. Some soldiers tried to add a little extra protection by placing sheets of plywood along the sides and stacking sandbags against them. It wasn't much, but it was something. Herzik had his little convoy line up behind the Bravo Company's armored Humvees and Bradleys. At least they'd be able to fight.

Corporal Forest Jostes, another of Herzik's soldiers, also volunteered for the casualty evacuation mission. Normally an artilleryman, Jostes jumped at the chance to serve as gunner, manning an M-240 machine gun mounted in the back of the last Humvee in Herzik's convoy. Back at the Fort Hood barracks, Jostes and Sheehan had lived just two doors down from each other; though they were always friendly, it was hard to imagine two more different personalities. While Sheehan kept almost entirely to himself, Jostes was the wisecracking prankster who loved to party. His supervisor had called him a "smart-ass" with an attitude problem, but he also knew that Jostes was one of the brightest soldiers in his unit. At twenty-one, he'd already made section chief in the Fire Direction Center of his field artillery regiment, supervising three soldiers. It was a position normally reserved for a staff sergeant four or five years his senior.

"Hey, who's going to soap my back tonight?" Forest Jostes would holler in the barracks shower, and the other guys would hoot in mock excitement. Jostes had so many girlfriends in and around Fort Hood that his friends couldn't keep them straight. With his tiny steel-rimmed glasses and prematurely receding hairline, he was hardly the most handsome soldier on post, but he always managed to show up at a military ball with a beautiful woman on his arm. His friends figured he had the right combination—bad-boy image and a charming wit. Women found him irresistible.

Corporal Jostes seemed destined for a military career, something his parents had half expected from the time he was seven years old and wrote in his school journal that he thought soldiers were "cool" because they drove around in "Geeps," with sunglasses and guns. At seventeen, before his senior year of high school in Albion, Illinois, Jostes had asked his parents to sign a paper allowing him to enlist in the Army National Guard. After the September 11 attacks two years later, he'd decided to join the army full-time. His mother, a devout evangelical Christian, told him she was putting his life "in God's hands."

Like Jostes, Casey Sheehan grew up in a religious household. His mother, Cindy, had been a youth minister, and his family, including a brother and two sisters, attended mass every Sunday. But while his family had drifted gradually away from the church, Casey had moved closer to it. In May 2000, he was attending Solano Community College in his hometown of Vacaville, California, and working as a stock clerk in a local department store. One day he visited an army recruiting office and enlisted. When Casey Sheehan went home, the news took his parents totally by surprise. His mother, a self-described liberal Democrat, was devastated by her son's decision.

He explained to his parents that signing up was a way to subsidize his education. But Casey was also a former Eagle Scout, and service in the U.S. Army emphasized the same values of service and discipline that had guided him in his scouting life. After his first tour ended, he reenlisted in August 2003, though by then he already knew the First Cavalry was due to be deployed to Iraq. Sheehan's parents, especially his mother, were critical of President Bush and didn't approve of the war, but they supported their son no matter what. Casey Sheehan might have been able to find a way to avoid serving in Iraq—two other soldiers in his battery fought the assignment—but he told his mother he was willing to go.

"Mom," he said, "this is what we trained for. I'm ready. The sooner I get there, the sooner I'll come home."

He spent Christmas 2003 with his family in Vacaville. He'd be gone at least a year, and Cindy Sheehan wanted to make it a special holiday. She prepared her son's favorite dish, macaroni and cheese, as well as ham and a turkey. Casey sat on the big white couch for a moment alone with his mother, telling her over and over that he would be okay. Cindy cried. She didn't want to make it hard for him, but she couldn't stop herself.

Forest Jostes had also managed a quick trip home, right at the end of February, just days before his unit shipped out. He drove straight from Texas to Illinois and spent three days with his mother and stepfather. They put on a celebration for his twenty-second birthday, which was actually two months later. Then his parents took him to the airport.

"Be sure and come home safe," Von Ibbotson, his stepfather, told him. "If anything were to happen to you, you'd break your mother's heart."

Diane Ibbotson held her son's shoulders and looked him in the eyes, telling him not to volunteer for any risky assignment, not to be a hero. No matter what, she said, we'll all see each other in heaven someday.

Forest Jostes had tried to call home as often as possible once his deployment began. The last time he spoke to his mother was the morning of April 3, when he used the last of his calling card.

"I just have a minute or two left," he told her, "so I wanted to say goodbye before I get cut off. I love you."

"I love you, too, Forest," she said. "We're praying for you."

★   ★   ★

BRIAN HERZIK TOOK A SEAT in the first Humvee, behind a wrecker going out to recover a disabled Humvee. They'd follow the Bravo Company armored vehicles. Behind Herzik was the LMTV. The last of Herzik's vehicles, a Humvee, brought up the rear.

First Sergeant Erik Smith, Charlie Battery's senior noncommissioned officer, counted the soldiers loading into the vehicles. He had more volunteers for the casualty evacuation mission than he had seats. He didn't want to overcrowd the vehicles, especially since they'd probably have to bring casualties back. When Casey Sheehan scrambled into the back of the LMTV, Smith held up a hand to stop him.

"Only six," Smith snapped. "Only six on the truck. Sheehan, you'll have to get out."

There were already four soldiers in the back of the truck—Specialist Chris Long, Specialist Keith Carter, Sergeant Brandon Morey, and a junior private whose job was generator technician—plus the driver and the truck commander. Sheehan picked up his M-16 and climbed reluctantly out of the truck. But as he walked away he noticed the junior private in the back. Sheehan told his first sergeant that he wanted to take the younger soldier's place.

Smith ordered the private out of the truck, and Sheehan climbed back in. He sat in front of the cargo compartment, just behind the cab on the driver's side. The truck had a canvas top, the side flaps rolled up and tied. Jostes jumped into the back of the Humvee behind Sheehan's LMTV and grabbed the M-240 machine gun. Another soldier in the Humvee was Specialist Joshua Cosme, who worked for Jostes in the Fire Direction Center. Though Cosme was just a year younger, he looked up to Jostes like a big brother. As their Humvee drove out the gate, Jostes winked at him and said, "Hey, Cosme, I said one for you."

"One what?" Cosme said.

"A prayer," Jostes answered.

The convoy turned south on Route Aeros, turning east into Sadr City and then north onto Route Bravo. Here the Bradleys would clear obstacles in the streets and go after the Mahdi militiamen who had made traffic on the nearby streets so dangerous. Wearing their night-vision goggles, the soldiers could see figures, weapons, and doorways through the familiar green haze. Moments after turning onto Route Bravo, the same street where U.S. military convoys had been ambushed hours earlier, gunfire erupted once again from the surrounding buildings. The Bradleys responded with their booming guns, and the soldiers in the Humvees and in the truck immediately returned fire, aiming at dark figures and at the muzzle flashes they made out on rooftops and in windows. In the trail Humvee, Jostes braced his feet and gripped the machine gun with both hands, firing ferociously at targets left and right.

IN THE NEXT VEHICLE FORWARD, shell casings were cascading across the bed of the LMTV. The soldiers were firing in all directions, trying to drive back the insurgents as the convoy snaked between the makeshift roadblocks. They were only minutes into the fighting when Casey Sheehan was thrown backward and slumped down in his seat. Through the eerie glow of the night-vision goggles, Sergeant Brandon Morey wasn't sure what was wrong.

"Are you okay?" he yelled. "Are you all right?"

Sheehan looked at him for a moment. Then his eyes rolled back and he fell over. While the other two soldiers continued to return fire, Morey dropped his weapon to attend to Sheehan. Feeling around in the darkness, he initially had trouble locating a wound; night-vision goggles are not designed for close-up inspections. Finally Morey's fingers touched the wetness that oozed from Sheehan's head, and he realized that something—a high-velocity round, fired apparently from above and behind—had pierced right through Sheehan's Kevlar helmet. The bullet exited his forehead and then ricocheted off the inside of the helmet, taking more tissue with it.

Morey snatched off the Kevlar and attempted to stanch the bleeding. He couldn't believe this could happen so quickly. Everyone was hollering and shooting and grabbing for bandages. Between the four soldiers, there were four combat lifesaving kits in the back of the truck, with many bandages, but the blood flow from Sheehan's head injuries seemed unstoppable. Morey kept talking to him, and for a few minutes Sheehan seemed to regain consciousness. But he never responded.

The LMTV commander tried to reach Captain Herzik in the Humvee just ahead, but there were so many people talking on the radios that he couldn't get through. Herzik had no idea a soldier had been hurt, but he told his driver to break away from Doug Chapman's Bravo Company convoy in front and turn west down a side street. Then the gunfire intensified. Only when his portion of the convoy was off on a side street did Herzik get word that Specialist Sheehan had been seriously injured and needed evacuation. Herzik immediately directed his convoy to a casualty collection point that had been set up at the corner of Route Delta and Route Silver. Four armored Humvees were parked there, two on either side of Delta, both facing south, toward the city, and two on Silver, one facing east, one west. Herzik radioed ahead. An ambulance was already at the casualty collection point with another injured soldier, but that soldier was only slightly injured, in good enough shape to await the arrival of Sheehan's convoy.

Herzik led his vehicles down side streets as fast as possible, trying to avoid the intense gunfire they'd just encountered on Route

Bravo. But just before reaching the casualty collection point, a single shot sounded, loud and sharp. The soldiers in the trail Humvee turned their guns toward the building where they'd heard the round. All except Forest Jostes. Specialist Cosme, sitting back-to-back with his friend in the dark, hollered over his shoulder.

"You okay?"

Jostes didn't answer. Cosme nudged him hard with his elbow. Still no response. Cosme turned and saw that Jostes had collapsed over his machine gun. "Jostes!" he shouted, grabbing him, trying to lift him upright. But Jostes just toppled into Cosme's lap. Rolling him over, Cosme saw that Jostes's face was a mass of raw flesh.

"Oh, shit! Oh, God!" he screamed, cradling Jostes in his arms. Cosme held his friend tight, sobbing under the soft glow of the moon.

The convoy pulled into the casualty collection point. Sergeant Morey and the other combat lifesavers moved Casey Sheehan into the ambulance. Sheehan was still breathing and moving, but he had lost a huge amount of blood and he was still unresponsive. Now Cosme ran up and told Morey that Jostes had also been hit in the head; within moments Jostes, Sheehan, and the injured soldier from another company were on the way to Camp War Eagle.

In the lead Humvee, Herzik was on the radio, talking while his eyes scanned for snipers. He told the TOC that an ambulance was on the way with Sheehan and the other injured soldier, unaware at that moment that Jostes, too, had been shot.

Specialist Chris Long, riding with Morey and Sheehan and Carter in the LMTV just ahead of Jostes's Humvee, learned that his best friend had been shot only when he saw soldiers lifting Forest Jostes out of the Humvee on a litter. When Long saw Jostes lying motionless, he felt a rage rise from deep within. Dashing back to Jostes's Humvee, Long jumped in and grabbed his friend's machine gun, then fired it blindly into the night.

When Herzik's Humvees and the ambulance came roaring into the front gate of Camp War Eagle a few minutes later, Lieutenant Joseph Esensten, one of Captain Herzik's platoon leaders, saw a soldier in the back of Jostes's Humvee pounding his fist into the side of the vehicle. He rushed to the aid station, stopping the first soldier he saw.

"What happened?" Esensten asked.

"Sir," the soldier said, tears streaming down his face, "you don't want to go out there."

A few minutes later, an order came down from the TOC: No more unarmored vehicles would be going into Sadr City.

MORE THAN EIGHT THOUSAND miles away, in Albion, Illinois, Diane and Von Ibbotson were eating breakfast at home with her two other sons, Forest Jostes's brothers. They'd been there early Saturday when Forest called from Iraq, but Diane hadn't bothered to wake them. After breakfast, they all went to church for the Palm Sunday service. This was a holy day, not a day to watch the news. Diane had prayed for her son, prayed for his safety just as she did every day. This Sunday morning she repeated again what she had told herself before Forest left. *He is in the Lord's hands now.*

WHEN CASEY SHEEHAN called home to Vacaville the night before leaving Fort Hood, his mother cried almost nonstop. Cindy Sheehan told her son she was crying because she missed him so much and could not imagine him being gone a year, but

Casey could tell she was also afraid. They talked about taking a vacation when Casey returned; he wanted to go to Disney World. Cindy said she'd always be proud of him, and she thanked him for being such a great son. The last time he called home was from Kuwait, just before his convoy left for Iraq, but by then he'd used up most of his calling-card minutes. They barely had time to speak. Through her tears, Cindy managed to tell Casey to be careful. And that she loved him.

That had been just five days earlier. On April 4, Cindy and Pat Sheehan were puttering around the house. The television was tuned to CNN when, around five p.m., the network reported that a big fight in Sadr City had left a number of U.S. servicemen dead. Cindy's heart shriveled.

"It's Casey," she told Pat.

"Don't be silly," he said. "I'm sure Casey is okay. There are a hundred and forty thousand U.S. military there. Look at the odds."

"No," Cindy Sheehan said. "I know he's dead."

★

Chapter 22

THE

SECOND

WAVE

2030 hours

How could it be? An Iraqi bus on base? The wounded and dead had arrived via every conceivable combat transport vehicle on this long night, but nothing like the rickety old white bus Trent Upton watched approaching him now. The terrified Iraqi driver pulled the bus near the aid station, where the wounded soldiers were then unloaded next to the growing pile of bloody boots. Upton was trying to keep track of the wounded and not think about the battle that raged just outside the gates; but seeing the bus brought the fight clearly into focus. If American troops had to commandeer a civilian vehicle to get help for the soldiers, Upton realized, this was a fight that had gotten out of control.

The first soldier carried off the bus was Specialist Tomas Young, paralyzed and staring blankly as he drifted in and out of consciousness. Upton thought he looked about as close to dead as a person could. Luke Fournier followed behind, his upper body a shredded scarlet mess. They kept coming, at least a half dozen more. Upton moved from soldier to soldier, keeping a thorough log of names of the wounded and the nature and extent of their injuries. The medical evacuation helicopters were coming in regularly; within minutes, Young and Fournier were stabilized and on the way to the combat support hospital in Baghdad.

Sergeant Robert Miltenberger, who'd flagged down the bus for his LMTV soldiers, arrived at Camp War Eagle about a half hour later and headed straight for the aid station. He was splattered from head to foot in the blood of his soldiers, soldiers whose lives he had worked so hard to save. He looked both frightening and achingly vulnerable, his skin so pale that he was almost luminous. A medic told him that Tomas Young and Luke Fournier had been stabilized and medevaced to the Green Zone hospital in Baghdad. There was no doubt in Miltenberger's mind that Tomas Young had been paralyzed by the gunshot that ripped through him, but at least he was alive. And the fact that Luke Fournier was still breathing was to Miltenburger nothing shy of a miracle.

But Miltenberger's relief was short-lived. Moments later a soldier brushed by him in the aid station and asked, "Did you hear about Arsiaga and Garza?"

The twins, Miltenberger thought. That was what he called Arsiaga and Garza, two platoon mates who looked so much alike that some people couldn't tell them apart.

Miltenberger braced himself.

Dead.

The soldiers gave Miltenberger the barest details. Arsiaga had been killed almost instantly. Garza had been declared dead shortly after he was medevaced out of Eagle base. Miltenberger said nothing. Only a twitch in his right eye betrayed any sign of emotion. He turned and walked through the darkness to the maintenance bay, where he and hundreds of other soldiers were sleeping until permanent quarters were completed. Even though covered in the gore of the injured, Miltenberger refused to change his clothes. He wanted to sleep with the smell of the battle, to feel the dried blood of his brothers. He wanted everyone who saw him to know the price of war. To remember.

CHAPLAIN RAMON PENA had been praying with the wounded soldiers for several hours now, trying to calm or encourage those who seemed in need, making a record of those he spoke to, and in some cases, administering last rites.

But it wasn't just the wounded the chaplain worried about. Many of the soldiers who'd escaped relatively unscathed were in bad shape. They'd seen friends and fellow soldiers ripped apart and dying, and no amount of training could properly prepare them for these realities of war. Private Cole Halliburton had walked out to the wreck of the Alpha Company LMTV to look for extra combat lifesaver kits. He had been in a Humvee several vehicles behind the LMTV during the firefight and knew men had died inside. But Halliburton was in no way prepared for what he saw when he bounded into the back. Floating amid the red-stained MRE boxes and water bottles was a Kevlar vest, completely soaked in blood. Tiny white pieces formed a pattern across it. The small chunks were everywhere. *Teeth,* Halliburton thought. *Someone lost his teeth.* He looked closer and then recoiled. These were not teeth. This was brain matter, soft and slippery and horrifying. He froze for at least five seconds, then grabbed the combat lifesaver kit, jumped out of the truck, and headed back to the aid station.

Chaplain Pena knew that this kind of horror, this grief, was so deep and so unique to the experience of battle that most of the soldiers might never be able to share the experience with loved ones. And though he encouraged the soldiers to cry, to let their emotions run free, he knew that, realistically, there wasn't a way to deal with it here. This wasn't an environment that accommodated emotional outbursts. The soldiers simply had to pick up their weapons and get back to work.

Captain David Mathias, the young pediatrician, had lost track of the number of soldiers he'd treated. Stepping briefly outside the aid station to check with his medics, he saw several tanks coming toward him through the darkness. A small band of soldiers carefully lowered the body of a dead soldier from the lead vehicle. As the men got close, Mathias could see right away who it was: Sergeant Eddie Chen. One of the few Chinese-Americans in the battalion, Chen stood out not only for his ethnicity but for his big, bold personality. Even the gentle and reserved Doc Mathias had enjoyed Chen's theatrical antics. They had shared laughs over the past few weeks; Mathias couldn't believe he was gone.

ALL NIGHT LONG, head physician Colonel Robert Gerhardt had been concerned about separating the dead from the wounded. The medical staff shared a deep respect for the dead but knew it was imperative to keep up the hopes of the seriously wounded. The doctors had all read the studies, but it didn't take a published medical report to convince them that it was profoundly traumatizing for a wounded soldier to stare at a dead one. So medics made a concerted effort to remove the dead from the aid station. Gerhardt had originally designated the aid station's broom closet as a temporary morgue. But as the night progressed there were too many dead; the closet was too small a space.

"I have to do something with these soldiers," Gerhardt said. It had been several hours, and Gerhardt knew the bodies would start to smell or decompose. He conferred with Upton, who ordered up a refrigerator truck. The bagged bodies of Hiller and Arsiaga were placed inside. Now Chen's body was brought into the truck with them.

The vehicles carrying Casey Sheehan and Forest Jostes arrived at Camp War Eagle within the hour. Both were struggling to stay alive and were brought straight to the aid station. Mathias worked feverishly over one of the young men before he even knew his name. Chaplain Pena was at his side, holding the soldier's hand and speaking in soft tones, kneading his fingers and palm as the soldier's grip grew weaker and weaker and then went limp altogether. Pena looked up at Mathias, who blinked heavily and shook his head slowly.

Pena offered a prayer. When he was finished, someone called out, "Does anyone know who this is?"

First Sergeant Erik Smith stood in the background, watching the doctors attend to Jostes. *His* soldier. Smith had come to the aid station to help, not sure exactly what he could do. Now he found himself staring at the blue flame tattoo on the arm of the dead young soldier.

"Yes," Smith said softly. "It's Forest Jostes." Then he began to choke up. "He's one of mine."

That's when Erik Smith spotted an uninjured soldier taking pictures of the scene inside the aid station. He grabbed the camera and hurled it against the side of the aid station. The camera shattered.

"Try doing something useful!" he screamed.

Colonel Gerhardt, meanwhile, was trying to save Casey Sheehan. Gerhardt saw that the gunshot wound to the head had pierced Sheehan's skull and skin multiple times because the bullet had ricocheted around inside Sheehan's helmet. He had been knocked unconscious the moment he was hit, but Gerhardt thought Sheehan's brain stem was intact, because he was moving and twitching. For now, though, it was critical that Gerhardt get a clear airway for Sheehan. A tracheotomy would take too long; instead he opted for a cricothyroidotomy. Gerhardt felt for the softer membrane of the cricoid cartilage below the Adam's apple, took a surgical knife, and sliced the skin of Sheehan's throat. He cut deeper into the airway, rotated his scalpel ninety degrees to open the incision, and inserted a breathing tube.

"Casey, stay with us!" shouted Captain Jeff Oliver. Oliver and another doctor, Captain Mario Caycedo, were both assisting Gerhardt in the small trauma room, all three men intent on getting Sheehan stabilized as fast as possible. He was, by far, the most critically injured; the other wounded men could wait.

Gerhardt gave Sheehan Dilantin, Valium, antibiotics, and morphine. His blood pressure was weak; Gerhardt tried to remain optimistic, but in his gut he knew Sheehan's chances were slim. There was also no telling how extensive the injuries to the brain were until a CT scan could be performed in Baghdad.

Captain Oliver glanced at Sheehan's dog tag. Catholic. Oliver was also Catholic. He knew Caycedo and Gerhardt were, too. "Casey, stay with us," Oliver shouted again. "Stay with us!" Oliver said a Hail Mary, just to himself.

Hail Mary, full of grace, the Lord is with Thee . . . This soldier was in trouble. *Mother of God, pray for us sinners, now and at the hour of our death.*

It was just the four of them there, with the same beliefs, the same hope, the same ideas of life and death. He really wanted this kid to make it.

"Stay with us, Casey," he said again.

GERHARDT KNEW HIS JOB was to get Sheehan stabilized and out to the helicopters. He wrapped his head wounds carefully for the ride. Because Sheehan was one of the last critically injured soldiers in the aid station, the doctor had spent more time with him than some of the others, but there was little more to be done. The breathing tube was working; Sheehan had a pulse, and his blood pressure was weak but stable. This was as good as it was going to get. The doctor watched as Sheehan was brought out to a waiting helicopter. Gerhardt breathed heavily. He hoped it would work out okay. *I'm forty-four, and I still believe in Santa Claus. I'm just going to keep believing this guy is going to make it.*

As midnight approached, Captain Trent Upton stood in a daze. The chaos was subsiding but the tally was ugly. Four soldiers— Stephen Hiller, Robert Arsiaga, Eddie Chen, and Forest Jostes— now lay dead in the refrigerated truck. More than sixty men had been wounded. It was a terrible night, and it was about to get worse. As Upton and Gerhardt were cleaning up some of the paperwork, they received shattering news. Specialist Ahmed Cason, who had given Upton the thumbs-up as he was loaded into a heli- copter, had died on the operating table in Baghdad. The bullet that hit Cason had torn through his liver. Trent Upton was shocked. Of the most serious injuries, Cason's had been the one he'd been most hopeful about. Upton had been the last person with Cason at Camp War Eagle, holding his hand till he'd been taken away in the helicopter.

Now Upton's emotions began spinning out of control. Would he ever be able to talk about this night? How could he ever tell his wife, Angie? Then he remembered: Today was her birthday. Poor Angie. He'd so wanted to call her that morning. But that was a lifetime ago. He wouldn't know what to say to her now.

Upton looked around at the bloody clothing and piles of dirty bandages that would have to be cleaned up in the morning. Per- sonal items would be stripped from the wounded and dead, to be accounted for and stored. Upton made a final check with the medics, crossed the dry moonlit field just outside the aid station, and headed to the TOC. The bulky body armor and Kevlar helmet he'd been wearing all day were stained with sweat, his boots and uniform smeared with dried blood. Upton walked heavily up the stairs to the small headquarters area and, helmet and vest still on, crawled under his desk. The bare concrete tiles were filthy but cool. He pulled his knees up, and closed his eyes.

Chapter 23

★

A KNOCK
ON THE
DOOR

10:00 p.m.

Fort Hood

LESLEY HILLER SAT IN FRONT of the TV on Sunday night, running her hand across the swell of her pregnant belly, unable to concentrate. She was bored and lonely—she hadn't heard from Dusty in three days, and she missed him terribly. She flipped from one station to another, looking for something to help pass the time. But there wasn't anything on, nothing good, anyway, and she refused to watch any of those cable shows so many of the other wives were glued to, day and night, for news about the war—she'd promised Dusty she wouldn't become obsessed in that way.

When the knock came, it was a momentary distraction. She got up and walked to the front door. This late—it was just after ten p.m.—Lesley figured it must be someone who was lost or had a flat tire maybe. She opened the door and saw an army chaplain. Another officer in uniform was with him. There wasn't a chance for either visitor to say a word.

"No!" Lesley Hiller yelled. She was frantic, panic-stricken. "You all got the wrong house!"

She slammed the door.

The officers stayed outside and began calling her name softly. After a moment she opened the door a crack.

"Are you Mrs. Hiller?" one of them asked.

She shook her head. "You have the wrong house," she insisted.

"Is your name Lesley?"

"No," she said again. "You got the wrong house!" Then she started to scream.

The officers followed Lesley Hiller into the house. She knew, of course, why they were there. She understood. It didn't matter how carefully or humanely the military tried to conduct such visits; in the end the news was the same. Your husband or your father or your son had been killed. The officers stayed long enough to offer their condolences and to explain that Dusty Hiller's body would be returned to the United States in a matter of days. Lesley Hiller wasn't listening; none of the details mattered. Stephen Hiller, just twenty-five, was dead. Her Dusty, her sweet husband, was gone.

AS ONE OF THE BASE'S Family Readiness Group's care teams, Aimee Randazzo and Vanessa Avalos had volunteered for exactly this sort of situation—to help some poor woman or family cope with the aftermath of a loss. As part of the close-knit core of First Cav officers' wives and families, they felt a duty to offer the sort of help and support they hoped someone would extend to them under similar circumstances.

The women had been given some basic training in grief counseling, but they'd never actually *done* it before. As they drove along the dark street and pulled up in front of Lesley Hiller's home, they felt nothing but dread at the thought of offering comfort to a woman who had just lost her husband. A woman they didn't even know: They had been given Lesley's name only moments before, after the official death notification was concluded. Their hearts ached—for Lesley and her children, but also for their *own* families. This could have been one of their husbands. It could have been someone else pulling up in front of either of their houses that night, instead of the other way around. Such thoughts and sympathies lay heavy in their hearts as they locked eyes on Lesley Hiller's doorstep. Finally, they rang the doorbell.

Lesley let them in, then went to the couch, cradling her youngest daughter. She sat shaking, eyes glazed and angry. No amount of training could have prepared Vanessa and Aimee for having to sit face-to-face with a fellow military wife who has just learned that she will never again see her husband. *A widow.* That's all Aimee Randazzo could think about when she saw Lesley's raw puffy eyes, the sleeping children, and the bulge in the young mother's stomach from the baby on the way. *She's a young widow now.* From this moment forward, there would be no father, no husband.

It can't get worse than this, Aimee thought.

Aimee and Vanessa struggled for words. Aimee walked toward a photo in the living room. "You have a beautiful family," she said.

Lesley squeezed the baby on her lap. "She looks just like my husband." That brought a new round of sobbing. She told Aimee and Vanessa that the rest of her family was far away, in Alabama, and she had to go see them as soon as possible. Lesley wanted to call her mom, wanted to be with her mom. Vanessa and Aimee felt helpless—didn't know whether to sit or stand, didn't know what to say, were afraid that anything they did say would sound stupid, or just make Lesley feel worse.

They didn't stay long. Lesley seemed to want them to leave. Aimee asked about upcoming doctors' appointments and if there was anything they could do. Lesley barely responded. Aimee and Vanessa knew that army officials would be there the next day to follow up with paperwork, and knew, too, that LeAnn Volesky would make sure Lesley didn't need anything else in the coming days. They let Lesley know that the FRG was there to help in any way, expressed their sincere sympathies, and said goodbye.

Before they'd even pulled away, Lesley was on the phone to her mother. Debbie Gillen answered almost immediately.

"Is everything okay?"

"It's Dusty. He's been killed."

Debbie was stunned into silence. Finally she spoke. "Are you sure? Are you positive?"

Everyone she'd speak to over the next several days would ask Lesley the same question, hoping there had been a mistake. Her father refused to believe the news.

"No, it didn't happen," he said when he got on the phone. Dusty had been like a son. Growing up, Dusty had hung around the house so much that Lesley used to tease him about it. *Why don't you go back to your own house?* she'd say. Both her parents had loved him deeply.

Lesley wanted to speak to Dusty's dad—the two had been estranged until a few years earlier—and the chaplain had said the father would be notified in a few hours. But there was a miscommunication; when Lesley called him, in the middle of the night, he hadn't heard a thing.

Dusty's stepmother, Glenda, answered the phone. Lesley told Glenda the news, and she in turn told Dusty's father. Almost as soon as she did, Glenda said she had to hang up. She thought her husband was having a heart attack.

Dusty's father recovered from the shock and called back later. He offered to come to Fort Hood to be with Lesley.

"I want to come home," Lesley muttered between tears.

"Are you coming home now?" he asked.

"As soon as I can."

They spoke for a while longer. Before they hung up, Dusty's father had one more question. "Are you sure that it was Dusty?"

LUPE GARZA HAD the first indication that something was wrong hours before Lesley Hiller heard the knock on her door. Lupe and her sister-in-law Kareena had been cleaning up their yard, blocks from Lesley's home. They were both tired, and they headed inside. It was nearly seven-thirty; the kids had to eat and get to bed. The phone was ringing. It was Lupe's mother, calling from Lubbock, Texas. "Someone from the Killeen Police Department just called looking for you," she said.

Her first thought was that they'd caught her driving without a license. *But how would they have caught her?* As she hung up, she had another thought.

"What if it's about Israel?" she asked Kareena.

Kareena, Israel's sister—she was the one who had introduced him to Lupe years before—assured Lupe that there was no way the Killeen police would be looking for her if it had to do with Israel. What she didn't know was that Dexter Jordan, the Fort Hood RDC, had been searching for Lupe Garza without success. A few hours later, Lupe's mom called back. Someone from Fort Hood was looking for her.

Suddenly, she felt nauseated. She wanted to know exactly what had been said.

"They said something about Israel coming home early," her mother said.

"That's not possible. Israel cannot come home early."

"That's what they said."

Lupe started to shake. Her knees were wobbling and she couldn't hold her hands still. "The only way Israel can come home early is if he's dead or injured," she told her mom. Then she hung up.

"Oh my God," Lupe mumbled to her sister-in-law. "I need to find LeAnn Volesky's number." Lupe was in the kitchen, frantically searching her files for an envelope that had important contact numbers, when the doorbell rang. She stopped and turned.

Kareena answered the door.

"It's for you," she said.

"Who is it?" she asked, wanting to hide.

Her sister-in-law didn't say anything, and Lupe started to walk out of the kitchen. It was the uniforms she saw, rather than any particular face.

Oh please God, let him be injured, she thought. *Please, God. Please let nothing be seriously wrong.*

"Are you Guadalupe Garza, ma'am?" one of the officers asked.

"Yes."

"Is your husband Israel Garza?"

"Yes."

"I'm sorry, ma'am. Your husband was killed . . ." His voice trailed off.

Lupe collapsed on the floor sobbing. She could barely breathe. "How did this happen?" she sobbed.

"Are you sure it's him?" Kareena asked. She knew that there were three Israel Garzas in the army. But the officers were sure.

"This can't happen, we have two young sons," Lupe said. She heard them say something about an ambush. "I don't understand," Lupe said. "How could it happen? He just got there."

The officers had no answers. They didn't know anything except what was written on the notification certificate—didn't know about the open truck, didn't know that doctors had tried to save

Israel Garza, that they had shouted encouragement even as he was loaded onto the helicopter for the short ride to the combat hospital. All they knew was that a fellow soldier had died.

The men wrote down phone numbers and instructions and then left Lupe Garza and her sister-in-law alone with their grief. Soon afterward people started knocking. The neighbors came. They had seen the car, the uniformed officers. Word traveled fast. People sat on the couch, they sat at the kitchen table, they hugged Lupe, holding her while she bawled.

"Oh my God," she asked. "How am I going to tell my family?"

With the exception of his sister, Israel wasn't close to his own family. It was Lupe's parents to whom Israel was the closest. When Lupe called her mother, she promised to be there first thing in the morning.

Then she dialed her brother Manny, a Marine who'd just returned from Iraq and who had a special bond with Israel. Manny, too, said he would be there in the morning.

Finally Lupe called Israel's mother, crying so much that Israel's mother couldn't make sense of what she was saying. "Slow down. Calm down. I can't understand you," she said.

Lupe's family came. Friends came. The care team came. She had so many people supporting her she barely noticed the care team. She just watched as all the food was brought over and piled on the counter and the table and in the fridge.

WHILE THE CARE TEAMS were out that night, LeAnn Volesky quietly cried in the soft glow of her living room. Christmas lights. She and Gary had left their big green plastic tree out—they had finally decided to buy a fake tree, so it would last longer—until he came home from Iraq. They loved Christmas, they loved the reflection of the white lights, so why not enjoy it all year? But it seemed such an anomaly tonight. Those peaceful little lights shining, so soon after she had watched four friends leave her house to offer support to two young widows.

She brought drinks out of the fridge for when the women came back. She didn't know what else to do.

When the group returned—they hadn't been gone long—LeAnn wanted to know if the widows had asked for anything. Did they need meals? Did they have questions? The notification officers would return to their houses the next day to go over paperwork and business. After that, they'd wait and see what came next, what was needed. It was almost eleven p.m., and the women were worn out. It was time to go home. LeAnn Volesky reached out to embrace the others. They were all going back to empty beds. LeAnn missed Gary so much. She couldn't imagine the pain he was in. She wanted to be next to him. Aimee wanted the same for Dylan. The women promised to reconnect in the morning.

HUNDREDS OF MILES from Fort Hood, nowhere near the care teams or the battalion headquarters, Allison Cason had finished cleaning up the kitchen at her parents' Alabama home. It was getting late and she was ready for bed. The kids were already asleep, exhausted after their great-grandfather's birthday celebration. Allison was turning off the lights when the doorbell rang.

She could see through the frosted glass of her parents' front door that there were three people standing outside. They were wearing uniforms. She headed for the door, thoughts flying in her head. Ahmed was coming home, she told herself. *Okay, he's been injured*, she thought. *He's hurt bad, but at least he's coming home.*

Allison asked the men to go around to the side door. There

was a tough lock on the front door; the other was easier to open. Or maybe she was just stalling. Allison Cason knew the men were there to see her, but she didn't associate the soldiers with bad news. Allison was thinking it was probably *a good thing*. If Ahmed was coming home, that meant he wouldn't have to deal with a whole year in Iraq, he wouldn't have to be at war. For those few final seconds, she actually felt relieved. Ahmed was coming home.

IT WAS TWO HOURS EARLIER on the West Coast, and Cindy Sheehan had been restless since she heard the CNN story about soldiers killed in Sadr City. She'd been certain that one of them was her son. But that was hours ago. If it really had been Casey, wouldn't she have heard by now? She even began to feel sorry for the mother whose child *had* died.

At about nine Cindy Sheehan took her two dogs out for a walk around the neighborhood. She led the dogs up the walkway and into the house. That's when she saw them. Three uniformed officers, standing in her living room. She fell to the floor, screaming.

Her husband, Pat, moved his gaze from his wife to the soldiers and then back. After several minutes Pat Sheehan began pleading. "You have to get up, Cindy." He sounded desperate. "These men need your Social Security number."

"Fuck them," Cindy yelled back, lifting her head off the floor. "What are you talking about? How did he die? How did my son die?"

One of the officers tried to explain, but he was using military lingo Cindy couldn't understand. How could a Humvee mechanic be killed *in combat*?

"Can you tell me that in real terms?" she howled. "Can you tell me what really happened to Casey?"

★   ★   ★

IN THE SMALL SOUTHERN Illinois town of Albion, the army officer and the sheriff who came to Diane and Von Ibbotson's door encountered an entirely different scene.

"Are you the mother of Corporal Forest Jostes?" the officer asked when Diane opened the door.

Diane nodded and invited the men inside. They all sat down, and then the officer began.

"I regret to inform you that your son—" he started.

Diane heard him say "was mortally wounded in battle." Everything else was a blur. Diane Ibbotson had no idea what was said after that, or how long the men stayed. Yet when the visitors were done, she smiled politely and thanked them for their kindness in delivering the news. She appreciated their coming. She was sure, she told them, that this was one of the hardest things they'd ever had to do. When they stood to leave, she put her arms around the officer.

She said, "I might not get the opportunity very soon to embrace a young man in uniform."

Chapter 24

★

DAYBREAK

April 5, 2004

Sadr City

GARY VOLESKY WALKED TOWARD a storage truck parked near the aid station at Camp War Eagle on Monday morning, shielding his eyes from the sun now creeping over the compound. The horizon that had energized him as he strode across the sand only twenty-four hours before, today left him dreading the day ahead. Eight men had died on the night he'd taken command of Sadr City; four of them lay in this refrigerated truck. Now, the fifth of April dawning, Volesky felt he needed to see their bodies, needed to spend time with his fallen soldiers. He'd promised their families that he'd bring all his soldiers home alive and safe—an absurdly optimistic promise, perhaps, even if for a "peacekeeping" mission—but he had believed in his own promise and was sickened now by the realization that he'd broken his word.

"Let's say goodbye to our boys," he said, putting his arm around Staff Sergeant Major Don Garner, walking beside him. Although he had been there just a short time, Garner was already considered the "mayor" of Camp War Eagle. He kept a close eye on the enlisted soldiers, and every soldier who had died the night before had been an enlisted man. Garner and Volesky embraced. Then they pulled open the truck door and walked inside. Four black body bags—the other four men had died in or en route to the Green Zone hospital—lay side by side at the far end of the truck, beneath the stark glare of a humming fluorescent light.

Eddie Chen. Stephen Hiller. Robert Arsiaga. Forest Jostes. Each man had died almost instantly. Garner leaned over the first bag, the one farthest to the left, and slowly pulled down the zipper. It was Arsiaga. He had died of a gunshot wound to the head. Volesky, who'd never lost a soldier in combat, knelt down and closed his eyes, touching Arsiaga's shoulder briefly.

"I'm sorry," he whispered.

Three of the four bags held the distinct outlines of lifeless bodies. One did not. An enormous and inexplicable mound rose in its middle, as though a beach ball had been stuffed inside. Garner reached for the zipper, working it carefully over the hump in the center. It was Eddie Chen, the muscles of his broad face locked and grim, his arms outstretched as if in a kind of imaginary embrace. He'd lain dead in the alley heat for hours, his body beginning to stiffen, and the other soldiers had raised his arms to lift him onto the tank when the rescue finally arrived. And there, frozen in rigor mortis, his arms had stayed.

Volesky had known Chen better than the other dead men. He ran his hand along Chen's arm, apologized to him, thanked him.

"Goodbye," he said softly.

Volesky unzipped the last two bags, revealing Forest Jostes and Dusty Hiller, and repeated the ritual. All four men were still in their bloody uniforms, though portions had been cut or ripped away during their last moments of life as fellow soldiers had fought to save them. After a few minutes Garner zipped the bags closed. Volesky and Garner both stood, humbled and over-whelmed. Volesky wondered if there was anything he could have done to mitigate the risk his soldiers had faced, and would continue to face. He took one last look. Then the two men turned and walked back to the TOC in silence.

In the densest urban terrain imaginable, in a city of two and a half million people, Volesky had sent several hundred men to face more than five thousand enemy fighters. Seven members of the incoming First Cavalry Division, and one from the outgoing First Armored Division, had been lost—killed in action. More than sixty had been wounded, several critically. Three Humvees were totally destroyed; four more Humvees plus four LMTVs were heavily damaged. Even the armored Bradleys—eight of them—had sustained damage, as had the big armored M-88 "recovery" vehicle.

The toll for the enemy had been much greater. The Iraqi Ministry of Health would eventually report that five hundred support-ers of Moqtada al-Sadr died in the fighting, but Volesky's soldiers thought the number was actually higher—they'd seen more than five hundred bodies in the streets. While the Sadr supporters included many civilians, Volesky was relieved that even the Iraqi Ministry of Health acknowledged that most of the Iraqi casualties were dressed in the black garb of the Mahdi militia.

In the meantime, on that Monday morning the fighting showed no sign of letting up. Volesky's men, many of whom had been fighting all night, were still coming under fire in Sadr City. After the Mahdi Army seized four Iraqi police stations, Volesky's men—fifteen of whom had been wounded in the initial battle and treated at Camp War Eagle, and had then returned to the fray—stormed in and recaptured the stations. Tanks and Bradleys established blocking positions around the police stations, engaging the droves of militia who advanced, yet again, behind women and children, lobbing grenades and spraying small-arms fire over their heads.

Tank Company Commander Steve Gventer, whose platoons fought to hold two of the police stations in Sadr City, wrote in his journal that night:

> Crowds of kids grew to crowds of teens and chanting gave way to rock throwing. One tank had every light, glass sight and external piece of equipment hit by rocks. Rocks, trash, dead animals and human feces were thrown on the vehicles and at the crews. We learned quickly that tanks up close are not good at dispersing crowds (unless they are shooting). It's amazing the lack of respect they [the Iraqis] have for tanks but how fast they scatter when a pistol is drawn or I chamber a shotgun shell. The "pump action" shot is well known, and young and old alike notice it. I hear the Iraqis say "Pump action?" all the time.

Volesky was back at the TOC when he heard the Black Hawks approaching the landing zone just outside. Emerging from the helicopters were Major General Peter Chiarelli, commanding general of the First Cavalry Division, and Major General Martin Dempsey, commanding general of the First Armored Division. Volesky understood full well the agonizing position Chiarelli was in: For the most part, these were his men doing the fighting, yet he wouldn't actually assume command for several more days. He trusted Dempsey in every way, but it had to be painful for Chiarelli to do nothing but watch.

A few hours earlier, Chiarelli had been in a tent in Baghdad when, via radio, he received word of the casualty count. *Eight dead.* He slipped outside the tent, looked through the darkness toward Sadr City, and wept uncontrollably. He thought of all those poor, brave men, so many of them so young, and imagined the agony of their deaths. He thought of their families, their wives and kids and parents—none of whom, probably, had any idea yet of what had transpired. He knew they were in their last hours of peace before a horrible heartbreak.

Chiarelli needed to talk this through with someone, but knew that his emotions were too raw now to turn to Beth, his wife, back in Fort Hood. Instead, he called Eric "Ric" Shinseki—his mentor and friend, a man who would understand better than most. Shinseki, a retired four-star general, had been chief of staff of the army and before that—like Chiarelli himself—commanding general of the First Cavalry Division. He'd done two tours in Vietnam, losing part of his leg to a land mine. But in recent years, he'd become known for something else altogether. In March 2003, just before U.S. forces invaded Iraq, General Shinseki had told the Senate Armed Services Committee that "something in the order of several hundred thousand soldiers" would be needed to stabilize Iraq after the initial phase of the war. Defense Secretary Donald Rumsfeld and Deputy Defense Secretary Paul Wolfowitz had publicly belittled the estimate, impugning Shinseki in the process. It would soon become clear how prescient Shinseki's forecast had been.

No one answered at Shinseki's house, but Chiarelli left a message, choking up throughout. "Sir, I had to talk to you," he said. "I wanted you to hear it from me. We were in a big fight tonight in Sadr City. We lost eight kids." And then, on the answering machine, Chiarelli began to weep.

Shinseki called back hours later. The two men talked about the loss, about the sudden and deadly direction of the war, about what would come next. "I know how shook up you are, Pete. Stay strong."

It was all Chiarelli needed to hear to regain his strength.

Now Chiarelli stepped out of his Black Hawk and, with Dempsey, quickly climbed the stairs to the Camp War Eagle TOC. There they found Gary Volesky, his gaze focused and intense, shrouded by the obvious worry and exhaustion that Chiarelli had expected to see. Volesky looked up to his commanding officer in much the same way Chiarelli looked up to General Shinseki.

"We'll make it through," Chiarelli said to Volesky as they embraced. Chiarelli was holding his battalion commander so tight that he was shaking. "Don't worry, we'll make it through." Volesky held on for only a moment, then assured Chiarelli he and his soldiers would be okay, before he began outlining the plan for retaking the city. There was much more to say, but for now they had to stay focused on the critical tasks at hand. Chiarelli gave Volesky's shoulders one last comforting slap and stepped out of the way, leaving Major General Dempsey and Volesky to work out the details of the morning's operations. Chiarelli headed over to the aid station.

There were mounds of bloodstained boots and body armor still outside. Chiarelli spotted a young sergeant nearby, his head bleeding, his uniform covered with filth; Chiarelli didn't know his name, and the soldier didn't offer it. He had one question for the general.

"Sir," he asked, "why didn't we bring all our tanks to Iraq?"

The inquiry left Chiarelli momentarily speechless. He felt like shouting, "I wanted to bring our tanks! I wanted more! I fought hard to bring them!" But the answer was complicated. At the time, Pentagon officials had thought the war was winding down; sending all the First Cavalry Division's tanks, they reasoned, would give the wrong message to the Iraqis—the message that the Americans were there as occupiers. Now, with a wounded soldier questioning that judgment, a soldier who was probably hurt in a soft-sided vehicle, Chiarelli gave the best answer he could.

"We didn't know," he said. "I wish we had the tanks, but we didn't know."

WHEN CHAPLAIN RAMON PENA arose from a few hours' sleep, the stark ugliness of the Sadr City fight was made even more so by the light of morning. Soldiers cleaned out the vehicles with a quiet solemnity, as if the events that had unfolded in each Humvee were playing out again before them. They gathered the litter of battle: tossing out spent shells, collecting blood-soaked bandages to be burned, and scrubbing away the last stains of the carnage.

Pena happened to notice one Alpha Company soldier making his way unsteadily toward one of the portable toilets. Virtually everyone carried some shadow from the night before, but this man seemed especially lost, dazed, despondent. As he pulled the stall door closed behind him, Pena sensed that something was wrong.

On a hunch, a chaplain's instinct, he approached the latrine. From inside he heard a soft, mournful crying. Without hesitation Pena yanked the door open.

The soldier had the barrel of his gun pointed directly at his head. When he saw the chaplain, he lowered the weapon, his hands shaking. "Sir, I was just looking at my wedding ring," he said.

Pena gently took the gun from the soldier's hand. "You need to come with me," he said.

Chapter 25

★

THE WAR
AT
HOME

April 5–11

Fort Hood

LEANN VOLESKY WOKE UP Monday morning after only two hours of sleep. Almost immediately she reached for the phone. Her eyes were raw and swollen from long bouts of crying; she could barely read the numbers on the keypad. But she needed to find out if there had been any progress on the notifications.

Black Sunday. That's what LeAnn and the women in the Family Readiness Group had already begun calling it. Within hours the death toll had risen from two to four to six and then finally to eight. Eight soldiers, four of whom had been married, four of whom had children. All of the men left grieving parents and siblings. All had been killed in a single evening. And then there were the wounded. Initial estimates had put the figure at several dozen; by the end of Sunday, the number had topped sixty. A large number of the soldiers were so seriously wounded that there was still a question as to whether or not they would make it.

The news of the battle was now nonstop fodder for the cable channels, with frightening but vague details about the casualties. There were no names, no specifics about the wounded or dead. That information hadn't yet been released. There was a reason. By Monday, seven of the families of the men killed in action had been notified; one had not. The family of Eddie Chen—the first of the men to die—couldn't be located. The phone numbers in Chen's records were outdated and out of service; to make matters worse, his parents lived halfway around the world, in Guam. This had left LeAnn Volesky and Connie Abrams in a terrible position. According to military protocol, no one was allowed to talk about what had happened or divulge the names of *any* of the dead or injured until *all* next of kin had been contacted. It seemed as though everyone at Fort Hood was speculating about what had happened—who had been hurt in Sadr City, who had died—but because the Chens hadn't been found, LeAnn and Connie could say nothing. As a consequence, families who hadn't already heard from their loved ones directly were in various states of panic.

Captain Dexter Jordan, Fort Hood's rear detachment commander, was struggling as well. He was getting calls from people around the country who had heard directly from the soldiers, if only briefly; now they wanted more information. "How is he?" they would ask. "When will he be flown home? Where will he be taken?" In some cases, Jordan himself hadn't been given the soldier's name. Other times he had no idea to whom he was talking or whether he could release the requested information.

Army rules and procedures hadn't kept pace with the changing realities of electronic communication. Iraq was America's first war in which e-mail was readily available. If circumstances permitted, the First Cavalry soldiers in Sadr City could share developments in real time with wives and parents back home. Within the Fort Hood community, meanwhile, news spread almost instantaneously via computers and cell phones. This speed, however, could create new challenges. In past wars, soldiers had always had some time to reflect on their traumatic combat experiences, to absorb the emotional shock and deal with some of the rawest aspects of their grief before sharing their stories with families back home. News from a war zone came in letters that took days or weeks to be delivered; now, deployed soldiers found that their spouses or parents expected to know immediately what had happened. For many it was a pressure they could not handle. A soldier seeing a buddy get shot in the head and die next to him in a pool of blood would create obvious difficulties in explaining the event to a wife who's cooking dinner for the kids thousands of miles away.

After the Sadr City battle of April 4, commanders imposed a partial communications blackout. An exception was made for wounded soldiers who wanted to call family members, though, so stories inevitably leaked out. LeAnn Volesky, Connie Abrams, and Dexter Jordan soon found it impossible to stay ahead of the informal network of families sharing news at Fort Hood. One wife of a wounded soldier, who received details of the Sadr City battle from her husband, then sent out an e-mail describing the numbers of dead and wounded, and appealed for support. Soon enough LeAnn's phone started ringing. *What do you know?* she was asked. *What do you need? What can we do?* Because LeAnn wasn't supposed to talk about anything, she couldn't even admit to needing help.

Before long, the stress and fear that many families felt was being directed at LeAnn Volesky, Connie Abrams, and Dexter Jordan, who were the main contacts for the First Brigade families.

As early as Sunday night, the three were being accused of deliberately withholding information from families. People grew angry with Jordan and frustrated with LeAnn and Connie, who in turn felt increasingly frustrated and helpless.

LeAnn's call to battalion headquarters on Monday morning changed nothing. Here it was, nearly twenty-four hours after Eddie Chen's death, and Chen's parents still could not be found. Captain Jordan had worked frantically all night—he never made it home—backtracking through all the paperwork that Chen had on file, but with no luck. Now Jordan was trying to find Chen's brother, who was also in the army, but even that was proving fruitless. Trying to track the families of the wounded proved equally difficult—there were so many that Jordan and his staff couldn't keep up.

Meanwhile the phone calls to LeAnn did not let up. Finally, she relented. After she conferred with Connie Abrams, the two women decided to take the rules into their own hands. This was their time to lead, to do what they thought was right to help the families. They agreed that they would not talk about details or mention names, but they realized that with the news spread far and wide, it was ridiculous not to acknowledge the gravity of the battle or that help would indeed be welcomed.

"Okay," LeAnn told one caller. "We need food for the families. We need food for the rear detachment commander." And so on. Then it dawned on her that they were going to need basic supplies for the wounded soldiers about to start returning to Fort Hood, who likely would be wearing and carrying next to nothing. They might not have shoes or shirts, much less toiletries, soap, blankets, or socks. And some of the families who lived out of town wouldn't be able to get to the hospitals with supplies before the wounded returned.

LeAnn didn't need to ask again. By late Monday, the operation was in full swing. Phones were ringing constantly; every few minutes someone would call or ring the doorbell. E-mails poured in. Women arrived, arms stacked with food, bags full of treats, clothing, and magazines. By the end of the day, LeAnn's kitchen counters, even the kitchen floor, were piled with casseroles, cakes, and salads. She couldn't keep the food moving out of her house fast enough. She started dropping some dishes off at battalion headquarters for the rear detachment staff. Jordan and the others had been grabbing quick naps on the couch and had had nearly nothing to eat since late Sunday morning.

Connie carried a load of food over to headquarters late Monday night. Having managed only a few minutes of sleep herself, she was in a daze. Walking into one of the rooms upstairs, she saw Dexter Jordan huddled over the phone. "Connie!" he said, clearly startled. "I'm talking to Abe." Connie had to stop herself from racing across the room and grabbing the receiver; she knew that Jordan had a job to do.

Jordan smiled at Connie Abrams, appreciating her restraint. Then he turned back to the call. Connie started moving away when she heard Jordan say, "Sir, do you want to talk to your wife?" There was a brief pause, and Jordan looked up somewhat embarrassed. "He says to tell you he's fine."

That was it. Connie knew then that Abe would not be able to speak to her about what had happened for days, if ever. He hadn't even taken command officially, yet he was clearly so overwhelmed that he couldn't spare a minute to talk to her. Without even hearing his voice, she knew that Abe's pain was enormous.

For the next several days Connie and LeAnn busied themselves by organizing the food and the teams who would distribute it. LeAnn's home was every bit as busy as her husband's battalion headquarters eight thousand miles away, and the job she and the other women had engaged was every bit as important. The women were in a combat mode of their own, staying focused and steady, working together, and watching one another's backs. They welcomed friends and fellow brigade families into LeAnn's home who just wanted to talk. Connie and LeAnn still couldn't say much about what they knew, and in fact they didn't know much. But they could listen. And while she listened, LeAnn turned to what she always turned to in times of stress: quilting. It had been her passion for fourteen years. Making intricate, colorful quilts had turned into a full-time hobby.

Just months earlier, LeAnn and another woman on post had started Operation Quilted Comfort, sewing quilts for the families of soldiers killed in Iraq. She never imagined that she would now be making quilts for her own 2-5 Cav families. Since Monday, LeAnn had been working on small squares—American flag squares—that would be part of the larger quilts. She wanted Lesley Hiller to be the first to receive one.

LeAnn called Lesley on Wednesday to ask if she could bring some food over. "Sure," was all Lesley said. When LeAnn arrived at the Hillers' house about half a mile from her own, she found Lesley outside, loading up her truck. Lesley barely looked up as LeAnn got out of her car and walked over to introduce herself. She felt almost sick looking at Lesley, watching her pack up her life, her babies, and any traces of her husband that she could carry back home. For an instant, LeAnn caught herself thinking, *Thank God it's not me and my family*. She imagined herself loading up Gary's things, carrying Alex out to the car, and then leaving their home—their *life*—behind. LeAnn immediately felt terrible for thinking that way—her heart went out to Lesley and her family, and she would have done anything at all to make Lesley's pain go away.

LeAnn could see instantly that Lesley was desperate to get out of Texas and back to her parents in Alabama. Even as LeAnn talked to her, tried to console her, Lesley did not pause from her packing. Pregnant, tired, and with her children in tow, Lesley apparently saw the move as a way to cope with Dusty's death, a way to keep moving forward, a way to avoid thinking about the new reality of her life. Just hours after the casualty assistance officers had delivered the news, she drove her truck down to the local service center, had the oil changed, and bought new tires. She told army officers who came back to assist her that her husband's funeral would be held in Alabama, not Texas, and that she wanted his body sent to his hometown of Opelika.

"When are you leaving?" one of the officers asked.

"As soon as you get off my couch," Lesley answered.

While Lesley continued to shuttle between the house and the car, LeAnn headed for the kitchen and placed the food she'd brought on a countertop. When Lesley came back inside, LeAnn offered her the flag square. In the swirl of moving boxes and suitcases, Lesley paused to finger the small stitched swatch of fabric.

"Thank you," she said to LeAnn, allowing herself to stop and sit for a moment. LeAnn asked if there was anything in particular from Dusty's life she wanted commemorated in the quilt she would be making. Lesley wanted his name, a First Cavalry patch, and the insignia of the Old Guard on the quilt. Dusty had been part of the historic ceremonial unit, whose duties had included guarding the Tomb of the Unknown Soldier at Arlington National Cemetery and escorting the bodies of deceased service members to grave sites. Yet Lesley didn't want Dusty buried at Arlington. She wanted him to come home.

On that Wednesday, April 7, she loaded her kids in her car and drove fourteen and a half hours to her parents' home in Alabama. By the time she arrived, the stress and terror the new widow was trying so hard to avoid had caught up with her. In three days, she had slept only eight hours. She was barely able to carry her children or even lift her head. A doctor told her she had walking pneumonia; but with children to care for and a funeral to arrange, she refused to check into the hospital.

ARLINGTON CEMETERY was exactly the place Eddie Chen's family wanted him to be buried, with all the ceremony and honors that the army would afford him. The army had finally reached Sergeant Chen's younger brother Virgil on Thursday, April 8. Virgil had been in the middle of training when a senior officer broke the news of Eddie's death. Virgil hadn't been on the official list of those who should be notified in case of Eddie's death, only his parents had. But since the parents could not be found, the army had to turn to Virgil. Leaving his name off the list had been an oversight by Eddie: The brothers had been close. When he heard the news, Virgil collapsed in tears. The boys, just a year apart, had joined the army within months of each other, seeing it as an experience they could share. Now Eddie was dead. Virgil knew exactly where to locate his parents. They had moved only days before, and the paperwork hadn't been updated. Virgil passed along their new address to Dexter Jordan and that of a family friend as well. Virgil himself left immediately for Guam to be with his parents, then accompanied them to Washington, D.C., for Eddie's funeral.

The final notification, of the Chen family, relieved LeAnn and Connie of the burden of keeping quiet. As soon as Captain Jordan gave the okay, LeAnn sent out an e-mail to the 2-5 Cav families. As she started to type the letter, LeAnn knew that she had to re-emphasize army protocol, the reason why she hadn't talked about what had happened in Sadr City any sooner than this. LeAnn still hadn't spoken to Gary, which in her mind meant she still hadn't heard "the real deal." She wanted the message to get through that rumors and misinformation are hurtful, scary, and can often be flat-out wrong. But at the same time she wanted to be compassionate.

Dear families of 2-5 Cav,

It is with the utmost sadness that I tell you that we have had some soldier casualties in 2-5 Cav. The families involved have all been notified so please keep them in your thoughts and prayers. If you would like to help any of these families with a gift of a meal, babysitting, lawn mowing or any other helpful support, please contact your FRG leader and let them know what you would like to offer. I am not publishing a list of these soldiers at this time to protect the privacy of the families. In the future, with their permission, I will let you know which families were affected.

I am truly sorry that we had to wait four days before we could contact you with this information. I know that some of you don't understand why, and some of you are just plain angry that we couldn't tell you any of this sooner. Please know that in the event of any casualties or wounded soldiers in a unit, "Next of Kin" MUST be notified in all cases before releasing ANY information to FRG members and the public. It took over 3 days to find the family members of one of our soldiers, and we could not publish any information about the incident until after ALL families were notified. I know how worried some of you must have been, but please remember, "No news is good news." The only reason there would be a delay in your notification of a death or injury is if we cannot find you because we don't have a current address or contact number.

There have been instances of family members who have been inadvertently notified of the death of a loved one by well meaning people (or the press) who were unaware that the family had not received official notification. Please put yourself in these families' places. Would YOU like to find out about the death of a husband, father, mother or child while watching the news, or from an acquaintance who calls to express their sympathy? That is why there are such strict rules about putting out information about the death of a soldier and why we had to wait to tell you any of this information. All we can ask is that you please be patient with the system we have to live with, and understand that we will tell you what we can as soon as we are given clearance to do so. We would never withhold information from you for any reason other than those stated above. A "negative report" was given to other battalions in the Division to let them know that the casualties were not from their units. We could not give a negative report to anyone in 2-5 Cav without violating Department of the Army rules. We will, likewise, receive a "negative report" if there are other battalions in the Division with casualties and that will be passed to you immediately.

We ask you to please NEVER pass on information that you have received from your soldier-spouse or friend to ANYONE. It is unfortunate that we have had instances of poor judgment on the part of some of our members. Graphic details of this operation were passed from soldiers in Iraq to family members back here, who then passed these graphic descriptions to other families who had not yet received information about their husbands. Another "well meaning" soldier wanted his wife to call the wife of another soldier to let her know that her husband had been hurt. This soldier was not on the wounded list and this wife would have been needlessly upset. I know that the soldiers mean well, but battle is confusing, and it is not the place of anyone but an official "notification team" to inform anyone of a death or injury. Mis-information is much more damaging than no information, and you can't take it back once it is done.

You can help us immensely by ensuring that your contact information kept with your FRG leader, and your husband's DD Form 93, contain current and correct information. Even if you are only away for a weekend, please file a valid phone number, and more importantly, a CORRECT ADDRESS with your FRG leader. This is so that we may pass GOOD news as well as bad.

I have had reports from several of the husbands that, in spite of our sad news, the Battalion remains motivated, focused, and that morale is high. They continue with operations in the vicinity of Sadr City, and are performing AWESOMELY. They are VERY busy doing what they do best—Soldiering! Communications have been restored and there are long lines of soldiers waiting to contact their families. Don't be worried if you haven't heard from them yet. You soon will.

We will be having a Battalion Information Meeting for all family members sometime next week. We should know sometime today (Wednesday) when and where that meeting will take place and your FRG leaders will send that info out to you.

I am so very proud to be a member of the Black Knight family. Thank you all for your help, your friendship, your laughter, your tears, and most of all your smiles!

Bless you all during this difficult time. Please do not hesitate to contact your FRG Leader, myself, or the rear detachment team if you have any questions.

Sincerely,

LeAnn Volesky

With communication lines now open, LeAnn would no longer have to watch her every word, dreading every telephone call from some soldier's wife with questions that could not be answered. She was at last able to play the leadership and support role for which she had been prepared.

AFTER SEEING LESLEY HILLER, LeAnn wanted to pay a visit to Lupe Garza and present her with a quilted flag square. She called ahead, not knowing how Lupe would react, and was surprised to have Lupe invite her to a small memorial gathering at her sister-in-law's house that same afternoon. Israel's funeral would come days later; first, Lupe wanted to celebrate his life. Photos of her husband were placed all around the house. Photographs of Israel smiling with his children, kissing his wife. Lupe tried to stay upbeat as friends arrived with salads, casseroles, and trays of cookies, determined to remember the best of her husband.

LeAnn stood in the living room, in a circle of women she had never met, holding hands with the people on either side. Joining everyone in a prayer led by the chaplain, LeAnn found herself completely wrapped up in the moment. She hadn't known what to expect when she walked into the house, but minutes later she saw a serene but strong young woman with two little babies and a dead husband, who lifted her head after the prayer was finished.

"Okay, enough of this," Lupe said. "Let's go eat."

LeAnn looked at the chaplain, who looked back at her. "God, what a woman," he said. In the midst of the sadness, loss, and tragedy, here was life: people gathered together, offering love and support. LeAnn felt as close to this military family as she possibly could. And that was truly the way she thought about it. This was her extended family.

★ ★ ★

ON THURSDAY NIGHT LeAnn went to the battalion head-quarters on post. It was late, past ten p.m., and way past Alex's bedtime. Alex had been wonderful these past few days. LeAnn hadn't given him any details about the battle, but because she was on the phone constantly he was largely left to play by himself. That morning he had asked LeAnn why she hadn't been playing with him. LeAnn looked him in the eyes and said, "Sweetheart, we've had some soldiers die, and we have some things that we need to take care of and people we need to help."

Alex looked up at his mother sweetly. "Okay," he said. "When you're done, will you come play with me?"

Now she loaded trays of food into the car and told Alex they needed to go for a quick ride. She wanted to check on Jordan and his staff, bring them something to eat, and see if she could do anything.

As she and Alex walked into the battalion office carrying the food, someone held out a telephone.

"I think you're going to want to talk to this person."

LeAnn was confused—she hadn't told anyone she was com-ing. It took her a few seconds to make the connection. "Oh, gosh," she said suddenly. "It's Gary!" Five or six soldiers were around her as she picked up the phone, yet when she looked up after saying hello, she was all alone.

"Are you okay?" she asked.

"I'm okay," he said. "I'm all right. Are you?"

WHAT LEANN AND CONNIE had to prepare for now was the arrival of the wounded, at least forty of whom would be return-ing to Fort Hood's Darnall Hospital on Friday.

Captain Jordan and his staff had been on the phone contacting families, keeping track of who would be meeting soldiers at the hospital, and helping with logistics. He needed to make sure people knew where to be and when. A decision was made to limit the people greeting soldiers at the hospital to family members only, with the exceptions of LeAnn, Connie, and Major General Chiarelli's wife, Beth. The hospital could not accommodate hundreds of people from the post or the Killeen community turning up to show support for the returning soldiers. Nice as the sentiment might be, it would only add to the chaos.

And there was plenty of chaos. When Beth Chiarelli walked up to the hospital entrance on Friday morning, she was stunned by the number of television cameras and reporters. The pain had all seemed so personal—a death in the *family*—that she had forgotten that the scope of the tragedy would attract the nation's attention. When she got inside Beth saw dozens of family members in the hospital lobby, leaning against the walls, staring off into the distance, or just sitting on the floor, exhausted. "How are you doing?" she asked as many as she could, knowing how nervous and worried they must be.

The long line of ambulances that had met the soldiers at the airfield began arriving at the hospital in the late afternoon. As each ambulance pulled up to the front of the hospital, the name of the soldier was announced. LeAnn, Connie, and Beth watched as family members stood in response to those announcements and headed for the front door of the hospital. Some ran, others hesitated. Was it a shattered leg? A face ripped apart? Would he be the *same?* Soldiers hobbled past on crutches or were pushed in wheelchairs, many with wounded arms in slings, some peering out through bloodied bandages. For many of these families, this was the moment of truth: Until they actually got to see their loved ones, there would be no way of really knowing what life going forward might be like. Connie Abrams began crying quietly as she saw one mother rush up to her son and hug him, a son, a soldier. Connie didn't know his name, only that he was one of Abe's soldiers. Connie, Beth, and LeAnn all wanted to offer support, but were mindful of not getting in the way.

Many of the soldiers were moved directly to their hospital rooms. Others, less seriously wounded, left immediately, driven to their homes hours away from the post, or to the barracks at Fort Hood. It was a world away from the fiery, smoky Sadr City scene they had been fighting in just days earlier.

"Do you need anything?" LeAnn asked, again and again, of every soldier she met. Some were nearly naked, with only blankets over their legs and anything from Iraq they might still be clinging to. She and Connie had put together hospital room welcome baskets, filled with magazines, toiletries, paper and pen to write home, and phone cards; they wanted the soldiers to have something they could call their own during those first few days in the often lonely hospital. Later that evening LeAnn would start distributing the clothes that women had raided from their husbands' closets, shirts freshly yanked off hangers, sweatshirts, T-shirts, shoes, and pants.

One family, husband and wife, had come to pick up their son at the hospital, then decided to take home with them several other injured soldiers who had nowhere to go but the base barracks. LeAnn and others collected linens, pillows, money, food, and clothing to help out.

Connie, LeAnn, and Beth stayed together in a corner of the lobby, away from the door. As more soldiers came in, Beth started to cry as well. All three watched as the wounded men hugged their wives, their mothers, their babies. Connie was amazed by what many said to her personally. "Mrs. Abrams," one soldier with a serious gunshot wound said, "ask your husband when I can come back." Soldiers who were still on crutches, some with mangled limbs, some barely able to walk without help, wanted to know when they could go back to fight. Many inquired about other soldiers, wanting to know if their buddies had made it home okay. Through their tears, LeAnn and Connie and Beth kept smiling, looking each soldier in the eye and offering a pat on the shoulder, the back, the arm. But to see so many wounded soldiers all at once was overwhelming. And this wasn't even all of them. For the next two days, the women returned to the hospital, checking on the families and the soldiers who continued to arrive.

On Easter Sunday, April 11, the women brought baskets full of chocolate, foil-wrapped bunnies, and hard-boiled eggs to the hospital. Some they had put together themselves; others were donated already assembled. And then they headed for church. It was hard to believe that a week before when the church bells had rung, the battle that would change their lives was just beginning. Shane Aguero was driving into an ambush, Gary Volesky was taking command, and Doc Mathias was just settling down to evening chow. Now, one week later, both Presidents Bush were on their way to Fort Hood to visit with the families and pray for the dead and wounded. Connie Abrams and the other FRG leaders had been asked to join the president and his family at the services. Connie and Robbie took a place in the second row.

"Who is that guy?" Robbie asked, once they had sat down. They were sitting directly behind the Bush family.

"That's the first President Bush," she said. George H. W. Bush turned around and shook Rob's hand. Then his son, George W. Bush, extended his hand. Robbie was glowing, thrilled to have had the chance to shake not one but two presidents' hands.

Captain Dexter Jordan was grateful to have been invited to the service as well. He looked forward to spending a few hours somewhere besides his office with one hand on the phone and the other sorting through papers and trying to jot down notes. He was meticulous about how he dressed that morning. When he got to the steps of the church, however, he was turned away. "No more room," he was told. Men with plastic cords hanging out of their ears glared at him. After the week he had just been through, Jordan couldn't even muster a plea or an explanation. He just turned around and walked away.

The day after Easter, hundreds of miles from Fort Hood, Stephen Hiller's body arrived in his Alabama hometown. Two men dressed in army uniforms accompanied the casket to the funeral home. Lesley was waiting. She moved toward the wooden box and started to lift the heavy lid.

"Ma'am," one of the men said gently. She ignored him, saying simply she wanted to see her husband's body. The escorts didn't dare stop her; but they warned her that if a soldier's body couldn't be cleaned up, it would be wrapped in a white sheet. If the body was presentable, the soldier would be wearing dress greens. Lesley lifted the casket lid slowly, waiting for a flash of color, a signal. With just the slightest bit of his body now exposed, she could see Dusty was wearing his greens.

The bullet that killed Dusty Hiller had ripped through an opening in his body armor, passing through his ribs on the left side, near the fourth rib down, tearing through his heart and both lungs, and then breaking his collarbone before exiting through his neck. Lesley tried to take some comfort in the knowledge that, in all likelihood, he had died instantly.

She stared at Dusty's face. Then a strange thought occurred to her, a thought that might seem irrational later, but that, at the moment, chilled her to the core. *Maybe,* she thought, *maybe it's Dusty's head on someone else's body.* He looked smaller. So Lesley reached into the coffin and touched Dusty's starched shirt. As the escorts looked at each other uncomfortably, Lesley's fingers moved across his chest, then began unbuttoning his shirt. In a moment she had it open.

"Ma'am," one of the escorts said again, "what are you doing?"

"I need to see a tattoo," she said. "I need to make sure this is my husband." She wasn't really talking to anyone.

"Ma'am, we're sure this is your husband."

That wasn't good enough for Lesley. She moved around to the other end of the casket and lifted the lid, down by Dusty's shoes. She started to pull at his pants, determined to find the evidence she needed. She had to find his tattoo, the one on his right calf. Finally she found it: a dragon, holding a crystal ball with a heart inside. He had gotten it just after they were married. Above the dragon was her name.

"That's me. Lesley," she said, touching her name on the tattoo. Now she knew for sure. "And this is my Dusty."

Epilogue

★

THE
ROAD
HOME

February 2005

Baghdad

DEEP INTO A LUKEWARM February night in 2005, Major General Peter Chiarelli sat behind the sagging piles of sandbags that fortified his Baghdad headquarters, staring at an inch-thick stack of index cards. The commander of the First Cavalry Division was only weeks away from the end of his year in Iraq, but the cards he was holding took him back to the beginning, to those first bloody days of April 2004.

Months earlier, Chiarelli had moved from the large tent where he'd lived and worked when he first arrived in Iraq; his new headquarters was inside a long row of buildings near the ornate Baghdad "water palaces" used by Saddam Hussein. The former Iraqi president, captured several months prior to the arrival of the First Cav, now sat alone in a prison cell within the same compound, surrounded by First Cavalry soldiers.

Chiarelli's own office bore no markings of war. A huge mahogany desk and conference table, shipped to Iraq aboard a military cargo plane, dominated the room. Computers and phones lined the desk, along with a cupful of candy for visitors. An American flag hung on the wall, and a half-empty box of Chiarelli's beloved cigars sat on a table underneath. It could have been the office of a patriotic executive in Cleveland. Only the fifty-four-year-old general himself, seated behind his desk long after midnight, provided clues that this was a combat zone. After a day in the field, a layer of dust covered Chiarelli's desert fatigues; a 9mm pistol hung from his shoulder holster; mud filled the crevices of his knee-high tanker boots. And then there were the index cards he held before him.

Chiarelli had asked his aide to prepare the cards, and he'd begun to put in extra hours memorizing the information they held. But now he was struggling. Though it had been a wrenching year full of pain and loss and heartache, he now realized he was still not prepared for the emotional wallop these cards delivered.

Each bore the name of a soldier. These men and women had come to Iraq thinking they would be part of a reconstruction mission, and had been sent back home in flag-draped coffins. Typed beneath each name were a few words about how the soldier had died and what family members were left behind. The fallen soldiers were all husbands or wives, fathers, mothers, sons, daughters. Many had been killed by an enemy they probably never saw.

Generals don't like to cry. But Chiarelli, a charismatic and physically imposing officer, had found himself crying often during his deployment. As he read the names of his fallen soldiers now, his eyes grew moist and his back stiffened. He had attended every memorial service in Iraq, save for one when his helicopter broke down and he couldn't get there in time. He wept on each occasion; this night was no different.

The cards for the soldiers killed on that first night of battle were at the top of the stack. Not since Vietnam had the First Cavalry suffered so many casualties in a single day. Number one was the card for Sergeant Eddie Chen, the first soldier shot that night. Next came the cards for specialists Stephen Hiller, Ahmed Cason, Robert Arsiaga, and Israel Garza. There were cards, too, for Corporal Forest Jostes and Specialist Casey Sheehan, who died within a few hours of each other; and for Mike Mitchell from the tank division.

For Chiarelli, that Sunday night in April had been the most difficult of the war. The families back in the States had been devastated by the losses, especially because they came so soon after their loved ones had left home.

Chiarelli had been in constant touch with his wife, Beth, who had helped care for the families. Like his soldiers in Iraq, the spouses at Fort Hood bonded together in tragedy. But those painful first days for the families and the soldiers were followed by many more. Chiarelli's First Cav soldiers had fought for eighty straight days to retake Sadr City. That fight was followed by another violent surge in August in Najaf, which brought on another sixty days of combat. And then there were the daily IEDs, the improvised explosive devices that killed more soldiers than anything else in Iraq.

The violence that began with the ambush of Lieutenant Shane Aguero's platoon claimed the lives of 168 soldiers from the First Cavalry Division over the course of the yearlong deployment and left about 1,900 wounded. By historical standards, the casualty toll was not so high. During the seven years the First Cav was deployed in Vietnam, from 1965 to 1972, the division lost more than 5,000 soldiers, with more than 26,000 wounded. More than 19,000 American soldiers died during just six weeks of fighting in the Battle of the Bulge in Belgium in World War II. But for General Chiarelli, the eight U.S. soldiers who died in Sadr City on the night of April 4, 2004, carried momentous significance. He had spent thirty-one years in the army, and until that night no soldier under his command had been killed in combat.

Black Sunday, Chiarelli realized, had marked a turning point for the U.S. military in Iraq. It was the day the war took a horribly unanticipated turn, shifting from a peacekeeping mission into a full-fledged fight against an insurgency. Across the country, facing a new enemy, the United States soon found itself, again and again, in the same position as Aguero's platoon in that Sadr City alley: ambushed, unprepared, bloodied, and alone. Chiarelli had brought his First Cavalry soldiers to Iraq with the expectation of a reconstruction and stabilization mission, one for which they would be welcomed by the Iraqi people. Instead, they were forced to fight a war to which their combat training did not apply. After Vietnam, the U.S. military had vowed never to wage a counter-insurgency war again—indeed had largely stopped preparing for the possibility. In the year since Chiarelli had arrived in Baghdad, however, he had learned what so many commanders before him learned, and always the hard way: The enemy has a vote.

Chiarelli hadn't personally known any of the soldiers who died on April 4, though by the end of the year their names were in-grained on his consciousness. It would take some work to learn the stories of the other 160 soldiers he had lost that year as the insurgency took root.

Halfway through the stack, Chiarelli came across the name of Captain Dennis Pintor. Everyone had known Pintor. The 1998 West Point graduate was a superb leader and a gifted athlete. He had been a company commander under Colonel Robert Abrams, and Chiarelli had heard the excruciating details of Pintor's death from Abrams himself, who had known Pintor since the young officer entered the army and had considered him a friend. Chiarelli recalled how Pintor's death had brought a replay of some of the horror Abrams had experienced in the Eagle base aid station on

April 4, the first time the brigade commander had seen any of his soldiers die.

On the October night in 2004 when a roadside bomb tore through Pintor's Humvee, Abrams was sitting in his base camp less than a mile away. Abrams had become accustomed to the sounds of war, but this blast was so powerful it shook the thick concrete walls of his headquarters, and he immediately inquired about the blast.

"Sir, it's bad," the voice on the radio said. "It's Dennis."

Abrams paused. "Dennis?" he barked. "Dennis Pintor?" His eyes filled with such intensity and pain that it was impossible for others in the room to look away. Initially refusing to believe that his friend had been killed, Abrams decided he had to see for himself. Forcing himself to stay calm, he walked quickly to the base medical station where the soldiers had been taken. For the next two hours, inside that trauma center, Abrams saw images that reminded him of the horrors of Black Sunday. The soldier who'd been next to Pintor in the Humvee was lying in pieces. Dead. His legs—boots still on—and his severed arm had been placed next to his body. Another soldier lay nearby, moaning in pain; he would die a day later.

Then he saw what he'd come to see, what he'd dreaded seeing: Pintor's lifeless remains, his body blown apart.

Dennis was gone.

Pintor's company had been so devastated by the loss of the three soldiers that night that Chiarelli himself boarded a helicopter and flew down to visit them. Inside a makeshift chapel, the general sat down with eighty young soldiers and talked intimately with them, saying how important their work was, how proud he was of them. Months later, in the stillness of his office, Chiarelli took another look at Pintor's card:

Survived by wife, Stacy, and four-year-old daughter, Rhea.

All the soldiers in Pintor's battalion knew about little Rhea. The young captain had used his home video camera to tape a skit for a going-away party for a fellow officer. On the night of the party, Pintor rewound the tape too far, and instead of seeing soldiers hamming it up, the partygoers saw Pintor's daughter happily collecting Easter eggs.

"There she is, ladies and gentlemen," Pintor had said, beaming. "Rhea Pintor waving to her daddy!" For a moment, the soldiers watching the video were taken back to their own loved ones.

Chiarelli would have no trouble recalling Stacy and Rhea Pintor. He thought again about some of the others who'd been left behind. Stephen Hiller's wife, Lesley, and their kids. Eddie Chen's parents, who thought their son would be attending law school after his stint in the army. Casey Sheehan's mother, Cindy, who'd become an outspoken antiwar protester in the months after her son's death and a vocal critic of the First Cavalry Division that Chiarelli led. He didn't judge her; he'd never lost a child, and he respected her right to grieve the way she wanted to grieve. He hoped to meet her at an upcoming memorial service at Fort Hood, to tell her that her son had died an honorable death, but he doubted she would come.

Chiarelli wanted to meet all the families, to know all the families. The thought of not recognizing a mother or a spouse or a child who'd lost a loved one sickened him. He thought of his own wife and the three children they had raised together. *If my child had been killed, I would expect his commander to know me, and to know how my son or daughter had died,* Chiarelli thought. *If it were my child, I wouldn't care much that there were 167 others. For me, there would be only one loss that really mattered.*

ON APRIL 4, 2006, exactly two years after Black Sunday, Chiarelli stood on the parade ground at Fort Hood, under a clear blue sky, facing the families of his fallen soldiers and those who had come to honor them. The "Gold Star" families—those who had lost a soldier in Iraq—sat together on folding chairs arranged in neat military rows. It was on this parade ground that many had said goodbye to their departing soldiers for the last time, and it was here that the fortunate ones had welcomed them back home. Behind Chiarelli was a magnificent black granite monument, etched with the names of 168 First Cavalry soldiers who had died in Iraq. In the preceding year, Chiarelli had taken operational command of all U.S. forces in Iraq, but he had returned to Fort Hood this day to dedicate the monument.

The First Cavalry Division band played Aaron Copland's "Fanfare for the Common Man." Then it was Chiarelli's turn to speak.

None of us here today will forget the sacrifices of these Americans. Pride is not a powerful enough word to describe how I feel about each of them. We remember them, not only for who they were, but also for what they stood for. They were rooted in duty, love of country and service to others. We pray that the families will find some measure of peace in knowing that their loved ones represent the very best this country has to offer, and that they lived and died as heroes. We hope their loved ones, the husbands, wives, fathers, mothers, children and friends, will find comfort in knowing we will never forget their sacrifice. I see their young faces in my mind's eye every day of my life. That will never change.

Lieutenant General Chiarelli met with as many families as he could after the memorial ceremony. Hours later, the general, still thinking of the soldiers' names on the black granite wall, kissed his wife goodbye, boarded a plane, and headed back to Baghdad.

APPENDIX

First Cavalry Division

The First Cavalry returned to the United States in March 2005. In November 2006 the division was redeployed to Iraq for another year. Many of the same soldiers who fought on April 4, 2004, have returned to Iraq as well.

Major General Peter Chiarelli gave up command of the First Cavalry Division in November 2005. He was promoted to lieutenant general that same month. He returned to Iraq in January 2006 for a second one-year deployment as the commander, Multi-National Corps–Iraq, operational commander for all U.S. troops in Iraq. General Chiarelli insisted on being called, day or night, whenever a U.S. service member was killed.

Beth Chiarelli moved to Germany (her twenty-sixth move since Lieutenant General Chiarelli joined the army) while her husband was on his second deployment to Iraq. She traveled extensively through Europe and frequently visited her three children—Erin, Peter Jr., and Patrick—back in the United States, and stayed in regular touch with the men and women of the First Cavalry Division.

FIRST BRIGADE COMBAT TEAM

COLONEL ROBERT "ABE" ABRAMS gave up command of the First Brigade Combat Team on July 12, 2005. The next day, he reported for duty as the chief of staff of the First Cavalry Division. In December 2005 he was reassigned to U.S. Army Europe, to serve as the executive officer to the commanding general of U.S. Army Europe.

CONNIE ABRAMS and Robert II moved to Heidelberg, Germany, with Abe. She and Beth Chiarelli were neighbors on the army post. "When we sign up to marry our husbands, we sign up to the army, too," she says. "This is their job. They're going to deploy, they're going to go to war, and you're just going to have to deal with it."

LIEUTENANT COLONEL ROBERT GERHARDT is a proud and devoted father to four children, and is currently an instructor and director of research at Brooke Army Medical Center in Texas. Bob and his wife, Denise, met while working in the emergency room at Darnall Hospital at Fort Hood and married in the base's Cavalry Post Chapel, on November 20, 1993. Denise served in the military for almost nineteen years as an army combat medic and as a flight medic. She also performed combat service during Operations Desert Shield/Desert Storm and ultimately became a brigade surgeon. Denise died in December 2005, after a long battle with chronic pancreatitis.

CAPTAIN DEXTER JORDAN was promoted to the rank of major on July 1, 2006, and is the battalion executive officer (XO) for an activated reserve unit.

2-5 CAVALRY BATTALION HEADQUARTERS AND HEADQUARTERS COMPANY

LIEUTENANT COLONEL GARY VOLESKY. Four months after the April 4 battle, in August 2004, Volesky led another rescue mission in Sadr City and earned a Silver Star for his efforts and bravery. After returning from Iraq in March 2005, Volesky and his family moved to Maxwell Air Force Base in Montgomery, Alabama, to attend the Air War College. He was promoted to colonel on June 1, 2006. He returned to Iraq in December 2006 for another yearlong deployment, as deputy chief of staff for III Corps.

LEANN VOLESKY, an avid quilter, is again living at Fort Hood with her son, Alex. She was reluctant to talk about her family's experiences surrounding April 4, but with Gary now back in Iraq, LeAnn talks more extensively with Alex abut his father's role in the war. Gary calls LeAnn "my heroine," and stresses the important partnership between soldiers and their wives, who "take care of all the issues at home, so we can focus on the mission in Iraq. We can't succeed without them."

CAPTAIN TRENT UPTON left the battalion S-1 position and took command of Alpha Company in June 2004. In January of 2006, he became the commander of Headquarters and Headquarters Troop, First Brigade, First Cavalry Division. He was promoted to major in July 2006. He was deployed to Iraq again in the fall of 2006.

ANGIE UPTON worked for several years as a county juvenile probation officer and later as a legal assistant in an attorney's office. The couple's first child was born in late 2006, just as Trent was scheduled to be redeployed for a year. Although they no longer live in the same area, Angie keeps in touch with Gina Denomy, Aimee Randazzo, and LeAnn Volesky.

CAPTAIN DYLAN RANDAZZO became an instructor at the Military Intelligence Captain's Career Course at the U.S. Army Intelligence Center at Fort Huachuca, Arizona.

AIMEE RANDAZZO was no longer involved with the Family Readiness Group once she moved to Arizona. But she still attends as many military family functions as possible while spending most of her time raising the couple's two young boys.

CAPTAIN DAVID MATHIAS returned home on R&R in September 2004 for the birth of his second son, Levi. Mathias served as chief of pediatrics at William Beaumont Army Medical Center in El Paso, and was promoted to major in June 2005. A year later, he left the army to work as a general pediatrician in Wisconsin.

CHAPLAIN (CAPTAIN) RAMON PENA is still a chaplain with the 2-5 Cav at Fort Hood. After returning to Fort Hood, he was surprised at how many of the soldiers remembered him from Sadr City. Specialist Sergio Estrella, Jr., was one of the soldiers Pena prayed with at the aid station that night; months later, Estrella would ask him to officiate at his wedding.

SERGEANT MICHAEL ADKINS was reassigned to Alpha Company in August 2004, where he served as a team leader. He went on to 2-5 Cav, serving as the sniper detachment sergeant, and was later promoted to staff sergeant.

ALPHA COMPANY

CAPTAIN GEORGE LEWIS left Alpha Company in June 2004 and served in the First Cavalry Headquarters in the Information Operations Cell until the division returned from Iraq. Back at Fort Hood he became the deputy public affairs officer for First Cav Division. He was promoted to major in October 2005. He says that even an emotional TV ad, especially one involving families, makes him think of Stephen Hiller dying beside him. His girlfriend, Elvy, broke up with him shortly after his return from Iraq.

SERGEANT FIRST CLASS REGINALD BUTLER became an instructor at the United States Military Academy in West Point, New York. He talks about his experiences in Iraq with young cadets almost every day and is diligent about keeping in touch with his fellow soldiers from Iraq. Butler's first wedding anniversary, April 4, 2004, was such a wrenching day that his wife refuses to celebrate the occasion.

STAFF SERGEANT EDWARD ELLIOTT was evacuated through Germany and treated at Walter Reed Hospital in Washington, D.C. Fulfilling a promise he and Staff Sergeant Reynolds made to each other to return to Iraq, both men were back in the country by June. Elliott remained in Alpha Company and was promoted to sergeant first class.

STAFF SERGEANT KENNETH PITTS became a drill sergeant. Since April 4, Pitts says, he's much more emotional than he used to be. He says he often starts crying while watching television and refuses to see violent movies. Pitts gets nervous driving down the street at night, especially when it's quiet. He asks his wife to talk to him and tell him stories, something that keeps his mind from wandering too far.

STAFF SERGEANT ROBERT MILTENBERGER was awarded a Silver Star for his efforts and commended, among other reasons, for "at one point during the fighting . . . applying first aid to three soldiers while maintaining fire against the enemy." But Miltenberger has never felt comfortable with the award. "I feel guilty because I wasn't shot, too. I didn't get hurt. I feel guilty they awarded me and didn't award everybody else." Months after the April 4 battle, Miltenberger, despondent and disturbed by everything around him, stood on a Sadr City street with his flak vest open, shouting, "Here I am. If you want me, here I am." He was later diagnosed with PTSD, and says no amount of therapy could make him stop thinking about that day. Miltenberger retired from the army in the spring of 2005, and returned to his home in Cameron, Louisiana. Five months later, he and his wife, Belinda, and their two children lost their home and most of their belongings during Hurricane Rita. He and Belinda grabbed wedding albums, photos, and some clothes and school supplies for the children. Belinda told her husband to take his Silver Star; he retrieved it from a closet shelf.

BELINDA MILTENBERGER knew little about April 4 until she ordered a tape of the ABC News *Nightline* broadcast in August 2004, which she had heard featured the story about the battle. She gathered her family together and watched her husband and other soldiers describe their experiences in great emotional detail. Sergeant Miltenberger had never before spoken of his experiences, and he cried throughout the TV interview. Belinda was devastated knowing that he had been through so much and shared so little, but the couple's marriage remains strong. The Miltenberger family is living in a FEMA trailer until their Louisiana home is rebuilt.

SERGEANT TIMOTHY APPLE was shot in the back, but the bullet stopped "just above my love handles." He has some permanent nerve damage and has been diagnosed with PTSD. Sometimes in his sleep he will squeeze his wife and shake uncontrollably. He works as an electrician with a construction company and has twin boys. Apple says he's still waiting for his Purple Heart certificate.

SERGEANT DAVID RYAN has had three surgeries to repair his left eye, and is legally blind on that side; he has little depth perception, and more surgeries ahead of him. When he was deployed, he and his wife were separating. He now has sole custody of his son. The events of April 4 "made a lot more of us sentimental," he says of himself and the other members of his unit. "It's like we're brothers now. We'd do anything for each other."

CORPORAL ALLAN ALEXANDER went on to become staff sergeant at Fort Hood. He was shot in the biceps and says he is about eighty percent recovered; he has slightly restricted movement. Alexander admits to suffering flashbacks and has trouble sleeping, but doesn't think it's PTSD. Married while he was in Iraq, Alexander later got divorced. "The army will do that to you."

SPECIALIST RAY FLORES didn't talk about April 4 for a year. By eerie coincidence, he was at a bar when a man came up to him and started talking about his cousin who had been killed in Iraq.

He was talking about SPC Israel Garza. "Oh my God," the man said. "You weren't on that vehicle, were you?"

PRIVATE FIRST CLASS JERRY BUNE moved to Colorado to be closer to friends and family. He left the military with PTSD and a forty-percent disability rating from the gunshot wound to the leg he sustained as the gunner on George Lewis's Humvee; his condition has since worsened to a seventy-percent rating. He works part-time at a Sears auto center and spends his free time restoring his own vehicles.

PRIVATE FIRST CLASS LUCAS FOURNIER was shot once in the left chest cavity and twice in his left shoulder. One bullet hit the ball and socket of his arm, and the other tore through his armpit. After ten days in the Baghdad Hospital, he was flown to Germany, and later to Walter Reed, where he stayed for a month while doctors reconstructed his left shoulder; the pain remains three years later. Fournier was medically discharged and went to work in a factory in Missouri. He got married in the fall of 2006. He says he has no signs of PTSD.

SPECIALIST TOMAS YOUNG was shot just underneath the left collarbone, where his Kevlar jacket stopped, and is paralyzed from the waist down. He has trouble sitting up in the morning. It takes him about forty-five minutes just to get upright. Young has been diagnosed with PTSD and depression and has been active in the antiwar movement. He and his wife, Brie, were married in August 2005. They started dating just before he left for Iraq, and spent their honeymoon in Crawford, Texas, protesting the war outside President Bush's ranch.

PRIVATE FIRST CLASS COLE HALLIBURTON was promoted to the rank of sergeant. He is currently serving as a recruiter in Austin, Texas. "No matter what your politics, the real reason we were fighting that day is because the guy next to you was."

PRIVATE PETER BAAH, originally from Ghana, became a U.S. citizen on May 17, 2006, and underwent a medical evaluation board in anticipation of a discharge from the U.S. Army. His index (trigger) finger still doesn't function, and his middle finger still contains shrapnel.

GUADALUPE "LUPE" GARZA, whose husband, Israel, died on April 4, was invited to join President Bush in church at Fort Hood's Easter Sunday service. She had little interest. *What can the president do to make me feel better?* she thought. Lupe's oldest son started having nightmares after his father died. He is in therapy now.

ALLISON CASON's husband, Ahmed, was buried at Jefferson Memorial Gardens in Hoover, Alabama, on the Monday after Easter. She wonders what she'll do when her son wants to go fishing one day or play sports. Allison is saving Ahmed's silver car for her daughter, so she can drive it when she turns sixteen. It's sitting in the garage. In the meantime, Allison plans to return to school to become a veterinarian.

LESLEY HILLER lives in Alabama, close to her parents, who are helping her raise her children. She says some days are still unbearable, but she's taking classes again and working on her education. Her son was born August 13, 2004—four months after her husband's death. She named him Stephen, after his father.

CHARLIE COMPANY

CAPTAIN TROY DENOMY remained in command of C/2-5 Cav until June 2005 and then became the assistant operations officer for 2-5 Cav. He was promoted to the rank of major in April 2006, and he is now serving as an assistant product manager in the Army Acquisition Corps in Maryland. He has recovered from his injuries to his back and shoulder.

GINA DENOMY is happy to be living in Maryland, just five hours from her family and away from the Texas heat, though she misses friends who are still there. Gina is raising the couple's son, Merrick, born just days before Troy began his yearlong deployment in 2004.

LIEUTENANT CLAY SPICER served as a military science professor for freshmen in the Corps of Cadets at Texas A&M University. He and his wife, DeLayne, had their first child on April 2, 2006, and brought her home on the morning of April 4. The couple relocated to McKinney, outside Dallas, where Clay works in the construction business with his father.

LIEUTENANT SHANE AGUERO became a mortar platoon leader on December 1, 2004. He was redeployed out of Iraq on the last flight out of Kuwait, approximately thirteen months after he arrived. Promoted to captain in December, Aguero volunteered to serve in Afghanistan as part of a reconstruction team. He currently serves as the executive officer and battalion S-3 for the organization. As for April 4, Aguero says, "It was like we're all on some drug called camaraderie. That day sealed that bond. For that entire year, there was never any fear if somebody got in some heavy fighting; there was a trust there that your brothers in arms would not only come to get you, they would rush to be there for you, regardless of the cost."

AMBER AGUERO. While Shane is in Afghanistan, Amber continues to live just outside Fort Hood with the couple's two children. She is completing studies in premed. She plans to attend medical school in 2007.

SERGEANT FIRST CLASS JERRY SWOPE received a Silver Star, the citation for which read: "[His] actions, more than any other single event, led to the overall survival of the platoon." With more than seventeen years in the army, Swope is stationed at Fort Bragg, working as an OCT (observer-controller-trainer) and teaching soldiers battlefield immersion. He's never really talked to his wife, Christine, about April 4.

STAFF SERGEANT ROBERT "BIG COUNTRY" REYNOLDS recovered from the massive wound to his thigh. He and Staff Sergeant Edward Elliott made a pact that they would return to duty in Iraq by July 1, 2004. They did.

SERGEANT ERIC BOURQUIN was promoted to the rank of staff sergeant and went on to serve as a drill sergeant in Fort Leonard Wood, Missouri. He and his wife had a son, Cannon, on June 22, 2006.

CORPORAL SHANE COLEMAN left the military to work for Sergeant Eric Bourquin's brother as a restaurant catering manager in Temple, Texas, and to continue his education.

TASK FORCE LANCER

JASSIM AL-LANI* has continued to work as an interpreter for the U.S. military in Sadr City. He is desperately trying to get a visa to live in the United States with his family because of the numerous death threats he has received.

CINDY SHEEHAN became a full-time antiwar activist and eventually an icon for the antiwar movement in the United States. She and her husband, Pat, divorced after more than twenty-seven years of marriage. Looking back on her son Casey's funeral, Cindy says, "The twenty-one-gun salute is so cruel and callous to me. My son was shot in the head. Here they are shooting. I believe I participated in the glorification of war and killing. If I had it to do over again, I wouldn't have done it that way."

C/2-37 AR

CHARLIE COMPANY 2/37 AR was extended in Iraq for an additional ninety days and returned to Germany in July 2004. During that time, they fought the Mahdi Army for one hundred days straight in Al-Kut, Najaf, and Kufa. The unit lost two more soldiers, First Lieutenant Ken Ballard and Private First Class Nick Zimmer.

CAPTAIN JOHN C. MOORE received a Silver Star for his efforts on April 4. He returned to Germany and married a German national, and began his career as a Russian foreign area officer. Fluent in German, he attended the Defense Language Institute

*Not his real name.

and learned Russian. Moore is currently at the George C. Marshall European Institute for Security Studies. He was promoted to the rank of major on July 1, 2006.

LIEUTENANT CHRISTOPHER DEAN received a Silver Star for his efforts on April 4. He was made a specialty platoon leader for the Task Force Mortar Platoon. He was promoted to captain and made the executive officer of Headquarters and Headquarters Company, 2-37 AR. In January 2006 he began a second tour in Iraq.

LIEUTENANT DAVE FITTRO commanded the 2-37 Task Force Scout Platoon after returning from Iraq. He was then the executive officer of Bravo Company, 2-37 AR. He served a second tour in Iraq with the 2-37 AR and was promoted to the rank of captain.

STAFF SERGEANT HENRY ELDRIDGE was promoted to the rank of sergeant first class. He lives at Fort Hood with his two daughters.

SERGEANT ERIK ALBERTSON is a recruiter in Fargo, North Dakota, where he is restless behind a desk. He lives a few hours from his family and keeps in close touch with the soldiers he was with on April 4.

★   ★   ★

MOQTADA AL-SADR continues to be a significant problem for U.S. forces in Iraq, as he gains both political and military power through his armed militia.

Acknowledgments

The story behind this battle was first told to me by General Jack Keane (U.S. Army, retired) during a dinner in Baghdad in July 2004. After a thirty-seven-year career in the military that began in Vietnam, General Keane knows the pain and intensity of war. And as an ABC News consultant for more than three years, he understands the power of a good story. Two days after that dinner, with the help of then Major General (now Lieutenant General) Peter Chiarelli, my crew and I flew to Sadr City to interview the soldiers of the First Cavalry Division for ABC News *Nightline* and ABC's *World News Tonight*. And for the first time since the battle, the platoon that had been pinned down returned to the alley to show us where the fight had unfolded. A few months later, when we returned to Sadr City to do follow-up interviews with the soldiers there, General Chiarelli suggested I talk to the families back at Fort Hood. Thus another *Nightline*, and this book, began.

There is no one who has given me more help on this book, both researching and reporting, than Bridget Samburg. She deserves an enormous amount of credit for telling this story. It simply could not have been done without her. What has inspired me most working with this fine reporter is her love for the story. She had never covered the military before, but she so quickly grasped not only the lingo but also the depth of the experience that these men and their families had been through. I cannot thank her enough for her outstanding work.

And Bridget and I know that the calcium in our bones was provided by retired Lieutenant Colonel Ginni Guiton. Ginni could motivate a tree stump. She has been a magnificent asset in putting this book together, from tracking down soldiers, to outlining the "order of march" in dizzying detail, to organizing, prodding, and generally being the person to whom we always turned for follow-up, help, or just a shoulder to lean on.

I also got help early on from the amazing Jennifer Hoar and Howard Rosenberg, as well as James Kitfield and David Chasteen.

During numerous trips to Iraq and to Fort Hood, I was helped immeasurably by Brigadier General William Troy, who has been a true friend. I also had the constant support of General George Casey, Major Tony Hale, Lieutenant General Tom Metz, Command Sergeant Major Neil Ciotola, Colonel Robert Abrams, Lieutenant Colonel James Hutton (the best public affairs officer in the Army), and Major Scott Bleichwehl (who is second in the PAO world only to Lieutenant Colonel Hutton). The First Cavalry Division, with General Chiarelli's blessing, could not have been more cooperative. The Fort Hood and Killeen communities were also most welcoming. I am especially grateful for the hospitality offered by Beth Chiarelli, Connie Abrams, Paula Troy, and Pam Metz. General Gordon Sulllivan and his wife, Gay, deserve much thanks as well.

My longtime producer at ABC News, Ely Brown, was a steady source of professional and personal strength on trips to Iraq. She demonstrated courage, good cheer in the worst of environments, and an innate ability to produce strong television. Needless to say, without the fine camera work (and friendship) of Mike Charlton, Bartley Price, and Doug Vogt, none of those ABC stories could have been told. No one is more courageous in war zones than photographers, and these three are the finest. For Doug, and for my friend and colleague Bob Woodruff, telling the stories of this war would result in terrible injuries in January 2005. Doug and his wife, Viviane, and Bob and his wife, Lee, have been a constant source of inspiration. Even with four children and a husband whom she has shepherded through a miraculously successful recovery, Lee, a gifted writer, managed to read my manuscript, offer helpful suggestions, and champion my efforts.

My three-way communications with the *New Yorker*'s Peter Boyer (whose writing leaves me in awe) and Marine Colonel Stephen Ganyard kept me laughing and stimulated. Colonel Ganyard, a fighter pilot and scholar, helped me understand the concept of assaulting through an ambush better than anyone on the ground ever has. Colonel Ganyard's fellow Marine, Nate Fick, was a great guide through the tricky world of book writing and the even trickier world of the military. Young Peter Chiarelli (the son of the general), a brilliant writer and producer, gave terrific suggestions upon reading the manuscript.

I owe so much to Gail Ross, at Gail Ross Literary Agency. She talked me into writing this book and was a strong and enduring advocate who made the whole process an adventure. Howard Yoon was a whiz at helping to craft a book proposal, and Kara Baskin offered much-needed help as well. I also thank agent Paul Julian for helping me through more than a few mazes.

At ABC News, senior broadcast producer Tom Nagorski has given me more guidance and encouragement than anyone. Tom, the author of his own extraordinary work of nonfiction, *Miracles on the Water,* was kind enough to read the manuscript and offer broad and detailed suggestions that were spot-on. He is a man I could not admire more. Help and encouragement also came from Brian Hartman, Luis Martinez, Robin Sproul, Dennis Dunlavey, Ian Cameron, Dennis Powell, Karen Travers, Stephanie Smith, David Kerley, George Stephanopoulos, Jon Garcia, Audrey Taylor, Larry Shaw, Ariane deVogue, Andrea Owen, Gerry Holmes, Dan Green, Mary Walsh, Mary Marsh, Leroy Sievers, Tom Bettag, and Katherine O'Hearn, who has been there for me from the beginning.

And thanks to David Westin, Paul Slavin, Mimi Gurbst, Jon Banner, and Charlie Gibson for supporting the many trips I have made to Iraq to tell the important stories of this war.

At Putnam, it was evident from the moment I met him that editor Dan Conaway was passionate about this story and would help in any way he could to make it the best it could be. His enthusiasm and that of publisher Ivan Held are the reasons I came to Putnam. Dan worked tirelessly to help this first-time author bring the story to life. I am grateful for his steady hand and his never-ending patience. And thanks especially to Rachel Holtzman, who has provided vital help with a smile.

Thanks also to my friends Nancy Crisman and Sunisa Mathews. And to Sheila Casey, Barbara Delinsky, Rosemary Mariner, Kim Holmes, Joel Bonder, and Dick and Judy Meltzer. And thanks and love to my mother, who has always encouraged me.

Most of all I thank my husband, Tom Gjelten. It was Tom who first thought this should be a book, and Tom who made all the sacrifices so that it became one. He could not have been more supportive or enthusiastic at every step (except for my frequent trips to Baghdad, which did not exactly thrill him). He offered his fine eye and storytelling skills to help me make this a better book, all while writing his own. And he picked up every ball I dropped at home. He learned an awful lot about eighth-grade and then ninth-grade math with my son, Jake, and a lot about law school and apartment woes from my daughter, Greta. As for Greta and Jake, they never wavered in their love and support, no matter how many football games or events I missed in the course of writing this. They fill up my heart. I could not be prouder.

A portion of the proceeds of this book has been given to Brooke Army Medical Center at Fort Sam Houston, Texas.

Remember.